THE GREAT
SCOTTISH
WITCH-HUNT

T0386379

The first history of the most intense period of witch-hunting in Scotland revealing the number of women and men strangled and burned alive at the stake.

Scotland, in common with the rest of Europe, was troubled from time to time by outbreaks of witchcraft which the authorities sought to contain and then to suppress, and the outbreak of 1658-1662 is generally agreed to represent the high-water mark of Scottish persecution.

These were peculiar years for Scotland. For nine years Scotland was effectively an English province with many English officials in charge. In 1660 this suddenly changed. So the threat to Church and state from a plague of witches was particularly disturbing. The tension between this English occupation and the revived fervour of Calvinist religion in the Scottish Church combined to produce a peculiar atmosphere in which the activities of witches drew hostile attention to an unprecedented degree.

THE GREAT SCOTTISH WITCH-HUNT

P. G. MAXWELL-STUART

The History Press

This edition first published 2007

Reprinted 2024

The History Press
97 St George's Place,
Cheltenham, Gloucestershire GL50 3QB
www.thehistorypress.co.uk

British Library Cataloguing in Publication Data.
A catalogue record for this book is available from the British Library.

ISBN 978 0 7524 4425 3

Typesetting and origination by
The History Press
Printed by TJ Books Limited, Padstow, Cornwall

Contents

ABOUT THE AUTHOR

P.G. Maxwell-Stuart is Lecturer in History at the University of St Andrews and is acknowledged expert on the occult. He is the author of *Witch Hunters*, *Witchcraft: A History*, *Wizards: A History*, *Ghosts: A History of Phantoms, Ghouls & Other Spirits of the Dead*, and *The Archbishops of Canterbury*, all published by Tempus. He has also written *The Occult in Early Modern Europe: A Documentary History*, and *Satan's Conspiracy: Magic and Witchcraft in Sixteenth Century Scotland*. He is currently writing a new history of the Devil for Tempus Publishing. He lives in St Andrews.

Author Note

Most of what follows is based upon unpublished manuscript material. My aim is similar to that I expressed in *Satan's Conspiracy*, which is the first volume in this history of Scottish magic and witchcraft – that is, to place new material in coherent fashion before the reader so that he or she may have a more detailed basis upon which to formulate future interpretation of this episode in Scottish history.

I have reluctantly rendered the Scots of the documents into modern English. Sums of money should be understood as referring to Scottish currency of the period, unless otherwise indicated.

I am grateful to the Staff of the University of St Andrews Library and of the National Archives of Scotland for their assistance, and to Jonathan Reeve of Tempus for his patience in waiting for the manuscript.

Introduction

Since September 1651, Scotland had been a country under occupation. By the end of the year, after great slaughter, the English had established garrisons the length of the eastern coast, from Edinburgh to Orkney, strongholds were contemplated and begun in Ayr, Perth, Leith, Inverlochy, and Inverness, and anyone wishing to travel from one part of Scotland to another needed a pass. There were no fewer than 10,000 troops in the country at any time, the Highlands were and continued to be in turmoil, and however keen the English were at first to annex their unruly conquest – a bill for which was introduced by John Lisle, the Lord Commissioner, on 30 September 1651 – the occupation was very, very expensive. The Kirk was riven with discord as rival presbyteries and assemblies jockeyed for power and endeavoured to catch the eye of the occupier. The civil administration worked, but intermittently; and so did the provision of justice which, between 1652 and 1655, was principally in English hands, too, and for a while at least, contemplated an amalgamation of both its law and practice with those of England, a plan much favoured by Baron Broghill, a young man whose conduct in Ireland had been such as to gain the trust and admiration of Oliver Cromwell. All in all, therefore, the condition of the Scottish state during the 1650s varied from more or less settled to more or less turbulent.

The tenor of the times may be gauged from a letter written by a Scots minister to one of his friends in London:

On the 20th of July last [1653], when our General Assembly was set in the ordinary time and place, [Edinburgh], Lieutenant-Colonel Cotterall beset the Church with some rates [companies] of musketeers and a troop of horse; himself entered the Assembly House and, immediately after Mr Dickson the Moderator his prayer, required audience; wherein he inquired, If we did sit there by the authority of the Parliament of the Commonwealth of England? or of the Commanders-in-Chief of the English forces? or of the English judges in Scotland? The Moderator replied, That we were an ecclesiastical synod, a spiritual court of Jesus Christ which meddled not with any thing civil; that our authority was from God, and established by the laws of the land yet standing unrepealed; that, by the Solemn League and Covenant, the most of the English army stood obliged to defend our General Assembly. When some speeches of this kind had passed, the Lieutenant-Colonel told us, his order was to dissolve us; whereupon he commanded all of us to follow him, else he would drag us out of the room... When he had led us a mile without the town, he then declared what further he had in commission, that we should not dare to meet any more above three in number; and that against eight o'clock tomorrow, we should depart the town under pain of being guilty of breaking the public peace: and the day following, by sound of trumpet, we were commanded off town under the pain of present imprisonment. Thus our General Assembly, the glory and strength of our Church upon earth, is, by your soldiery, crushed and trod underfoot, without the least provocation from us at this time, either in word or deed.[1]

We have, then, a country with a distinctive but fissiparous religious tradition invaded by another; an alien civil and legal tradition imposed, with greater or less efficiency, by force; armed resistance by parts of the country with a quite different set of traditions from the rest; an invader with constant problems of his own; and the outbreak of what looks like a series of atrocities. The situation, *mutatis mutandis*, may sound familiar. This is the background to the apparent swell of witchcraft which broke out into what seemed to be a period of more intensive prosecution than Scotland had known before, a period often, but misleadingly, called 'the great Scottish witch-hunt'. But who were these witches, what had they been doing, and how different were 1658–1662 from the years preceding them?

The practice of magic, both beneficial and malevolent, and the consultation of specialist magical practitioners was going on all the time; that is to say, magic in almost any one of its multifarious forms was readily available to everyone, no matter what his or her rank, profession or religion, as a practical means of solving an immediate problem. It might be the only means used; it might be one of several, such as medicine or prayer. But its ready availability meant that people tended to take it for granted. Consulting a magical practitioner might rouse a certain anxiety, just as nowadays a visit to one's doctor may prove to be a somewhat unsettling experience. But just as no one regards going to the surgery as a bizarre thing to do, or the doctor as a mysteriously aberrant individual, because everyone accepts that medicine and medical practice represent a rational method of trying to deal with one kind of predicament, so no one in the early modern period regarded a magical practitioner as weird or unnatural, because magic, given the premises of the world-view generally held at that time, was entirely rational. The shift in outlook we have to make in order to try to understand the earlier past may be difficult, but it is essential we make it, otherwise we shall fail to look at our subject with early modern eyes – the only way in which we can hope to do it justice.

The Kirk was governed by three principal bodies: the synod, the presbytery, and the local kirk session. When episcopacy was reintroduced into Scotland, the archbishop or bishop generally acted as chairman of the relevant synod. The synod usually met twice a year, in April and October, for about two or three days on each occasion. Its role was to oversee Kirk discipline, especially in difficult cases referred to it from the presbyteries, and to make sure that ministers were doing their job properly and conforming to what was expected of them, particularly in matters of personal behaviour. Next in line came the presbyteries. These consisted of a minister and principal elder from each of the parishes under each presbytery's control, and therefore the size of the presbytery session depended on the number of parishes within its bounds and the attendance rate of those entitled to be present. The presbytery of St Andrews, for example, had twenty parishes; the presbytery of Dunfermline, nine.

Presbytery sessions were usually held once a month, and more or less did for their jurisdiction what the synods did for theirs. Finally, the basic and most important tier of ecclesiastical government was the kirk session. It consisted of the minister, elected elders, and elected deacons – the latter, officials who looked after the temporal affairs of the congregation – and met once a week to oversee almost every aspect of the parishioners' public and private conduct.

Consequently, a large number of people in any given parish could expect to come before the session at some time in their lives, to answer for such offences as laying out washing on the Sabbath, falling asleep in church, fornication, adultery, violence (public or domestic), slander, theft, 'superstitious' behaviour, consulting magical operators, or being a witch and practising some form of witchcraft. The penalties a kirk session could exact ranged, according to the nature of the offence which had been proved against the individual, from a reprimand in private before the session or in public before the Sunday congregation, to confinement in the jougs (a hinged iron collar attached by a chain to a wall or post, and locked round the offender's neck), and imprisonment, usually in the local tolbooth or the steeple of the church or, sometimes, if neither of these was available, in a secure room in someone's house. Some people may have found the experience of appearing in front of the kirk session intimidating, and curbed their ways sufficiently to ensure they were not seen before it again. Others, however, both women and men, were not so cowed, and their names crop up in the records time after time. Familiarity with one's judges obviously works both ways, and although most people conformed to the session's edict and performed their penance in the end, it sometimes took a very long time indeed for the culprit to give in and express any kind of repentance.

Now, there are instances of name-calling, consulting, charming, and witchcraft recorded in kirk and presbytery session minutes throughout 1658.[2] Bad-tempered exchanges between women frequently included one woman's calling another 'witch', not usually a serious matter in the end, as investigation tended to prove. Thus, at the end of September the kirk session of Trinity Church in Edinburgh heard that Janet Scot, wife of James Anderson, had called Janet Scot, wife of George Mossman, a witch, adding that she hoped in God to see her burned and to see her arse shine upon the wall of the castle, and that Janet [Mossman] should not treat her as she [Janet Mossman] had treated Helen Shorteous whose child had died – a clear implication that Janet [Mossman] had killed the child by magic. Two other women testified they had heard Janet [Anderson] say all this, but the session clearly did not believe that the accusation of Janet [Mossman's] being a witch was sustainable, because Janet [Anderson] was simply required to kneel down and ask Janet [Mossman's] pardon, and suffer a sharp rebuke from the minister. Name-calling, arising as it usually did in the course of personal quarrels, commonly between neighbours, was, in fact, most often treated as slander and the party judged most at fault – and sometimes this meant both parties equally – made to apologise publicly to the other. The ministers seem to have been more concerned to restore communal equilibrium than to pursue what they and most other people in the parish would have known was a charge spoken more in anger than in the cold heat of intentional accusation.

Nevertheless, name-calling was always taken seriously in case the accusation turn out to be true. So calling someone a witch could pose a potentially grave threat to the person on the receiving end of the insult, which is probably why she (or sometimes he) complained to the kirk authorities. In March, for example, Isobel Craig in Dirleton, a village about two-and-a-half miles west-south-west of North Berwick, was accused of calling Margaret Martin a witch, and inquiries extending into April revealed it had been part of a rather more sinister quarrel. The two women were in the local mill to have their corn ground, when for some reason Margaret tried to throw Isobel's corn out of the hopper. High words followed. The exact sequence of events is not clear from the record, but at one point in the exchange Margaret said to Isobel, 'May the Devil bewitch your senses from you, and may lice eat all your flesh!' and Isobel called Margaret a witch and drew blood by scratching her. If this is indeed the order in which things happened, the scratching could be significant, because drawing blood thus from a witch provided counter-magic to her malefice, and Margaret's curse would also be significant because of Isobel's reaction. Had Margaret already had the reputation of being a witch, her curse could have been taken less as an expression of bad temper and more as an effective magical formula. Hence Isobel's calling her a witch and seeking to counteract the bewitchment by scratching Margaret.

Consulting was equally fraught with possible danger. On 16 May, James Martin testified to the kirk session of Haddington that Marion Young had sent for him because she wanted him to help her find out who had stolen some money from her. Marion wrote down the names of Isobel Hunter's servants and James took the list to Mrs Kirkby, an English woman living in Musselburgh. Kirkby (her Christian name is not recorded) took him into a room where there was another man and a woman – neither their names nor their functions are ever explained – and then read the fiftieth psalm. The theme of the psalm is that God will reward those who obey His commandments, but will punish severely those who break them and do wrong. It may also be significant, in view of the current and frequent accusation that witches made a covenant with Satan, that the psalm makes two references to humanity's covenant with God. Either now, or just before the reading of the psalm, a key was placed on the page, perhaps at verse 18 which begins, 'When thou sawest a thief', and then James began to read the servants' names from his piece of paper. As soon as he came to 'John Cathcart', the session was told, the key turned round, a sign that the thief had been discovered.

The session wanted to know how James knew that Mrs Kirkby was a magical practitioner and James answered that Marion had told him she had seen her perform this divination once before, in Isobel Hunter's house. (Whether this was part of the same case of theft, or another, is not made clear.) Further inquiry elicited from Marion herself that Isobel Smith, her mistress, had recommended Mrs Kirkby. It was now 23 May and the record shows that Marion had been arrested and put in prison, probably the tolbooth in Haddington, then a three-storeyed building with accommodation for prisoners at street level. She was left there until 20 June, when she said it was Janet Acheson who had recommended she go to Mrs Kirkby. A week later, Janet Acheson agreed she had seen Mrs Kirkby 'turn the key' in John MacCail's house and had told Marion about it; but she denied she had advised her to consult Mrs Kirkby about her own loss. On 4 July, Marion stuck to her version of events, and Janet Acheson stuck to hers, although she added the intriguing detail that Isobel Smith had been visiting the tolbooth at a time when Mrs Kirkby was in her house, turning the key to find out who had stolen money from *her*, and that when she came home, Mrs Kirkby offered to reveal who had taken the money, but Isobel said she already knew.

A small deputation, including the minister and the baillie (a local official with special responsibility for the administration of justice in the town), was then sent to question Isobel, and reported that she admitted she was actually present at the turning of the key, but that she claimed she was an unwilling spectator, saying it was done in someone else's house and that she had not urged Marion to consult Mrs Kirkby at all. By this time, Marion must have been liberated from the tolbooth, probably on caution [bail], because when she was summoned to attend the kirk session on 18 July, she did not turn up. Further sessions on 25 July and 1 August saw the parties more or less repeating what they had said before, but Marion added that Isobel had told her there was no evil in going to Mrs Kirkby, while James and Janet denied ever hearing Isobel saying anything of the sort. The minister, Robert Ker, was then absent until 22 August when Marion's case was referred to the presbytery for advice. This frequently happened when kirk sessions were not quite certain what to do anent a particular matter, and at the end of the month the presbytery suggested Marion should satisfy in sackcloth before the congregation. This meant she would have to wear a cloak of coarse fabric – the Presbyterian equivalent of the Spanish *san benito*, the tabard of the convicted heretic – stand in front of her entire community at Sunday service, confess her sin, and receive a public rebuke from Mr Ker. Marion was taken aback at the sentence, although she could scarcely have been surprised by it. Such public humiliations were the most common feature of Kirk discipline at the time. She may have protested, because David Young (perhaps her husband) was obliged to stand surety to the session for her compliance – not a usual requirement. James Martin, too, was warned he was going to be disciplined for going to Mrs Kirkby at Marion's request. On 12 September, Marion came to the session and pleaded with it not to make her stand in front of the congregation in sackcloth, and her earnest exhibition of sorrow and guilt was partly successful. The session agreed to release her from the obligation to wear sackcloth, but insisted she make a public avowal of her sin and ask God's forgiveness for it, a penance she is recorded as having performed on 26 September. James Martin, however, was not so pliable. He did not turn up at the session on 12 September, and when he did appear on 19 September, he received a sharp rebuke and was then sent to prison for defying the minister and elders.

The whole affair had lasted for four-and-a-half months, with the kirk session tenaciously pursuing witnesses and examining and re-examining all those concerned until it was satisfied it had got to the bottom of the business. This is typical of the Kirk's procedure in such matters; and if we remember that the 1563 Witchcraft Act was still in force, we can understand the Kirk's rigour but also acknowledge its relative mildness in dealing with magicians and their clients. For the Witchcraft Act imposed the death penalty not only on practitioners of magic but also on any who ventured to use their skills. Under contemporary criminal legislation, therefore, Mrs Kirkby and Marion and James should have been executed. A fairly short period in prison and an hour or two of carefully calculated embarrassment might thus have been considered preferable.

Charming was another magical activity the Kirk sought to suppress. Sometimes it was interpreted as witchcraft, sometimes not; but to the authorities charming represented the living remains of what they called 'superstition' which they were keen to eradicate from their communities in order to replace it with 'godly religion', and therefore instances of its use, when reported, were investigated with rigour. On 6 June 1658, for example, Margaret Imrie was fetched before the kirk session of Dunbarny, a village of south-east Perthshire, to answer charges of trying to cure her daughter by magical means. The story, as it emerged piece by piece under protracted questioning, was a complex one and reveals an interesting picture of magical working in everyday life at village level. Margaret Imrie's daughter, Janet, became ill and so Margaret sent George Brown to Isobel MacKinlay who lived in Dunning, a good ten miles or so south-west of Dunbarny, with instructions to ask her 'if she knew whether her daughter had gotten a glisk of ill wind or no'. A 'glisk' is a short space of time, or something of small duration: but it also means 'a glance', and the obvious implication of this – and perhaps the most likely reason Margaret sent to someone she knew to be a charmer – is that she was worried that Janet's illness might have been caused by the evil eye, a corrosive, deadly look from someone with magical powers, willing to exercise them for malevolent reasons. George took with him some 'bear' (inferior barley) by way of payment, and one of Janet's head-scarves which Isobel could use as a sympathetic link for divination, just as a modern medium may employ for the same purpose something which belongs or has once belonged to the subject of her or his inquiry.

Isobel confirmed that Janet was indeed suffering from a glisk of ill wind, and recommended a charm to chase it away.

Precisely how the charm was supposed to be performed is not altogether clear. According to George's testimony, they were supposed to take a pair of blankets and put Janet through them three times, throwing a stone or a clod of earth after her on each occasion. Margaret Imrie denied using a stone or clod, but mentioned that 'a knot was cast on [the blankets], as on a sowing sheet', which means that they were tied in such a way as to form a kind of bag, just as a 'sowing sheet' was made by folding a piece of canvas into a large pouch to hold corn-seed, the pouch then being hung round the neck of the person sowing. This, however, does not make much sense, because Janet could not have been passed through it. If, on the other hand, each end of each blanket had been knotted together to form a big circle, Janet could certainly have passed through that, and so could a stone: and we know from elsewhere that sick people were frequently made to go through a circle made from the intertwined branches of particular plants. This, then, is more probably what was recommended and done. But, as in cures effected by overt witchcraft, the illness did not merely disappear. It had to go somewhere, and in this case passed into the body of Margaret Dick's son, Hugh Scot. Margaret Dick was Margaret Imrie's mother-in-law, and Hugh Scot was Margaret Dick's son. He fell ill, we are told, 'on Saturday, the first night after the charm was used by Margaret Imrie, and the said Margaret Imrie's daughter was well the time of his sickness, and he never grew better till she grew sick again'.

A session on 20 June elicited further information. What made Margaret Imrie think Isobel was a charmer? Because two years before, when Margaret Dick's daughter, Christian Scot, had been ill, Margaret Dick had sent George Brown to ask her what to do. On that occasion, Isobel had been paid with a measure of peas, and had given George three small stones to put in Christian's hair (or in her bed, according to a later statement). When Ninian Balmain, Margaret Imrie's husband, had been ill, was he put through the blankets, too? Margaret said no, but admitted that Margaret Dick had sent Bessie Balmain (presumably Ninian's sister) to consult Isobel about his case. This evidence of an active magical operator not far away, and what appeared to be frequent consultation of her by more than one member of a local family, gave the kirk session pause, and it spent three weeks thinking about the problem. The various parties reconvened on 13 July when Isobel MacKinlay herself turned up to be grilled by the minister and elders. Asked about the points already alleged against her during the sessions held in June, she denied them all. She also denied advising the two Margarets to wash Janet's feet in the mill stream, and to take her to church after she had been put through the blankets; and no, she had not said that Janet would die if her milk dried up.

She and George Brown were then brought face to face. This confronting was a very common technique used both by kirk sessions and by the criminal courts to see whether both sides or either would stick to their versions of what they had alleged the other had said or done. As soon as Isobel and George met thus, Isobel caved in and admitted everything in detail, including her warning to George on one occasion that he should take heed nothing bad happen to him on his way home. (Was this a magical threat, or was it no more than a friendly warning to watch out for the usual kind of hazards any traveller might meet?)

Isobel had agreed, among so much else, that Bessie Balmain had indeed come to consult her when Ninian Balmain was ill, so Bessie was summoned to appear in front of the session on 25 July. Bessie's evidence complicated the story still further. According to her, William Imrie (possibly Margaret Imrie's father) had sent her to Isobel along with one of Ninian's shirts, and Isobel had told her to wash it, put a live chicken through it, and then dress Ninian in it. The chicken, like the stone or clod in Janet's case, was clearly to serve as a vehicle to which the illness could be transferred and so disposed of; the washing, too, almost certainly referred to the magical practice of washing a shirt in clean, south-running water – a prescription frequently given by magical operators such as Isobel – and then putting it, still wet, on the patient. George Brown, said Bessie, had given Isobel's name to the local troopers (a reminder that Scotland was under military occupation), and had advised her (Bessie) to say that Bessie Flockhart and Eppie Scot, both of whom were now dead, had recommended she go to consult Isobel. Blaming the dead was, of course, a simple device to deflect blame from the living. Margaret Imrie, asked on the same day if she had given Bessie one of her husband's shirts, denied it and said it was Ninian's mother who had given the shirt to Bessie. Ninian's mother was conveniently dead at the time of the questioning.

The session had not forgotten that Margaret Dick's son, Hugh Scot, had had Janet's illness magically thrown upon him by Isobel's charm. So on 1 August, Hugh was brought before the session, where he denied his wife had been charmed and put the suggestion down to gossip. Ninian Balmain almost supported him, saying that on the night the charm was being used, Hugh had said to him, 'I don't know if anything is being done in my house tonight', to which Ninian replied he should beware of it. But Ninian flatly denied to the minister and elders that he knew anything about what was done to him while he was ill. The session had heard enough, at least for the time being, and suspended both Margarets, George Brown, and Hugh Scot from the sacrament because of their involvement in these magical operations. It also submitted the affair to the presbytery for further advice.

On 7 August, Robert Young, who had been minister of Dunbarny since 1647, reported that the presbytery had accepted Ninian's plea of ignorance. For the rest, however, inquisition ground on and on. On 5 September, both Margarets and George admitted consulting, but Hugh persisted in his denials. On 19 September, his sister, Christian Scot, who had also been a subject for consultation with Isobel, was finally brought in for questioning, but said that her mother, Margaret Dick, had offered to charm her but she had refused. Hugh Scot failed to turn up to this session – no reason is given for his absence – and indeed drops out of the record entirely until, ten months later, on 30 July 1659 he was rebuked by the minister in front of the session (but not the congregation) for taking part in the charming of his wife, and was then re-admitted to the sacrament. The others, however, were not to enjoy any respite. On 3 October, Bessie Balmain was asked if she had recommended anyone else to make use of charming, and admitted she had told Agnes Dron and John Wright, Agnes's husband, that his illness was just like Ninian's. So via Bessie they consulted Isobel, who told them to wash his shirt in the water below the mill. John Wright was summoned and agreed that the facts were so. At the end of the month, Agnes made her appearance and admitted likewise. On 19 December, Margaret Imrie confessed her sin in sackcloth before the congregation, and was then received into communion with the Kirk again. Margaret Dick and George Brown, however, were not so easy to bring to repentance. It took until 29 May 1659 before George made his public confession, and Margaret, in spite of three separate summonses during August and September, stayed away, appearing on 11 September only to say she had not been well. It is possible this was true, of course, but on 25 September she came before the session, giving no sign of recognition she had done anything wrong; so the session postponed her case for a fortnight, presumably to give her time to change her mind. But this she did not do until 11 December, and even then something must have been unsatisfactory, because the prospect of her doing public penance dragged on into March 1660, when it is recorded she was sick, until finally, on 15 July the record tells us that 'Margaret Dick signified her repentance for charming before the congregation, as she was ordained, and was received'. It had taken over two years to bring her to this conclusion. Bessie Balmain, for whatever reason, took a day or two longer, the presbytery records showing that it was not until 18 July that the presbytery recommended to the parish of Forgandenny, where she was then resident, that she do penance in sackcloth for her sin of charming. This, however, was just the presbytery record. We do not know when, or indeed if, Bessie did as she was told.

One or two points are worth making anent this affair. The tenacity of the Kirk in pursuing its inquiries is typical of its determination to discover the entire truth of complaints or allegations brought before it – not just those involving magic, but other offences too, such as slander or adultery or infanticide. Church records give little evidence of any partial animus against magical practitioners in particular, and indeed illustrate the concern of Kirk officials generally to do justice in as far as they could. In this, they resemble the officials of the various Catholic Inquisitions who, like them, were eager to save souls and redeem any offences which may have been committed against God, and who had a tendency to regard witches, especially if they were women, as silly and misguided rather than viciously malevolent. The Inquisitions, like the Scottish Kirk, also placed a high value on procedural propriety; so the notion that either they or the Kirk were committed to persecution, or conducted their business without proper regard to the requirements of either legal or natural justice is, in the main, mistaken. Unlike Inquisitorial records, however, those of the kirk and presbytery sessions tend to be somewhat sketchy. The detailed circumstances of each inquiry, fully known to or quickly discovered by the minister and elders, are therefore missing, and it is often difficult for us to follow exactly what had been going on prior to the accused's appearances before the session. But we may reasonably presume, because of the evident thoroughness with which examinations were carried out, that the truth, or at least something very close to it, usually came out in the end. So when Margaret Imrie, Margaret Dick, and the others finally admitted they actually had used the charms recommended by Isobel MacKinlay, there is a good chance their admissions were truthful and that, in consequence, their subsequent punishment was justified.

One can always speculate, of course, on such things as official pressure, their neighbours' disapproval, the shame of being barred from communion – a potent consideration in close-knit rural communities in which standing, credit, and respect are intimately bound up with adherence to the expectations of one's neighbours. But speculation needs to be founded on evidence, otherwise it is pointless, and in most cases, including those we have looked at here, evidence of undue or harsh pressure is largely missing. So verdicts of 'guilty' should be allowed to stand unless we have very good reason to call them into question. Anent this general point, it is also worth bearing in mind that people did not always automatically cave in to whatever pressures may have been exerted to get them to confess and conform. Neither Hugh Scot nor George Brown, for example, readily acceded to the Kirk's sentence, and if it be argued they were men and perhaps less easily intimidated than women, one should note that Margaret Dick and Bessie Balmain held out much longer than either of them. Nor were Margaret or Bessie unique in this respect, as we shall see. So if a member of a congregation thought that she or he had been hard done by in a disciplinary hearing by the session, it was not uncommon for that person to disregard summonses to appear, or to fight a rearguard action against the requirement to be publicly humiliated. Consequently, the Kirk could not take for granted in any given case that either the imposition of Church discipline on the one hand, or the surrender of long-cherished beliefs and practices on the other, were easily or even permanently achieved.

It is also worth noting how readily – if we accept the basic truth of the narrative – the people involved in the Dunbarny case consulted a magical practitioner, particularly when they had to travel some distance to get to her. There may not have been such a person in Dunbarny at the time, of course, or Isobel may have accumulated a reputation as the kind of healer Margaret Imrie and her various relatives were looking for, or they may not have wanted their neighbours to know they were consulting a charmer, and so chose to go to one living ten miles or so away. In this latter case, one motive may have been nervousness lest their neighbours elect to give the name 'witchcraft' to what was only magical healing. Healing by magic was bad enough and would certainly attract the disapproval and censure of the Kirk. An accusation of witchcraft, however, would put the accused parties in serious jeopardy of being handed over to the civil magistrate, and from there the step to a criminal court was very short. Yet Margaret and the others were willing to take a risk, and to take it on several occasions. Their confidence or hope in the charmer's abilities or knowledge overrode any hesitations they may have experienced; and, of course, after they had consulted Isobel once and got away with it, they may have felt somewhat bolder the second and third times. Indeed, the narrative leads one to wonder if it was not actually a neighbour's complaint which led to their several interrogations by the Kirk, but a pettish or angry gesture by George Brown who gave Isobel's name to troopers after one of his visits to her.

This business of handing in someone's name to the authorities is known as 'delation' and was a very frequent cause of arrest and inquisition for witchcraft. It happened more than once, for example, to John Corse and his wife, Margaret Beveridge. Isobel Prop in Dysart, a coastal town in the Kingdom of Fife, had been arrested for witchcraft and imprisoned in the tolbooth of the town. While there, she delated John and Margaret who were thereupon brought to the tolbooth on 25 October 1643 to be questioned by the town baillies, two of the kirk elders, and James Craig, the kirk precentor (the man who led the singing during church serv-ices). Isobel confessed to being a witch and was later executed, so her testimony was grave and potentially very dangerous for both John and Margaret. But nothing seems to have come of it, for we find the self-same delation repeated, again in Dysart, on 16 December 1647, when Grissell Rankin confessed she was a witch and named them as witches, too. Once more, Grissell was executed but John and Margaret seem to have escaped at least the most serious consequences of being delated. Indeed, three years later John gave fifty merks to the kirk in Auchtermuchty and was thanked for it officially, as a minute for 8 December 1650 records, in which we learn he was a meal-maker and a burgess of Dyce. He was thus clearly a man with a degree of social status within his community, since the burgess was a free citizen of a burgh, with full municipal rights, and should be accounted a member of the upper ranks of urban society. The 'meal' he dealt was oatmeal – other types of grain were designated by their particular name in Scotland – and he would have bought it in bulk, ground it to flour, and then sold it to individual customers. The merk was minted as a silver coin during this period, and while it is impossible to give it a modern equivalent value, we can perhaps gain some notion of what fifty merks represented from a document of 1611, relating to the regulation of wages in Fife. This tells us that six merks (or £4 Scots) was supposed to be six months' wages for the lower grade of agricultural servants. John Corse's gift, therefore, represents four times the regulated annual wage of such a worker in Fife forty years earlier.[3]

But the fact that both he and his wife had been delated twice in what may have been their native parish – a Robert Corse and a Robert Beveridge are both recorded as living in Dysart in 1630 – was sufficient to store up trouble and, sure enough, on 12 December 1657, John appeared before the kirk session and not only confessed that he himself was a witch, but delated his wife Margaret, too, along with another woman, Margaret Williamson. We know that Margaret Beveridge was arrested and imprisoned. It seems reasonable to suggest that, under the circumstances, the other two were arrested and imprisoned as well. John then came before the session again on 16 December, and furnished details of how he came to be a witch. (These I have transposed into the first person.)

About eighteen years ago [c.1639], I was at Balbirnie Mill. Two men approached me. One of them was carrying a book. I told him to enter my name in his book, but he said he would not until he saw which way I was going to go. Ten days later they both came there again, and asked me for several things which I refused to give them. The Devil answered that flesh and blood had not given me that [? stubbornness]. Later on, I came to the village of Galatown at about nine or ten at night. There I met a number of women and said I wanted to go to Robert Lessel's house. They said they had already been there and had come from it.

I was transported to the west end of the town, I don't know how. When I arrived at my own house, I found Agnes Halket and Margaret Williamson

(Robert Swyne's wife) sitting there with the door barred shut. I asked, 'How did you get in?' and they said, 'Through the lock'. The Devil, looking like a black man, was in my house. Margaret Williamson called me outside. I asked her if that was her husband, and she said, 'Yes'. The Devil then vanished from my sight. Margaret told me to open the door, and I told him to leave as she was coming in.

Later on, Margaret Williamson took me to the Three Trees. The Devil was there and said to [the women], 'What's that you've brought me now?' Margaret answered, 'A man who has a good reputation upon earth'. The Devil said, 'Why have you brought me this older man?' He'll [just] go back again'. They asked what they should do with me and the Devil said, 'Take him back the way he came. He'll bring shame on you all'. Then the women called out, 'The time is passing. Mark him!' The Devil marked me on my right cheek. I renounced my baptism, and put one hand on the crown of my head and the other on the sole of my foot, and gave everything between my hands to the Devil.

This confession was made to and witnessed by James Wilson, the minister, Andrew Bond, the schoolmaster, James Craig, the precentor, and James Johnston, who is designated as a 'wright', and was probably one of the kirk elders. James Craig, we may recall, was precentor at the time of John and Margaret's delation in 1643. Is there some connection to be made between the arrest in 1657 and that previous incident? Unfortunately, the evidence allows us to do no more than ask that question.

Three weeks later, on 7 January 1658, John appeared before the minister and William Gay and repeated his allegation that his wife Margaret was also a witch. Referring back to the time they were in Auchtermuchty, he said that one night in *c.*1651 she and Margaret Williamson came to his bedside, and that when he himself 'entered in covenant with the Devil', his wife and Margaret Williamson and Agnes Halket were present. After he had made the pact, the Devil said to him, 'What do you want in return for this gift you have given me?' John answered, 'Nothing', and his wife said, 'What will you do with the various people who owe you money?' Next day, his wife said to him that she had got her revenge on him. John also told the minister and William Gay that Janet Ross, who was herself delated as a witch, asked him one day if there were any rats in the house after his wife had left, and advised him to stay in the house till his wife came back. John answered he saw only one rat, a very big one, sitting on top of the chest. He went to brush it off and it ran away, and Janet said, 'That rat was your wife'. It looks as though most of this information is a kind of appendage to his December testimony. The dating to *c.*1651, and Margaret Beveridge's reference to John's good reputation which his generosity in 1650 would have confirmed, if not initiated, suggest that John's becoming a witch took place in or near Auchtermuchty. The anecdote about his wife's shape-changing, however, is new and there are no clear indications about when this alleged incident is supposed to have taken place.

A week later, on 14 January, Margaret Beveridge came before the session. We are told she had been imprisoned 'for witchcraft', which may mean she had been arrested on specific charges of working magic, but is more likely to mean she had been detained on suspicion of being a witch. She confessed that this indeed was the case, and that she had met the Devil (who was wearing black clothes) at the Three Trees. She also met him in her own house – a detail which tallies with part of her husband's December evidence – at which time he seems to have had a distinctive physical defect, a cloven or, as we might say, a hare-lip. Margaret renounced her baptism and gave herself to the Devil with the same containing gestures John had used – this method was very common, and appears over and over again in seventeenth-century Scottish testimonies – but said she felt afraid when he gave her the mark. She also delated Margaret Williamson, and said that Margaret had vanished from her on two separate occasions, once on the moor and once while dancing at the Three Trees. She added that it was light that night. One can supply the likely preceding question from the session: since it was night-time, how did she know Margaret had vanished and not simply left?

Her confession was witnessed by two baillies and two ministers, James Wilson and Robert Honyman, both of Dysart, who also noted that by the time they were signing the written account of these proceedings, Margaret had gone back on what she had said 'without any torturing' to the session, and was now denying it altogether. I shall return to that phrase about torturing, but for the moment it is more useful to pursue the remaining testimonies so that we have a complete picture of what the records tell us was said by the principal parties. On 17 January, John was summoned to the session yet again, and more or less repeated what he had told it before: Margaret Williamson had called him out of his house and accompanied him to the Three Trees where the Devil was in company with a number of witches; John gave himself to the Devil; the Devil asked him what he wanted in return and he said, 'Nothing'. John also said that the Devil came to him once at Balbirnie Mill, and turned away from him 'like a brussell coke', that is, a bristle-cock. This may be a reference to shape-changing, but is perhaps more likely to describe the Devil's manner of leaving, offended, angry, arrogant. A few new assertions, however, make their appearance. This departure by the Devil is one of them. John also said that Margaret Williamson made a complaint about him to the Devil, and that when the witches asked him to dance, he said he could not; and then one of them cried out, 'The time is running away! Mark him, mark him!' whereupon the Devil threw him to the ground at his feet, and marked him.

On 21 January, a Crispin Swyne came to Dysart kirk session and told it that about five years before (c.1653), he met John Corse in Falkland, and that John had told him he [John] would do him an ill turn; and Crispin claimed that, as a result of this, he 'became distracted', a phrase meaning anything from troubled to raving mad. It may be pertinent here to remember that Margaret Williamson's husband was a Robert Swyne, so Crispin may have been a relation – Robert's brother, perhaps, or son – and therefore a man with both a family as well as a personal animus against John. This piece of information was written down by James Craig, described here as 'clerk to the session', who may or may not have been the same as James Craig the precentor. Then, on 22 January, John appeared one final time before the session and unburdened himself of a number of new and interesting statements. First, 'to convince his wife Margaret Beveridge of her sin of witchcraft', he said that in about 1656 the Devil stayed in his house all night. He looked like a man with a hare-lip, and Margaret tried to tell John that this was her brother-in-law and (for some unexplained reason) made them share a bed. John, however, maintained that the man was not Margaret's brother-in-law, but one of the men who had once tried to tempt him – perhaps a reference to the incident at Balbirnie Mill in c.1639. John, the record says, 'further desired his wife to confess, that she might get her soul saved'. It is not clear from this whether she was present at the session and John was addressing her directly, or whether he was explaining to the minister and elders why he was apparently so keen to 'convince' her of her sin. 'Convince' is ambiguous. Was he trying to demonstrate to her in the teeth of her intransigence that what she had been doing was wicked, or was he trying to get her convicted as a witch by the session in order to give the minister an opportunity to lead her back to God? His evidence is partial, of course. He may have been wanting to throw some kind of favourable gloss on his own case by suggesting that his motives anent his wife were Christian and charitable, or, of course, the face-value of his words may represent their genuine worth. It is impossible to be sure from so cursory a remark.

Secondly, John returned to his time in Auchtermuchty and said that while he was engaged in buying corn, Margaret came to him 'in another likeness than her own', something he had never spoken about before. When asked what she was like, he said her complexion was much darker than usual. She also said to him, 'Tie up the mouth of your sack before you pay for the corn'. This sounds like a warning to him not to be dishonest, not to try to slip more corn into the sack after he had paid for a certain weight. Apart from the reference to Margaret's unusually dark complexion (which scarcely amounts to the magical shape-change suggested by 'another likeness than her own'), however, this revelation has nothing to do with witchcraft or being a witch, and, indeed, is rather odd. Why would John want to suggest to the session that his wife (or even some other woman rather like her) suspected he was trying to cheat his customer and came forward to warn him not to do so? But John's third confession to the minister and elders may reveal that he was trying to clear his conscience of past wrong-doing, for he admitted that he had twice committed fornication, and three or four times adultery, once with a woman from Dundee, and twice or thrice with a Katharine Ross in Dysart.

All these confessions by both John and Margaret appear as extracts from the session records copied and signed as documents to be presented to the Court of Justiciary in Edinburgh. The dossier is dated 2 February 1658 and labelled 'Confession, John Corse, warlock'. A further record tells us he was executed. Margaret's fate is not known, and neither Margaret Williamson nor Agnes Halket appear elsewhere, so we have no idea whether they were pursued or not. But as for John, an assize [jury] listened to the evidence we have, and probably to much more of which the record has not survived, and found itself sufficiently convinced of his culpability to declare him guilty. Is there anything in the testimonies we have which may furnish some kind of clue to that fatal verdict?

The first thing one has to acknowledge is the difficulty inherent in reading such manuscript accounts, be they kirk and presbytery session records or summaries of criminal trials. Such records are hardly objective, for example, and are liable to omit as much as they include. Court records frequently give an abbreviated version of the evidence which was presented to the court on the day of trial. This means we are reading the résumé of a narrative which has already been through several stages of question and answer over what could have been a long period of time. There are instances of accused persons' spending weeks or even months either in prison or on caution [bail], and naturally there is every chance that during the interval the accused may alter or expand or (as in Margaret Beveridge's case) deny an earlier version of events. Kirk session records often help one to follow the narrative a little more easily, because one can see its outlines, and sometimes its details, developing or changing over time. Even so, there is no telling whether the record of a person's interrogation by the minister and elders was written down immediately, or reconstructed later from notes or memory when the clerk to the session decided to bring the session-book up to date. Speculation, therefore, should necessarily be tentative and kept to a minimum.

According to John's testimony, he and his wife were not on the best of terms. The day after he had given himself to the Devil, his wife said she had got her revenge on him. It is a strong statement. Revenge for what? Not for his fornications and adulteries, if we are to believe John when he says he had never confessed them before. Auchtermuchty and Dysart were both small places. Had word of his offences leaked out, he would have been in trouble before December 1657, and his adultery in Dundee was far enough removed, perhaps, for him to have escaped a revelation in Dysart. So if these immoralities were indeed confessed for the first time in January 1658, and if – a crucial 'if' – Margaret Beveridge had not known about them before, her revenge would have been taken for some other offence, an offence of which we know nothing because the record does not provide anything which might offer an adequate explanation. But there is, of course, always the possibility that Margaret never said anything of the kind, and the statement is just part of John's attempt to shift some of the burden of accusation from himself to her, since it certainly looks as though he is trying to portray himself as a victim.

Puzzles indeed increase as we look at the record. John's testimony in December contains episodes which are, on preliminary reading, odd. His encounter with two men who approached *him* has the appearance of some sort of business meeting, with John eager to join some kind of a consortium and the others not keen until they had proof of his worth and reliability, until the record identifies one of the men as the Devil. Was this John's original statement, or was it put into his head by a question from one of his interrogators? The Devil's remark that 'flesh and blood did not give you that' is reminiscent of 'flesh and blood have not revealed it unto thee' (*Matthew* 16.17), and more distantly of 'we wrestle not against flesh and blood, but against Principalities, against Powers, against the rulers of the darkness of this world' (*Ephesians* 6.12) – Biblical echoes which John, certainly, could have carried in his head, but which could also have come readily from the minister, James Wilson, or James Craig, the precentor. Similarly, when John met some women in Galatown, said he wanted to go to Robert Lessel's house, and was told the women had already been there and come away, there is nothing to suggest that these were witches except the following sentence – 'I was transported to the west end of the town, I don't know how'. In the record, this reads as though it happened straight away in Galatown, and implies that the women were somehow responsible. In fact, it could be an entirely separate incident and the reason for its inclusion at this point is lost to us. The word 'thereafter' which occurs several times in the narrative is no guide to anything like precise timing, and we are here faced with one of the difficulties attendant upon trying to interpret what survives for us to read. Our tendency is to want to make sense of the testimony by pulling it together and interpreting it as a concerted whole, a tendency which we probably ought to resist. The record of someone's confession (to any offence, not simply witchcraft) may be fragmentary for all kinds of circumstantial reasons about which we know nothing, and the evidence, of which the remaining records were only a part, was such as made sense to a contemporary assize, some of whose members, at least, would be acquainted with, or indeed have intimate knowledge of, those very same circumstances.

The only real clue we have to John and Margaret's finding themselves investigated for a third time on the charge of being witches is that simple fact – that it was the third time. We have noted, too, the apparent presence of a James Craig from the start. Whatever or whoever precipitated the accusation this final time, the previous occasions are likely to have told against them, on the principle of no smoke without fire. People were not silly. They could tell the difference between malicious gossip and serious delation. The number of times kirk sessions dealt with name-calling between angry neighbours is very high and, since the members of the sessions were well acquainted with local details which escape us, such as a person's reputation, common behaviour, financial and marital circumstances, and so forth, they were able to judge how far to press their investigations into charges of witchcraft or being a witch. Dysart knew, or thought it knew, enough to pursue both John and Margaret as far as the criminal court and therefore must have been in possession of evidence it regarded as substantial. Dysart itself was not in the grip of anything remotely like witch fever at the time, and so it cannot be suggested the town was persecuting rather than prosecuting the couple. But being a witch was a serious offence. Substitute the word 'paedophile' for 'witch', and gauge the effect of such a charge in a small community these days. So there can be little doubt that Dysart believed it was protecting itself against two heinously wicked people when it sent them on to Edinburgh.

This brings us to a final, but significant point about John and Margaret's case. Their testimonies describe how the two of them became witches, but say nothing at all about any magic they may have practised later. Now, this difference is important, for unless we are to assume that whole swathes of evidence relating to their maleficent activities have either been lost or were not included in the material sent forward to the Court of Justiciary – a somewhat unlikely assumption – we are presented with people whose offence was becoming a witch and not actually practis-ing witchcraft. It may seem, of course, that the two should, indeed must, go together; but in fact the two offences are not the same. Becoming a witch was in essence apostasy from the Christian religion. The Jesuit Martín Del Rio, one of the great European authorities on all the occult arts, whose work was known and used in Scotland, was perfectly clear on this point. 'Workers of harmful magic [*malefici*] or witches [*lamiae*] withdraw from God by a deliberate denial of God and the Faith. This is apostasy'. Practising magic of any kind, on the other hand, tended to be seen more as an expression of idolatry, and again Del Rio is forthright: 'All forbidden magic is tacit idolatry'.[4] Now, one of the most potent influences in Scotland during this period was the effect of the Solemn

League and Covenant, a declaration made in 1643 by 'the noblemen, barons, knights, gentlemen, citizens, burgesses, ministers of the Gospel, and commons of all sorts, in the kingdoms of Scotland, England, and Ireland' that they would seek to preserve their version of Christianity against its enemies and extirpate not only Catholicism and Anglicanism, but also 'superstition, heresy, schism, profaneness, and whatsoever shall be found to be contrary to sound doctrine and the power of godliness'. Such a declaration is likely to create an embattled section of society which sees divagations from its accepted modes of thinking and belief as heretical at best and apostatical at worst, and therefore there may have been elements in Scottish society more primed in these post-Covenant decades to point an accusing finger at those they suspected of abandoning Christianity altogether by handing themselves over to Satan. Whether the accused went on to take advantage of his or her apostasy, and persuade the Evil Spirit to enable them to work wonders beyond natural human ability, was almost irrelevant. This merely added to the number of their crimes. Becoming a witch was crime enough in itself to warrant the severest punishment according to either the Biblical or the criminal law prescribed for such people.

The Covenant – and we should bear in mind that there had already been one expression of this kind of religious solidarity in 1638 – drew together the godly, and thereby separated them, in their own perception, from the ungodly, just as the witches' covenant drew together adherents of the Devil and thereby separated them from faithful Christians. Presbyterians in general, and Covenanters in particular, were led by the powerful dictates of their religious convictions to live in a world in which there was no middle ground between right and wrong. Everything was an expression of one or the other. The National Covenant of 1638, for example, begins with a ringing declaration of this sense of personally determined certitude: 'We, all and every one of us underwritten, protest that, after long and due examination of our own consciences in matters of true and false religion, we are now thoroughly resolved in the truth by the Word and Spirit of God'.[5] With Scotland itself conquered by the English, the Kirk in a collapse of bitterly feuding factions, and many people both high and low, minister and layperson, motivated by an inner certainty that they were a godly few embattled against constant assaults by enemies of every kind, post-Covenant Scots found themselves in a period of intense and increasing agitation, a psychological state rachetted almost to distraction by the constant stream of sermons to which everyone was subjected. The diary of Sir Archibald Johnston of Wariston gives us examples of the effects of this kind of religious bombardment.

> After sermon, in my sister's gallery, I got floods of tears remembering first the seventh verse of the forty-sixth Psalm... At night, I meditated on the forenoon's sermon and had religious dreams. On Monday morning, I got many tears, acknowledging and blessing God for turning my affliction to the sensible [deeply feeling] weal of my soul and increase of graces in me... Then I meditated on the afternoon's sermon and read the seventh chapter of *Deuteronomy*... At night, I meditated on the eighth chapter of *Deuteronomy*... I found my heart melt unto floods of tears... On Tuesday... At night, I got abundance of tears, meditating on [Henry] Scudder his treatise on fasting.

Now, Sir Archibald had been one of those responsible for the drafting of both the National Covenant and the Solemn League and Covenant, a man, therefore, of the strictest religious scruples and principles – in August 1654 he noted he had spoken sharply to his wife and daughter because they had been dancing at a wedding – and yet he did not hesitate to record that he was accustomed to use divination, (one of the occult sciences especially condemned by all writers on demonology and witchcraft as especially pernicious), as a means of guiding his mind when he was in doubt over what to do on a given occasion. On 11 August 1654, for example, he wrote:

> I fell on ejaculating for the Lord's settling my mind about my going, and thought I was in perplexity these two days and would never be clear anent the Lord's mind whether to abide or stay but by trying by the lot, whether I should cast the lot anent my going or not; and, if it was not to cast, to take it for not going, which was the common advice of folk. And so, after prayer and laying my hand on my Bible and on my covenant with the Lord, and earnest conjuring [invoking] of the Lord my God as he loved Jesus Christ, the Son of His love, that he would direct me aright, that if the lot was to cast and then to go, I might find his special protection... and if it was not to cast or casting not to go, he would let me find

his gracious direction in it… after some conjuring ejaculations, I drew the lot and it was not to cast and so to stay.[6]

A village magical operator, casting lots on behalf of one of his clients, would scarcely have done less; but he would certainly have found himself in front of his kirk session on charges which might turn serious, should his client or a neighbour be so affected by a sermon that she decided to complain to the authorities; and, to be fair, so too would Sir Archibald had any of his associates called into question the desirability of what he was doing. But if Sir Archibald, for all his genuine religious enthusiasm, could permit himself the use of what were, in essence, magical methods to determine a course of action – and he admits to doing so on at least six occasions in a twelve-month period – it is scarcely surprising that others less socially advantaged and perhaps less religiously exalted thought no shame or difficulty in employing both these and similar practices. Was this hypocrisy on Sir Archibald's part? Not necessarily. The intense religious circumambience of his casting, the presence of the Bible and (most significantly because of the multiple associations of the word) his covenant, may well have quietened any notion he may have had that the practice was in any way similar to those of the diviners. They, after all, were ungodly: he was not.

We can see, therefore, a number of themes which need to be explored further. The post-Covenant decades, and the 1650s in particular, constituted a period during which people's personal, religious, and political self-awareness existed in a hothouse atmosphere created by a combination of military invasion, foreign occupation, and internal religious fissiparousness; and it is this which forms the peculiar circumambience of prosecutions for magical activity throughout these years. The peroration of the Solemn League and Covenant gave expression to the mood: 'Because these kingdoms are guilty of many sins and provocations against God, and his Son, Jesus Christ, as is too manifest by our present distresses and dangers, the fruits thereof; we profess and declare before God and the world our unfeigned desire to be humbled for our sins'. What is more, the very idea of a covenant was, as Ian Bostridge has pointed out, 'a vital part of [Scottish] political theory and theology' at this time, while 'covenant-breaking [was] condemned and associated with diabolical forces'.[7] It is thus no accident that during a Royalist pageant in Linlithgow, an arch, bearing the text 'Rebellion is the Mother of Witchcraft' and showing an old woman holding the covenant, was burned.

'Magical activity', of course, is a blanket term which covers a very wide range of offences under the law, and Stuart MacDonald has suggested that one may detect two kinds of prosecution directed at two different kinds of magical activity: one driven by the accused's local community, members of which were taking steps to resolve grievances caused by what they perceived as acts of personal animosity expressed through magical actions; the other caused more by specific tensions within the secular or ecclesiastical élites who gave vent to their frustrations, whether political or religious in origin, by seeking to excise from the wider community individuals and groups of people whom they regarded as inimical to the social or political or religious advancement of the nation towards their envisioned utopia.[8] These two kinds of prosecution, however – supposing for the moment that there were indeed two kinds – clearly proceeded for the most part at different paces at different times and in different locations, although a degree of overlapping here and there is only to be expected.

We have already seen that kirk and presbytery sessions tended to deal with the various complaints about alleged magical activity which came before them according to ecclesiastical and not secular discipline, as one might expect. Accused persons, even when adjudged guilty, were not automatically handed over to the secular arm for further trial, depending, of course, on the nature of the alleged offence; and the Witchcraft Act of 1563 thus did not often intrude into the deliberations of ministers and kirk elders. So two sets of trial and two sets of penalties were in operation at any given time. On the one hand, small local groups sought to humiliate the guilty, bring them to repentance, and thereby reintegrate them into the godly society; on the other, the criminal courts passed the death sentence on those found guilty by an assize, in an effort to purge and purify the state by radical surgery. Witch-prosecution was therefore a much more complex process than has sometimes been allowed, and part of our task will be to set out some of the complexities so that a more subtle apprehension of these episodes can begin to be seized. It will also be necessary to investigate the role of Satan and the question of torture, two major aspects of evidence produced for witch trials not only in Scotland but in many places all over Europe, to see what their role may have been. The results of such investigation may not be quite what is commonly asserted.

CHAPTER ONE

1657: Neither Devil Nor Hunt

As far as witches and witchcraft were concerned, the authorities would not have found 1657 especially taxing.[1] In February, John Cock complained to the Canongate kirk session that William Braidie had called his mother a witch; in Dirleton, Elspeth Darge told the March session that Jean Nicholson had called her, her mother, and her grandmother witches, and Margaret Kemp that Marion Henderson had said she was a 'fairy lady runt that the Devil rode on'. In Dalkeith Agnes Hunter and Isobel Boyd, her mother, were found guilty of calling Christian Douglas a witch and were referred to the town baillies for civil punishment, a proceeding which argues that they may have caused trouble before and that the kirk session had run out of patience with them. In May, John Wadie gave in a bill to the Carrington session, asserting that James Nisbet had called him a warlock; and in Inchture and Rossie, Agnes Hately said that Elspeth Milner and Elspeth Moncur had called her a witch. All these incidents of name-calling, save that in Dalkeith, were settled by the usual Sunday humiliation and the parties being required to reconcile themselves, one with the other. Inchture and Rossie, however, had trouble with Elspeth Milner who refused to acknowledge she had done anything wrong, and declined to turn up for punishment until the end of September – a potentially dangerous defiance, because kirk sessions were by no means reluctant to refer

recalcitrant individuals, not just to the baillies but to the civil magistrate to ensure the authorities' will be obeyed, as when South Leith
in Edinburgh referred Marion Gotterstoun and Catharine Cowan in
December 1659 for calling Margaret Telfer a witch, and in November
1661 Jean Duncan who had garnered the reputation of being a witch
after an unstated period of name-calling.

In January, Falkland busied itself mightily with Grissell Hutchin and
Margaret Walker who were in the habit of sending people to Airth, a
small village in east Stirlingshire, where there was a spring known as the
'Lady well', whose waters were deemed to have curative powers. Several
people had been persuaded to go there, recite the Creed, leave money
and perhaps a napkin, and bring home some water without letting it
touch the ground; and the kirk session was much perturbed until the
middle of May when, at the end of five months' inquisition of everyone even remotely concerned, the congregation was warned en masse
not to go to the well, under pain of ecclesiastical censure. (Falkland was
not the only parish to be troubled by what looks like a combination of
ancient superstition and Catholic pilgrimage, of course. Dunfermline,
for example, censured Andrew Burns in August 1648 for allowing his
wife to go to a similar well and spend the night in the grounds of an
abandoned Catholic chapel to seek cure for what is called her 'madness';
and in April the following year, the two men who accompanied her
there, clearly acting as minders or nurses, were also obliged to make public repentance for doing so.) In January 1657 Margaret Palmer in Kelso
was accused by Janet Murray of charming her own son who, presumably,
was sick. Apparently Janet had peered through a hole in the adjoining
wall of their houses, and both seen and heard the procedure. When asked
if she had heard any words of the charm, Janet told the session she saw
Margaret 'rapping and gaping and holding up her hands and mutter-
ing with herself, but knew not the words'. Margaret then said she came
into Janet's house, still gaping and yawning, and Janet remarked that she
had been at no good. Accused of charming her son, however, Margaret
was not abashed and said she would do it again. In February, John Mill
and Isobel MacKie came before the kirk session in Inverurie on charges
of charming, while in June, the kirk session of Elgin issued an appeal
from the pulpit, 'that any that knows anything of William Donaldson for
charming, let them declare it to the ministers or elders'.

'Charming' was a very broad term and covered a wide spectrum of magical practices, as can be seen, for example, in Petty kirk session's prohibition in April that same year of the use of needfire, fire produced by the vigorous rubbing of dry wood, which was supposed to have magical properties and to be efficacious in curing or preventing disease in cattle, or ensuring success in fishing, and Humbie's investigation of Agnes Gourlay's 'charming' which consisted of her preventing cows from producing cream in their milk, a piece of maleficent magic which, had the kirk session chosen to view it so, was proximate to witchcraft. That September, the presbytery of Dunoon moved to stamp out a particular practice within its bounds, having heard the case of Marie MacIldowie, a midwife, who had charmed a child by putting a rope or cord of plaited straw around its waist, then cut the straw into three pieces and cast them into the fire. Dunoon chose simply to require Marie to undergo public penance, but William Donaldson had been playing with fire if he did perform any kind of charm, regardless of whether it was with good or ill intent, for the kirk session of Elgin was not inclined to be patient. In January that year, James Stronach was called before it because he claimed to have been frightened by witches when he was out walking near a deep pool known as the 'Order Pot'. He had seen neither man nor woman, but 'there was a great wind, and he was once driven back, and it continued till he passed the gibbet'. Whether the session took him seriously or dismissed him as a time-waster, we do not know; but it still readily referred him to the local justice of the peace. Margaret Palmer from Kelso, too, for all her bravado, had stirred up a hornets' nest for herself. On 11 November the previous year (1656), she had actually come to Janet Murray and asked her to go to the far end of the town and bring her a clean shirt to put on, because 'she feared that Janet Thomson would delate her and cause her to be brought before the judges' as a witch.

In Cullen in Forfarshire, Margaret Philp, wife of Gilbert Imblaugh, was arrested on charges of witchcraft in January. The justice ordered her release until advice had been sought from the presbytery of Ruthven – by the look of it, an instance of a state official's insisting upon the Kirk's following the proper ecclesiastical procedure before he would hear the case himself. This was done, and then in February, he and the minister of Cullen and several kirk elders met in the tolbooth of Cullen to hear the evidence against her. Such a meeting in such a place constituted something between a kirk session and a civil court hearing, so the evidence against Margaret must have been considered rather too serious for the session to deal with alone. This evidence consisted of a number of allegations by her own servant, Isobel Imblaugh, who, judging by her surname, may have been related in some way to her husband. The burden of Isobel's testimony was that Margaret had had dealings with a spirit in the form of a hare. Isobel said she saw this spirit and heard it say, more than once, 'Give me that cross-eyed witch, Maggie Soullie, for she is mine', to which Margaret replied, 'Go away, Satan, common lying thief!' The spirit asked Margaret for food, and Isobel saw her put out a bannock (a round, flat cake often made from oatmeal), a drink of unfermented beer, and a piece of meat, all of which, Margaret had told her, were gone the following morning. According to Isobel, Margaret had threatened her and told her not to tell anyone what she had seen and heard. Isobel then went off to fetch some water, and on her return saw Margaret flying above the house.

Margaret's husband, Gilbert Imblaugh, confirmed everything 'except that in particular anent the hare'. This is perhaps an important reservation, because it leaves open the possibility that Margaret was acting under the inspiration of a spirit-guide whom she heard and maybe saw herself, but whose alleged existence had to be reported by her to other people. There are one or two clues which lead to this tentative conclusion. When Margaret was examined by the presbytery, she confessed 'that the voice that spoke to her was the voice of the Devil'. If we allow that this identification of the voice may have owed more to the examining ministers than to Margaret herself, we are still left with a voice; and we find that several of the reported conversations between Margaret and the spirit were reported by Margaret who is saying, in effect, that she frequently heard a voice which badgered her, or told her to do something. It told her, for example, to buy some plaiding and a headdress and some pins for Isobel, which she duly did. Did Margaret talk out loud to the spirit, and supply its answers? Some modern mediums under the influence of their personal spirit-guide speak in voices quite unlike their own. Did Isobel hear Margaret sometimes speaking naturally, and sometimes in a different voice? It would account for her saying she heard both Margaret and the spirit. None of this accounts for what she said she saw, of course, but we may care to ask ourselves what it was she actually did see. A hare

entered the house, lapped up some unfermented beer in a bowl, leaped
about, and then jumped through the window. (Isobel says it did so 'in
the form of a cloud', but this may be a piece of gratuitous identification
of Margaret as a witch, suggesting that the hare was not actually real,
just as her claim that she saw Margaret flying above the house is meant
to confirm Margaret's status as a witch, since, notoriously, witches fly).
Isobel also saw Margaret leave out food and drink – an action which is
suggestive of the common custom of providing sustenance for fairies
– but relied on Margaret to tell her they had disappeared the next morning. So what she actually *saw* was very little, and (flying apart) none of it
particularly surprising.

One is reminded, *mutatis mutandis*, of Elizabeth Dunlop from Lyne in
Ayrshire, who was tried for witchcraft in 1576, and Alison Pearson from
Boarhill in Fife, who was similarly tried in 1588. Both women claimed
to have dealings with a non-human entity which was either identifiable
with a *sìth* [fairy], or closely associated therewith. So we can venture that
Margaret's spirit may have belonged to this stratum of belief which was
common all over Scotland throughout this period. Whether it saw fairy
belief or witchcraft or a mixture of the two, however, the presbytery took
Margaret's case very seriously. It ordered her immediate excommunication
– not a usual proceeding. Excommunications had grave consequences for
the individual concerned, for he or she would then be shunned by the
whole community and ordinary living become nearly impossible. So a
person under threat would normally be given warning of the penalty and
allowed a protracted period of weeks or even months to reflect on what
it meant and ask for forgiveness and reconciliation. Margaret's summary
punishment is thus a measure of the reaction her case evoked.

One consequence of this is that we should not attempt to brush aside
the recorded evidence as though it were the result of simple foolishness
or spite or ignorance. Nor should we fall back on the tired old war-
horses of torture, sleep-deprivation, or ill-treatment to help us explain
away the narrative. There is no indication that Margaret suffered any of
these, and we are not entitled to assume that she did, just because such
experiences would suit our *soi-disant* rationalising impulses. Kirk records
– and we shall see many examples of this – indicate a high degree of
caution and care for justice among the authorities who were accustomed
to hear accusations of name-calling, charming, and witchcraft; and it is

worth remembering that when ministers met at the frequent presbytery sessions which were held in various places within their areas of responsibility, they would have had ample chance to exchange views about such matters in general, as well as to air opinions and seek advice on individual cases. At a distance of well over three centuries, it is impossible for us to be sure how many of the details of the case against Margaret Philp her interrogators took seriously, and how many they dismissed or treated as dubious. But their final verdict is most unlikely to have been one based on unthinking credulousness, and we should be prepared to accept that, and the consequences for our understanding of Scottish witch-prosecutions in general.

Kirk records turn quiet until June, when Canisbay in Caithness heard that Donald Lyall's wife (unnamed) and Margaret Water had been depriving Isobel MacBeath of her breast-milk, killing Andrew Water's geese and rendering his hens sterile and his cows unable to give milk, and killing one of Thomas Robson's cows and making another ill, until he went to the two women and objected, whereupon the sick cow made a recovery.[2] Then in August appeared a case which lasted until the beginning of 1658, making its way from the kirk session and presbytery of Dalkeith to the High Court of Justiciary in Edinburgh. Catharine Cass from Lugton, a village in the parish of Dalkeith, had been arrested in the early part of August after being delated to the kirk session as a witch by Isobel Mow, wife of Thomas Wood, an indweller [inhabitant] of Lugton. On 17 August, information was laid before justices of the peace, who heard six points against her: two involved the death of one George Richardson who fell sick after a quarrel with Catharine and, on his death-bed, blamed her for killing him. Some time later, his son John was drinking in Ronald Forrester's house when Catharine burst in, furious that John's brother and her son had been fighting, and threatened he should go the same way as his father. Whereupon John got to his feet and slashed her face with a knife. Now, it was fairly common practice to cut a witch so that her blood might act as counter-magic to some malefice of her own, as, for example, happened in 1633 when James Wilson from Kirkcaldy said of Alison Dick, 'Yon same witch thief is going betwixt me and the boat. I must have blood of her', and he went and struck her, and made her bleed. But in Catharine's particular instance, when it is clear the two parties were in a state of high emotion, it may be that John's action was merely violent and not intended to be apotropaic. Catharine, it seems, was not dismayed by this and said, 'Go and draw out as many dead horses as was drawn out before', and the next morning, says the record, 'two of his horses were found dead in the stable, which took their suppers well enough the night before'. A third point charged that Thomas Davidson's dog had uncovered some raw meat beneath a cherry tree in his yard. Casting raw meat could be taken as a sign of witchcraft, so it is not surprising that Thomas's wife made quite a fuss when she found out. Catharine, alerted by her exclamations, looked over the dyke [low boundary wall] and said, 'What the Devil's the matter? They're only seeking the fruit of your trees! What's the matter?' Whereupon the trees died and bore neither fruit nor leaves thereafter.

Now, Catharine was engaged to be married. She had a written agreement to that effect from John Merrylees, which she kept safe in her purse, remarking to him on one occasion, 'As long as I have your bond in my purse, you will never have power to marry any other woman but me'. Incensed by this, John managed to get the paper out of her purse and threw it on the fire, at which Catharine threatened him with ruination. 'You will never have food and clothing both at one time and, go where you will, the wind shall still blow in your face'. The other witness to this, apart from Merrylees himself, was one Ronald Forrester who attested to a number of charges against Catharine, including an odd reminiscence he and Catharine had once had. She said to him, 'Do you remember the night awhile back, when a good many cats came into your house? You said to John Merrylees, "Get up and see if you can catch some of them"', but John refused to do so. Catharine then said, 'Although John had no respect for my withered face, if I had not been there and defended him, they would have choked him'. Is this a woman who knows she has the reputation of being a witch and cannot help turning an ordinary incident to her advantage by reminding people that she has magical powers? However dangerous such an unguarded boast might be, it could bolster her self-confidence, especially, as seems possible from her reference to her withered (that is, wrinkled or weather-beaten) face, she was an older woman engaged to be married to a younger man and wanted to assert herself a little in his eyes, as a woman of status.

Catharine, indeed, seems to have been given to dropping such remarks. She called on Agnes Davidson with a request which was refused, but then, on meeting Agnes later, said, 'If you hadn't come when I called on you, you would have been as guilty of witchcraft as I'. She also told Walter Turnbull that she had beggared John Young (Agnes's husband) by killing his horses; that the Devil had struck Nicholas Somerville blind as he ran down the stair, because Nicholas had angered her; that she was his (Walter's) enemy, and that an unnamed 'we' had power over his goods but not his person; that she deserved to be burned because she had caused her husband's death; and that it was a woman in Muntounhall who first taught her to be a witch. So when the justices of the peace heard from Walter Turnbull that Catharine had been heard to say, 'God help poor Laird Watson, for when he is in a good mood, he says to his barley, "Come up, my dears!" But I say it won't come up well this year, for I and another three danced upon it', they would perhaps have taken this as a clear admission that Catharine certainly was a witch, since she had not been in the least averse from claiming to be one in front of other people.

This business of boasting or showing off was not particularly unusual, and although Catharine's behaviour brought her into conflict with her neighbours and, finally, in front of a criminal court, we should not assume therefrom that she was weak in the head. A deep-seated realisation that much of her reputation actually rested on her own hints may account for her begging the presbytery on 24 August to send for 'the man who tries the witches', so that he might test whether she was a witch or not. The ministers seem to have agreed, because a document dated 28 August records that John Kincaid, 'tryer of the witch's mark, after incalling upon the name of the Lord by Mr. Hugh Campbell, minister in Dalkeith, gave his oath of fidelity in trying of Catharine Cass, whether she had the witch's mark or not; and after trial, the said John Kincaid gave his great oath that he had found two witch's marks upon the said Catharine Cass, one upon the inside of her left thigh, and another upon her shoulder'. The document is signed with his initials (so clearly he did not know how to write even his own signature), and witnessed by five others, including two justices of the peace, the chamberlain William Scott, Hugh Campbell, the minister, and John Simson, public notary. Again, Catharine's request to be tested was by no means unusual, for many other accused persons did the like, and indicates either self-confidence in her own innocence or a brazen hope that she could face down such a trial.

One or two points are worth noting about this case. The presbytery heard thirteen charges against her, nine of which involved two witnesses, Ronald Forrester and Walter Turnbull, and three which came from John Richardson whose father George, he said, had blamed Catharine for inflicting him with the illness which led to his death. The bulk of the evidence therefore rested upon three people who were supported in some instances and not in others by additional witnesses. Seven witnesses altogether were questioned closely by the presbyters, and in only two instances did a majority agree that Catharine had done or said what she was accused of. The first relates to the incident of John Merrylees's snatching and burning his written promise of marriage – although Thomas Davidson thought Catharine had stolen the paper from Merrylees and then given it back to him; and the second involves Catharine's trying to borrow from Agnes Davidson, meeting her later, and making the odd remark that if Agnes had refused to come out of her house, she would have been as guilty of witchcraft as Catharine herself. Five witnesses in the first instance and four in the second, however, also agreed that both occasions took place during Catharine's 'distraction'. What this distraction was is not explained. It kept her in bed at one point, and she also had a surgeon to bleed her for it; but 'distraction' can refer to anything from genuine madness to temporary inebriation. The seventh charge against Catharine, for example, has one of her neighbours, John Speir, drinking ale which he had brought into her house for her mother's benefit. After drinking it, 'he became mad for three hours', and his wife came in and uttered a dire threat to Catharine that if her husband did not recover, it would be 'a dear sickness to Lugton. Whereupon the said Catharine went up and saw the said John, and he became well'. The wife's implication that Catharine had made him ill by magic and could therefore cure him is clear enough. But so is the meaning of 'mad' in this particular context.

Catharine's distraction, however, is likely to have been the result or accompaniment of a fever – one notices she was bled for it, and that no one suggested she was suffering from any kind of bewitchment – and it is significant that one or two witnesses at least in relation to six of the points against her testified that she was acting or speaking 'at the time of her distraction'. These included her burning the bond of betrothal, her remarks to Agnes Davidson, two instances of her confessing she had killed someone's horses, and both her direct claims to be a witch – the remark about dancing with others in Laird Watson's barley-field, and her claim to have been taught witchcraft by a woman from Muntounhall. But before we seize on her illness as a 'rational' explanation for both her reputation and the subsequent accusations against her, it is best to remember that there were seven other charges which had nothing to do with her distraction, that not every witness to the six charges I mentioned attributed them to her illness, and that even if several of her remarks did spring from this temporary disorder, it does not mean to say they were necessarily untrue in substance or merely figments of a fevered imagination.

Hearsay also played a significant role in the various testimonies. Isobel Mow, for example, who was the principal accuser before the presbytery on 23 August, when asked 'if she knew the foresaid delations of her own certain knowledge, or if she had them only by information, answered she knew none of them, but had them all by information', and named seven others as those who had told her about Catharine's alleged mis-sayings and misdoings. What was her motive in doing so? The surviving records do not provide an answer, or even allow us to guess – another example of local information which would have been known to many, if not all of those concerned, and which may have influenced their deliberations one way or another, absence of which ought to act as a brake on our desire to provide a complete or 'rational' explanation for what was going on. The seven witnesses named by Isobel Mow were not unanimous on every particular. A variable majority – six out of seven, five out of seven, four out of seven – agreed on some points of the dittay; but three points – two relating to her part in George Richardson's death and her threat to his son, and one of the discovery of raw meat under a cherry tree – were alleged by a single witness. So the testimonies varied both in quality and support, a common feature of the evidence presented to both ecclesiastical and to criminal sessions. Again, this should not be taken as a sign of unreliability: merely that witchcraft trials were like any other and did not necessarily draw witnesses into an unnatural or con-spiratorial uniformity of malice against the accused. Indeed, there was a formal requirement made of every witness before either type of ses-sion that he or she take an oath that his or her evidence would be given without personal malice, an assurance we ought to accept, just as we accept the general validity of modern oaths to tell the truth, the whole truth, and nothing but the truth.

Catharine's case lingered throughout the autumn and early winter of 1657, largely because she persisted in denying the whole of her dittay and partly because the ministers, despite frequent confabulations, were unable to make up their minds what to do about her. Clergymen had been appointed on more than one occasion to have private conference with her and persuade her to plead guilty, but still she refused to co-operate, so the session decided to hand her over to the justices of the peace, with a recommendation 'that they may take such course with her as they shall think fit'. To our ears, this may sound sinister, as though it were a hint to subject her to torture; but, as we shall see later, it was by no means an easy matter to obtain the necessary legal permission to use torture, and there is much to let us think that actually torture played little, if any, part in the examination of Scottish witches at this time. There is no evidence either way in Catharine's case, and we are certainly not entitled to assume it was or must have been used. What *is* worth remarking is Catharine's refusal to be brow-beaten into a confession. Scottish women were by no means overawed by male authority, and we shall find them fully prepared to resist it when they thought it was unjust or unfair. Catharine's protestations of innocence, therefore, indicate that, even in the climate of physical discomfort which her imprisonment would have entailed, and under the psychological pressure of frequent visits from ministers, she was not prepared to buckle. Whether this indicates her actual guilt or innocence, of course, is impossible to tell.

On 30 December, six witnesses came in front of the justices of the peace to pay the court £5 sterling to ensure that they would turn up to her trial, which was set for the first Tuesday in January, and on 1 January 1658 six more did the same on the same conditions. This last document, 'bond by the witnesses against Catharine Cass', is dated 2 February, and notes that three witnesses, most significant of them, perhaps, Ronald Forrester, did not appear. Since Ronald was one of the principal witnesses against her, Catharine's chances of surviving her trial were thus increased. But we do not actually know what happened to her.[3]

This is in contrast to Agnes Robert from Linlithgow, who was pricked by Kincaid on 13 June 1657 and found to have a single witch's mark on the small of her back. She was released on caution [bail] on 6 October when neither pursuer [prosecuting counsel] nor witnesses (twenty-one of whom had been summoned to attend her trial in August) appeared before the court to offer any charge or evidence against her.[4] The discovery of a mark was therefore not necessarily fatal to the accused, nor did the authorities take it alone as sufficient proof of a person's being a witch. On the other hand, it might contribute to a prisoner's despair at her condition. Janet Bruce from Tranent in East Lothian was tested by Kincaid (who also came from Tranent) on 22 June, and four insensitive spots were found upon her body, the pin being sunk in to a depth of two-and-one-eighth inches, as the relevant document informs us. On 30 June, Kincaid deponed further that in his opinion these marks were diabolical in origin. At some time during the week between her being tested and this declaration by Kincaid, however, Janet seems to have tried to commit suicide, for William Forrester, a surgeon from Tranent, testified that Janet had got hold of poison which had caused her body to swell, and that if she had not vomited it up, she would have died. Consequently, she was able to stand trial on 4 August, when she was found innocent of fourteen out of the fifteen charges against her, although the assize was split on that single article and convicted her only by a plurality of votes.

That one item is rather odd. Janet, it was said, agreed to cure a sick woman but demanded to be given a child in return. When this was refused, she asked for clothing which was given to her; but later on, having invited the sick woman's husband to take supper with her, Janet renewed her request for a child in return for curing his wife, a request he rejected, saying that 'he hoped in God that He had not given him that bairn to be given to the Devil'. So the supper remained uneaten and the wife uncured. Did John Frame, the husband, interpret Janet's demand in the worst possible light because she had some kind of reputation as a magical healer, and did Janet really ask for the child as a potential sacrifice? Normally one would not ask such a question, but item 13 on her dittay includes the information that a year before, Janet had come to the house of one Marion Hamilton, declaring that she could cure any disease, and was invited to cure Marion of persistent flatulence. Janet promised a cure and was paid three dollars [slang term for five-shilling pieces]. But one of Marion's neighbours told her that Janet was a witch, so Marion and a man went after her to take back the money. They overtook her about a mile from her own house, struggled with her without success, but managed to remove her plaid, and, tied up in one corner of it they found 'the flesh and bones of dead children', and that 'there was the thigh and arm whole, as yet unconsumed'. 'Unconsumed' here almost certainly means that the flesh had not yet dropped away from the bone, rather than 'uneaten'.[5] The charge may appear to be extraordinary, but it was not unique. The Old Kirk session of Peebles heard from Janet Haddon on 17 November 1675 that she had heard a man say that the woman who came in to Baillie Rush's house was surely a devil, and when he was asked how he knew that, the man replied that he smelled it and that the woman was carrying raw meat around with her. So the direct accusation that Janet was carrying round pieces of children's bodies implied maleficent magic as clearly as though the word 'witchcraft' itself had appeared in the dittay. Yet the assize found her not guilty on this point, though by how many votes is not recorded. Had some version of this incident reached John Frame and so caused him to misinterpret whatever exactly it was that Janet was asking him for? What happened to Janet, convicted of only a single item on her dittay, we do not know. The court delayed pronouncing sentence until 6 October, and there the records fall silent.[6]

The geographical spread of these cases is wide. Five took place either in Edinburgh itself or in East Lothian; the rest are scattered over what one may roughly call 'the central belt' (Forfar, Perth, Stirling, Argyll), with one or two much further north in Aberdeenshire, Elgin, Inverness, and Caithness. The numbers involved are small: sixteen altogether, of whom four were men, and one other man who claimed he had been frightened by witches. The social status of those involved is uncertain. Marie MacIldowie was a midwife, and Margaret Philp had a servant, but that tells us very little. The context of the various accusations suggests that the defendants and their accusers belonged largely to the petite bourgeoisie and lower class, but such an impressionistic observation must be treated with some caution.[7] The Kirk authorities clearly took pains to investigate any accusation of magical or 'superstitious' dealing with great care, and weighed the reliability of witnesses and their evidence before coming to a conclusion. It is also clear that the Kirk would pursue even name-calling until it was satisfied that the parties concerned were penitent, publicly humiliating them as a way of demonstrating the spiritual discipline it was intent on imposing on all its members. The majority of offences dealt with by kirk and presbytery sessions during 1657 included name-calling, charming, and 'superstitious' pilgrimage in search of a cure. Four only were accusations of witchcraft, and one of those (Margaret Philp) involved traffic with a spirit in circumstances which could be interpreted as self-delusion as easily as actual communion with a non-human entity, although Margaret's excommunication suggests that the presbytery saw her offence as the latter rather than the former. Only one of these cases, that of Catharine Cass, made its way from Kirk hands into the criminal court, and in no case was the Devil even mentioned, let alone an active participant; nor was there any suggestion of a covenant with evil. As far as the ecclesiastical courts were concerned, 1657 scarcely looked like the initial stages of a widespread, serious outbreak of covenanting witchcraft.

Secular law-courts, however, saw something of a flurry. Since 'witchcrafts, sorcery, and necromancy' and the consultation of anyone claiming to exercise powers or abilities in those operations had been criminal acts since 1563, and subject to the death penalty, accused persons were liable to find themselves in front of a criminal court, perhaps after appearing before a kirk or presbytery session, perhaps not. In practice, the most important of these courts, subject to the Privy Council itself, was the Court of Justiciary sitting in Edinburgh ('High Court' after 1672). There were also justice airs, circuit courts which travelled north, west and south, and met in such places as Aberdeen, Dumfries and Jedburgh. Commissions were issued to give authority to hold courts, either to try individuals or to try a range of offences.[8] Thus, in March 1657, commissions to try 'treason, murder, slaughter, mutilation, fire-raising, theft, robbery, adultery, incest, witchcrafts, charmings, bigamy, etc.' were issued for the shires of Lanark, Renfrew and Dumbarton; in April, for Selkirk and Jedburgh; and in August, for Kincardine; while on 25 July 1661, in phraseology which was standard for this kind of document, the Privy Council, 'informed by petitions from heritors [land-owners] and others within the parishes of Musselburgh, Dalkeith, Newbattle, Newton, and Duddingston that there are a great many persons, both men and women, within the said bounds who are imprisoned, as having confessed, or witnesses led against them for the abominable sin of witchcraft, and being most desirous that the land may be purged of that horrid sin', authorised:

Mr Alexander Colville of Blair, Mr George MacKenzie, and Mr John Cunningham, justice deputes, or any two of them, to meet at Musselburgh upon Monday next, and thereafter to appoint their own times of meeting, and then and there to sit and hold courts for all legal trial of so many of the said persons… and to proceed against them according to the law and practice of the kingdom.

Just such a personal commission was requested in February 1657 for Bessie Carnochan who had been examined by two justices of the peace in the kirk at Twynholm, a village three miles from Kirkcudbright, on 12 June 1656.[9] On that occasion, twenty-six articles were laid against her, which resulted in her being imprisoned in October. Further inquiries must have been made, for she was examined again on 11 December in the same place by the same magistrates, and a further eleven articles were added to her dittay. Bessie finally came to trial in May 1657. She did not necessarily remain in prison all that time. Accused persons could be let out on caution [bail] if a relative or friend was willing to post it. That said, however, Bessie does not seem to have been a woman with personal resources at her disposal; her husband was a cottar, a tenant on a farm, who had a cottage and perhaps a small plot of land which he rented from the farmer. Nor, indeed, does she appear to have had many friends. So on balance, the likelihood may be that she was not restored to liberty after October, although it is interesting that she was not put in prison for the four months following her initial interrogation which had revealed a remarkably large number of serious accusations against her. Speculation about her treatment during those four months is probably better not made.

The preface to her dittay is worth noting, because it is fairly typical of its kind.

You are indicted and accused, for as much as by the divine laws, and Acts of Parliament of this nation, the crime of witchcraft and sorcery is punished by death: nevertheless, it is of verity that you, the said Bessie Carnochan, having shaken off all fear of God, reverence to this divine law and Acts of Parliament of this nation, have these many years bygone taken yourself to the service of the Devil, the enemy of Man's salvation, entered in paction with him, renounced your baptism, received his mark, and with his assistance, by your sorcery and witchcraft, have committed many

malefices [acts of harmful magic], laid on divers sicknesses and diseases
upon sundry [of] the people within this nation and have occasioned many
of their deaths: also by your sorcery and witchcraft, you have taken off
diseases off a great many people, (as by the following articles does appear):
and you are a common and notorious witch and sorcerer, and have acted
and committed several and many witchcrafts.

It should be noted, first of all, that Bessie's articles contain instances of her
laying on and taking off illness, eleven of them relating to human beings,
and nine to her laying illness on humans without subsequently providing
a cure. Eight accusations say that her maleficent magic killed its object,
whether human or animal. So that part of the preface relating to her dittay
is mirrored by a majority of the articles. She also ruined the brewing of
John MacKie and Thomas MacGowan, and dried up Grissell Dalziel's cow
so that it gave no milk – a standard piece of harmful magic attributed to
witches. That Bessie was 'a common and notorious witch' is suggested not
only by the fact that twenty-one people came forward to testify against
her, but also by the wording or implication of at least three articles. The last
(no. 38) tells us that Bessie often used to come to Grissell Dalziel while she
was alone, and say, 'Doozy kittie, you sit pining and hungering in a house'.
'Doozy' is the English word 'dozy', meaning 'lethargic' or, by extension,
'somewhat stupid'; and 'kittie' is an epithet for a brainless young woman –
a word generally used in disparagement, and suggesting that the woman is
of doubtful character. Grissell, according to her own evidence, replied that
she was not well and therefore unable to look after herself. To this Bessie
said, 'If you would do as I do, you need not want'. But Grissell answered
immediately, 'God keep me from doing as you do!' What did they mean
by this exchange? It may be explained by article 11. Alison MacRobert
testified that she and Bessie were out walking one day, and when Bessie
noticed she was sunk in thought 'by reason of great want', she said, 'Alison,
if you would do as I advise, it would go better with you'. Alison asked
what she meant and alleged that Bessie answered, 'If you would believe
in my god, you would never want'. Alison asked who that god was, and
Bessie replied, 'The king of all devils is my god'.

Can we believe it? Bessie confessed to her kirk minister that she was
the Devil's servant, and did so before her imprisonment; so the likelihood
is that she produced her evidence without torture, physical constraint,

or ill-treatment. Now, what she said, regardless of her motive in saying it, was, as far as she was concerned, either basically true or a mischievous lie; and so anent this point it is worth noting that her remark does have its parallel in one attributed to Alison Dick, accused of witchcraft before Old Kirkcaldy kirk session on 8 October 1633, who was supposed to have said, 'There is none that does me wrong but I go to my god and complains upon them, and within four and twenty hours I will get amends of them'.[10] It is also worth noting that Katharine Thomson alleged that the women of Borgue were milking their cows one day when Bessie turned up, and as soon as the women saw her they said to one another, 'There's Bessie! All the milk will not go home this day, for Bessie is casting her peats [throwing them into a heap to dry]'; and sure enough, milk disappeared from a full cog [wooden tub], even though (Katharine alleged) the women had kept their eyes on it all the time. But whether Bessie did indeed steal the milk undetected is beside the point. The women expected some of their milk to disappear, and the thrust of the whole evidence is not that Bessie was a thief, but that she was a witch. Her reputation as such thus seems to have been known and well-established not only in her home village of Twynholm, but also three miles away in Borgue where one or two of the witnesses against her were normally resident.

Did Bessie deliberately contribute to this reputation? William Martin from Borgue testified that he had once said jokingly to her that she was a witch, and that Bessie replied she had some skill indeed, but that she had got it from the fairies. Perhaps the man from Borgue was more willing than the women to make light of her reputation, or perhaps the incident goes back to a time when Bessie had just begun to be known or suspected as a witch. But Marion MacNaughtrie who was moving to live in Borgue was told (she said) by Bessie that it would not be good for her health, 'and the very first day, as she was carrying water from the from the well, there came seven ravens with hideous noise and lighted on the house, dabbing with their heads and wings hard upon it'. Next day, Bessie came and asked Marion if she had seen the ravens, and explained that they were not actually ravens but seven devils. Asked how she knew that, she answered she had it from the fairies – 'and since that time, the said Marion very seldom has her health'. This is not the first time we have found an accused witch associated with fairies. Margaret Philp, we may recall, left out food and drink at night, an action which may be inter-preted as maintaining the *sìthean*, and Catharine Cass, too, was not averse from dropping hints to other people about her magical abilities. Bessie, therefore, is credited with behaviour similar to that of other women from other parts of Scotland, accused of witchcraft in 1657.

Accusations against her, as we have seen, fall into two groups. The first (articles 1-26) left her at liberty, but the second (articles 27-38) caused her to be imprisoned. The first had been heard in 12 June 1656, the second was presented on 11 December before the same justices of the peace. Is there anything in the new evidence gathered during those intervening months, which might cause the justices to deprive Bessie of her freedom? Not as far as one can see. The charges contain a mix-ture of laying on and taking off illness, as before, of malicious acts such as drying up a cow's milk and ruining a man's brewing business, and of Bessie's hinting she had preternatural powers. Article 27 brings in the Devil, but not in such a way as to make a special enormity of the charge. John MacGowan and Bessie MacHimson, his wife, alleged that once, when Bessie Carnochan was in their house, their daughter said to her, 'If I were William Henry, you would go to the session for laying sickness on his wife, because everyone blames you for it'. Bessie replied, 'The great Devil may take your wits from you, and you may say I did it!' The next night, the girl went out of doors and saw a big, frightening 'black man' in the yard; whereupon she came back indoors 'distracted', and continued in that state a long time, crying out that Bessie was lying on top of her and holding her down. Bessie then visited her several times and prayed for her, saying, 'God send her her health', after which the girl recovered – 'by your witchcraft', as the dittay expresses it.

The ambiguity of 'may' in Bessie's apparent imprecation is interesting. Are we to understand that she magically cursed the girl and gave her permission to say that she (Bessie) had caused her distraction; or does the 'may' in both sentences amount to ironical observation – it is quite possible that the Devil may make you mad, and if he does, it is equally possible you will blame me for it? What, too, are we to make of the girl's reaction to her fright at seeing a large, dark figure in the yard? The sensation of having a heavy weight on one's chest – sometimes called 'the night hag' – is often described in witch trials and attributed to the accused person's sitting on the victim's chest while she or he is asleep.

Such a reaction is perfectly comprehensible in terms of sudden stress, but it passes once the sufferer has had a chance to calm down. It is not prolonged. One cannot help having a suspicion, therefore, that the girl may have been acting after the genuineness of her original unpleasant experience. She obviously bore a personal dislike of Bessie – hence her remarks about William Henry and his wife – and the prolongation of her symptoms, and her attributing them to Bessie, may have owed much to spite and a wish to cause her trouble. On the other hand, of course, since Bessie had a reputation as a witch, the girl may have been quite genuine throughout, the sight of Bessie bringing on sufficient stress each time to cause a re-occurrence of the smothering sensation, and only after several visits during which nothing untoward happened did the girl cease these distressing reactions at the sight of her: hence the cure. Interpretation of such instances is difficult, and it is always tempting for the modern commentator to choose a superficially 'rationalist' explanation, forgetting that the people he or she is describing were likely to be absolutely genuine in their beliefs in a universe quite different from ours, and that their reactions to it make perfectly good sense in their own terms, even if he or she does not like or accept either those terms or that universe. Article 27 may thus have been more damaging to Bessie than we realise, precisely because the participants were speaking the truth as they saw it.

How far do the charges laid against her conform to those listed in the preface to her dittay? First, she is accused of wilfully breaking the 1563 Witchcraft Act. This forbade the use of 'witchcrafts, sorcery, and necromancy', the claim to possess skill therein or knowledge thereof, and the consultation of anyone professing to use witchcraft, sorcery, or necromancy.[11] By 'witchcrafts', the Act is likely to have meant acts of harmful magic or acts of beneficent magic allied to the former (such as removing an illness which had been laid on by harmful magic), both of which kinds were open to interpretation as magic performed with the assistance of an evil spirit. Hence, 'charming', not overtly referred to by the Act, was liable to be included under the head of 'witchcraft' if it was thought that the person accused was achieving her or his preternatural effects with demonic help, or if the person accused had other, overt acts of witchcraft included in her or his dittay. Clearly all Bessie's alleged activities came under this general heading. The 'sorcery' of the

Act may be there simply because of lawyers' verbosity; but since the word is derived from the Latin *sortilegium*, meaning 'casting lots to fore-tell the future', it may well retain something of this distinctive force in the Act which goes on to condemn the 'seeker of the response or consultation'. A 'response' implies a question, and answering questions about the future was always considered to be one of the most useful skills of a magical operator. Indeed, Heinrich Institoris, author of the highly influential *Malleus Maleficarum*, saw prediction as characteristic of a *malefica*, 'a female worker of harmful magic' or 'witch'.[12]

'Necromancy' was, of course, a particular technique of divination whereby a dead body was temporarily resurrected and the revived person constrained to answer questions put to him or her. Necromancy is not alleged of Bessie, but neither is sorcery in the restricted sense of *sortile-gium*. Her 'sorcery', then, if we are to go by the items listed in her dittay, was either the same as her witchcraft, or it can be detected as something distinct from it. However, the phrase 'by your sorcery and witchcraft' appears at the end of twenty-six out of thirty-two items on her dittay. 'Witchcraft and sorcery' appears once, 'witchcraft' alone after two items, and 'sorcery' alone after three. These three involve (a) laying on an illness, (b) laying on and taking off an illness, and (c) ruining someone's brewing business. The two references to witchcraft alone involve her (a) laying on and taking off an illness, and (b) drying up a cow's milk. In other words, there does not seem to be any distinction between Bessie's witchcraft and her sorcery, so it looks as though the wording of the charge owes more to legal prolixity than to precise definition.

So in as much as the evidence could prove that Bessie had disobeyed the law in committing acts of witchcraft/sorcery and thereby had been 'a common witch and sorcerer', it would have shown that she was guilty as charged. But the preface to her dittay also alleges that she had been the Devil's servant for years, had made a pact with him – the word is 'pact', not 'covenant' – renounced her baptism, and received the Devil's mark; and none of these actually appears in the separate charges against her. The first three might be inferred from them, of course, since she alleg-edly admitted to working her magic with the aid of the Devil whom she called her 'god', and this would suppose she had entered into an agree-ment with him to be his servant, which in turn would suppose she had renounced her baptism. A mark, however, is scarcely a supposition. Was she pricked? We do not know. Pricking seems to have been a frequent feature of the examination process, but it was not an integral part of it, so we have no certain knowledge in Bessie's case. Was she tortured before, after, or during imprisonment? We do not know. Again, torture was not invariably used in cases of Scottish witchcraft, and we are not entitled merely to assume that she was. All we know, apart from the details provided in the justices' application for a commission to try her and the items listed in her dittay, is that the assize [jury], by unanimous vote, found her guilty of ten of the charges against her. On another – laying on and taking off illness from John Herries's horse – a unanimous vote declared her not guilty. For the remaining twenty-seven charges we have no record of what her assize concluded, but we do know that she was executed at Dumfries, along with another witch, Euphame MacClean, on 13 May.

The preface to the dittays of Elizabeth Maxwell and Euphame MacThynne who were tried in Dumfries in May 1657 are cast in very much the same terms as Bessie's.[13] There were twelve items in Elizabeth's dittay. Seven accused her of laying on illness and causing both humans and animals to die; three said she laid on illness and took it off again; one had her kill three children magically, while the fourth recovered only because other witches were able to lift the illness laid on by Elizabeth; and one article said she had ruined a woman's brewing business. According to the record – and we must be careful to remember that it is, by its nature, a hostile document – Elizabeth seems to have been a distinctly unpleasant woman, quite prepared to kill her own stepson by magic and then, having been imprisoned by Thomas MacBrain, the baillie, at the request of the minister in Dumfries, to turn a fatal current of magic against Thomas himself who died two years later. One William Gladstone, too, suffered at her hands. The relevant items (nos 9 and 10), say that William saw her one night, 'riding upon a cat and leading two in your hand', whereupon he called out to her, 'Mistress, I know you well'. He fell feverishly sick that night, but Elizabeth allowed him to recover, possibly because his wife went and told his sister who then said, 'Oh my brother, I vow to have him burned that has thus wrong him!', shouting it out so that Elizabeth, who was present, should not fail to hear. The cure, however, turned out to be only a respite, for some time later she afflicted him again and this time he died, accusing her of having killed him.

Why would William have thought he saw Elizabeth riding upon a cat – always supposing he did and that the witness or witnesses reporting this to the court were not lying? This is always a possibility, of course, but so is the chance he had said it in good faith either during the period of his feverish illness or at some other time when he was in perfectly good health. Scottish witches, it must be said, did not usually ride upon cats. They were sometimes accused of appearing to people in the form of cats or, like Isobel Young from Dunbar in 1629, of sacrificing them to the Devil. A divination ceremony (*taghairm*) practised in the Gaidhealtachd and in northern parts of the Lowlands roasted cats alive over a period of several days in the belief that at the end of it demons would appear in the shape of cats and answer the participants' questions. But none of these traditions has the witch actually riding the cat. Such a concept seems to belong rather more to early-sixteenth-century Germany. Ulrich Molitor's witchcraft treatise *De laniis et phitonicis mulieribus*, first published in 1489 and illustrated by a number of fairly crude woodcuts, went through many editions, as well as being translated from Latin into German. In the German edition of 1545, one chapter has been slightly altered. From its original reference to women riding to feasts (that is, by implication, the Sabbat) on a stick or a wolf, the text now runs 'on a stick or a cat', and the relevant woodcut shows a fully-clothed woman riding on an indeterminate creature which, presumably, is meant to represent a cat, although the possible attempt to suggest that the creature is demonic rather than natural has led to a somewhat extraordinary likeness. We may also note a mid-sixteenth-century imitation of a painting by Lucas Cranach the Elder (*Melencolia*, 1528) which includes a naked woman standing upon the back of an unmistakable cat, both flying with companions in the midst of a cloud over an empty rural scene. We thus have evidence for a German tradition of witches riding upon cats, but clearly this does not necessarily translate into a Scottish equivalent. So although the implication of William Gladstone's reported sighting is evident enough, the form his sighting took is rather puzzling.

Elizabeth's case never came to a verdict, for a marginal note in the record tells us she died in prison. Euphame MacThynne, charged in Dumfries the same month, had fourteen items alleged against her although, according to notations in the record, two of them were withdrawn for reasons which are not explained. One of these (no. 10) says that she was walking one day with her son and Janet Hastie and came across a mole. Euphame said to her son, 'Have you a knife?' He said, no, and thus the mole escaped. Euphame then said to Janet, ' If you find a mole, get hold of her and cut off three of her feet. Let her go while she is still alive, and send the three feet to me'. Some time later, Janet must have run across a mole, for she sent three of its feet to Euphame and, not long after, Janet's father contracted such an infection in his foot that it rotted from him and afterwards he died. A note tells us that the article was not proven. The actual verdict 'not proven' was not formally introduced into Scottish legal procedure until the early eighteenth century, so this note does not record a vote by the assize. It may explain why the article was withdrawn, but without further information we cannot be sure. Article 6 tells us that during a visit by 'the man... that did brodd [prick] the women suspect of witchcraft', Euphame went to William Waugh and his wife, Janet Edgar, and asked them to hide her in their barn. This they agreed to do, and she remained in concealment for several days. Why were they willing to hide her? There is no evidence they did so from fear of her as a witch. Euphame did say that if they agreed to hide her, 'it should never be forgotten, and [she] would do them a good turn for it', but this phraseology does not necessarily imply *magical* benefit to them. They could have consented out of simple compassion or fellow-feeling. We do not know. A marginal note says, 'By which you declare yourself to be guilty of the abominable sin of witchcraft', presumably because the writer assumed an innocent woman would not have felt the need to hide herself from a witch-pricker. A different hand, however, adds that the article is 'to be [with]drawn', and so it is likely that Euphame never stood trial for it. Again, we do not know why.

That she had some kind of reputation for being a witch, however, seems probable. Four witnesses were found to allege that during a quarrel between Adam Barton, John Barton his son, Roger Huddleston (Euphame's husband), and Euphame herself, John struck Euphame on her forehead and drew blood, after which he went 'mad' until Euphame came and cured him. But the cure was actually just a magical transference, for Adam soon after contracted an infection in his leg, 'so that it rotted from him and he died'. Now, John Barton's blow could simply have been delivered in anger – another article tells us that Roger Neilson hit her after she had uttered some malicious speeches against him, so this was not her only taste of violence – but we also need to bear in mind that making a witch bleed was a piece of counter-magic against her own malefice, and since we do not know why the four of them were quarrelling, we cannot be certain it was not over some alleged act of witchcraft the others had thought was hers. When John went 'mad', the family sent for Euphame to cure him, thereby clearly indicating they thought she was responsible. The assize, however, unanimously found her not guilty; but one of the witnesses was dead by the time the case came to trial, and two, a man and his wife, did not turn up, the wife (interestingly enough) being fined 200 merks – over £135 Scots, or the equivalent of about thirty years' wages of an agricultural servant – leaving John Barton himself as the only witness present. So either the assize did not believe his testimony, or it considered him too biased a witness to provide satisfactory evidence. If, then, he did not strike her deliberately to draw blood as apotropaic magic, the assize was not willing to press a connection, in this instance at least, between Euphame's reputation and Adam Barton's illness and death. The verdict, however, does not necessarily mean that the assize did not believe she was a witch at all.

Euphame was accused of laying on and taking off illness in two items on her dittay, and was acquitted of both. Six items alleged she had laid on an illness which was followed by the death of the object of her malefice, and she was acquitted of four of these. Four items alleged she had ruined malt or milk or brewing, or had made someone's ale mysteriously vanish, and she was acquitted of three of these. The acquittals were all unanimous. The three charges of which she was found guilty produced mixed verdicts: that is to say, she was 'fylit' by a majority vote. One of these items said she had ruined someone's malt; a second, that she had laid on an illness of which the victim died; and a third, that she had done the same to a servant of that same victim. The second item has one or two distinctive features. Euphame, Robert Kennan, and others had been present when men had fished Lag Hall Water for their breakfast and the fish they had caught were being distributed. There was one spare, which Euphame asked for, but which Robert decided to give to the men who had done the fishing. Euphame was annoyed and threatened to do Robert an ill turn, and the next day, when the men were drawing their net from the water, they found it contained no fish 'but a great toad, such as they had never seen before for greatness'; and that same day Robert fell seriously

ill. Three days later, Sir Robert Grierson, the laird of Lag, came to visit
him, but before he could arrive Robert died, 'like unto a mad man, being
held up in people's arms'; and no sooner was he dead than the fishermen
at Lag Hall Water began to draw an abundance of fish again. A different
hand in the record notes that this incident happened 'in August 1649 or
thereby'. It was attested by eight witnesses, two of whom also said they
had heard Euphame's husband, Roger Huddleston, say to her afterwards,
'I thought I had told you not to have anything to do with that man',
adding 'thief', which at first sight looks as though it refers to Euphame,
but is more likely to be directed at Robert who had deprived Euphame
of the fish she had requested.

About a fortnight after Robert died, Elspeth Edgar, his servant, said to
Euphame while they were both loading beer on to a cart, 'Ill sight light
upon that witch-face for dividing me and my dear master!' to which
Euphame, looking over her shoulder, replied, 'I shall remember that, and
I shall deal with you, if I can'. Whereupon, before Elspeth had finished
loading beer on to the cart, she felt pains shooting through her body and
was obliged to go home and take to her bed where, a short time later,
she died. Now, other articles charged Euphame with similar offences,
and yet the assize found her not guilty of them; so what was it in these
three which made the difference? In the end, we cannot know, because
there must have been so many attendant details which have not been
recorded and yet were known to all those involved, any of which could
have explained the assizors' decision. But there is one link between the
first and second items – the third is really an appendage of the second –
which may or may not be significant: the person of Sir Robert Grierson.
The Griersons were the most notable family in the area, having occupied their seat at Lag Hall since the mid-fifteenth century. Not only had
he intended to visit Robert Kennan whom he must have known local
gossip was saying had been bewitched by Euphame, but when Mary
Lachlieson had her malt ruined, blaming Euphame for the disaster, Mary
set out the mixture upon the highway, 'so that all people might behold
it; who all said that looked thereupon that it was bewitched'. Sir Robert
Grierson happened to be coming from the church. He stopped and put
his stick in the vessel, and the stuff gurgled and stuck to it, like lumps of
starch. 'Then [he] also said that it was witched'. This is powerful testimony, for Sir Robert was a man of status and influence, and although he

was not alive in 1657 to present his opinion to the court, the fact that he had expressed himself on the subject was bound to have carried some weight. Three of the witnesses against Euphame in the case of Robert Kennan and his servant were Griers, too: Bessie, John, and Agnes. Now, the names 'Grier' and 'Grierson' were more or less interchangeable at the time, so it is possible that the Griers were related to or connected with Sir Robert, however distantly, in which case one might think the weight of his pronouncement in one case, and the combination of Griers in the others could have been sufficient to sway Euphame's assize. But if it did, it did not sway everyone, for Euphame was convicted of these charges by a plurality, not a unanimity, of votes. Social influence, therefore, may have had its limits. What happened to Euphame is not recorded. She may have been executed on the strength of these three guilty verdicts, but it is probably best not to take such an outcome for granted.

A third case relevant to May 1657 is that of Janet Tulloch, whose name first appears on the Renfrew Dittay Roll of 1656.[14] She had spent a long time in prison, according to a note in the record, having confessed to witchcraft before magistrates in Renfrew as early as 1650, although it is not necessary to assume she had been imprisoned all that time. Accused persons could be let out on caution [bail], and six years is an unusually long period for anyone to remain in a tolbooth on charges of witchcraft. It is not, however, impossible, and we do know that the original record of her confession, taken down by the local minister, was lost after he died, so that she and the witnesses had to be examined again. The minister in question was John Maule, who took up the Renfrew ministry in 1650 and died on 29 April 1653. Janet's case, then, must have been one of the earliest he heard, because she appeared before the magistrates that same year; and the date of his death indicates that Janet was in prison in 1653, since he examined her while she was in the tolbooth. 1653 until 1656 thus represents the minimum time she spent there. On 1 July 1656 she appeared before the kirk session and denied causing illness and death to Adam and Janet Knox and James Wray, and breaking the laird of Fulbar's leg by magic. At some point she was pricked and a mark discovered. On 15 January 1657 the details of her case were again rehearsed before the presbytery, after which the ministers recommended she be sent to the civil magistrate for trial. On 1 May a court held in Paisley sent her forward again, to be tried in Glasgow, and a note tells us she was convicted and executed.

Janet had been delated by Thomas Leitch, a confessing warlock whom she had helped escape from prison and for whom she along with two others, had stood caution when, for reasons we do not know, he was granted his cautionary freedom. She was also delated by Janet Montgomerie, a witch who later suffered execution, although the wording of the document suggests that Thomas simply alleged that Janet Montgomerie had delated her. The preface to her dittay mentioned the usual offences – disobedience to God's law and the Act of Parliament, 'paction and covenant' with Satan, renunciation of her baptism and acceptance of a new name ('Crooning', which in Scots refers to bellowing like a bull, or whining, or purring, or wheedling: clearly it has some reference to her way of talking), and reception of the Devil's mark – and that she had attended several meetings with the Devil, 'and had contrived sundry malefices', which were then listed.

The bulk of the document which deals with testimony against her at the hearing in Renfrew on 15 January, however, relates to something quite different. The evidence comes from her time in the tolbooth at Renfrew. James Paterson, for example, testified that 'one night, when he was waking Janet Tulloch, together with one John Paterson (now dead), they being at their own prayers and the night being calm, the tolbooth shook the space one would go a pair of butts' – about seventy yards – 'and after they had done, about midnight they heard a number of cats coming up upon them, screeching and crying, Janet having knelt down with the rest as it were in prayer'. James called out to her and she yawned twice before she answered. 'What's the matter with you?' he asked. 'Didn't you see?' she replied. 'There was a big thing like a large mouse or rat, trying to get into my mouth', and she panted heavily. James then opined that it was a devil who had been trying to get inside her to make her deny (that is, refuse to do something – in this instance, presumably to pray), adding the curious non-sequitur, 'Janet, you are not a witch, but some spirit has told you how to get possessions and money'; to which Janet said that there was a little man who came to her and told her how and where she would get them, and that she always followed his advice and was successful. This whole conversation she then repeated next morning in the presence of the minister, the baillie, and several other people.

What does James mean by 'waking' Janet? One's immediate inclination, perhaps, is to take this as a reference to deliberate sleep-deprivation, but I think this may be a mistake. James and John were at their prayers, and the intention seems to have been to wake Janet – so the implication is that she was asleep, not being kept awake – to let her, or oblige her, to pray with them. She is said to have sat down with the others, as it were to pray. 'Sitting' here means 'sitting upon one's knees' as the regular Scots expression has it, and thus indicates kneeling. Accused witches, for example, are often described as sitting upon their knees to utter curses or imprecations against those who had angered them. It is difficult to follow the sequence of events from the curtailed account in the dittay. Did the shaking of the tolbooth take place while the men were at their prayers, while they were waking Janet, or after she had kneeled down and joined them in their devotions? (Why, one must also ask, were they occupying themselves with prayer during the night-time? Was this a regular occurrence when men were guarding suspect witches, or were James and John particularly devout, or had they been instructed by the minister to observe regular devotions to protect them against Janet's possible malign influence, or provide her with a worthy Christian example?) They had all finished praying when they heard the sound of screeching cats. Why does the account mention at this particular point Janet's praying with James and John? Is it poor sentence construction, or are readers and hearers meant to make a connection between Janet's praying and the screeching of the cats? In the latter case, is the screeching of the cats meant to represent the sound of demons shrieking with rage that she has abandoned them and reverted to her previous Christian state, or are we to infer that Janet's prayers were still diabolic in character and that therefore the appearance of the yowling cats happened in answer, so to speak, to her ambiguous devotion?

Andrew Love (since deceased) deponed that one night Janet started to tremble as she lay in the tolbooth. He asked her what was the matter, and she told him it was a spirit. Was it a good spirit or an evil one? he asked, and she replied it was 'doubtless' – that is, certainly or, perhaps, probably – evil. Andrew testified she was in the same state next morning at nine o'clock, and he asked her how long it was since she had been visited by the spirit. Janet answered it was some months ago, but Andrew could not remember how many she had said. Very soon after Andrew died, the laird of Fulbar and the minister, John Maule, asked her what the spirit was, and she said it came to her in the form of a mouse or rat and was certainly/probably evil. Asked how long it had been troubling her, she answered a year or two. (This disparity between what she told them and what she told Andrew argues that the conversation with the laird and minister took place much later than that with Andrew). The laird 'posed her hard', that is, clearly, sought to make her view of the spirit conform to standard witchcraft theory, for eventually she told him 'she knew it was the Devil, and that he made her renounce her baptism, and gave her a new name, calling her *Crooning*, and that he had carnal copulation with her, and that he gave her a mark'. It is interesting to note that the record makes it clear it was the layman, not the minister, who was keen to cast Janet in the traditional witch-mould. Perhaps he bore a grudge because of his broken leg. On the other hand, he may have believed she really was a witch and that her version of the spirit was merely an attempt to fudge or dodge the issue.

John Somerville, town baillie at the time, more or less repeated what the laird had deponed, but when asked about John Paterson's evidence, said his memory was not particularly clear but that he did recall there was a spirit in the form of a mouse or rat which came and troubled Janet from time to time. John Stevenson, however, searched his memory and produce a slightly different recollection. He said that when Janet was lying in her bed, 'there came a spirit and cried "Janet!" twice or thrice'. Asked whom she thought it was, Janet said she thought it was her husband who had died some time before. Mice and rats in a tolbooth are scarcely an unusual phenomenon. Did one run across her face, and did she manage to catch it and hold it out for James Paterson to see? If so, his reaction was odd, for the record makes him say three things which do not quite hang together: (a) 'the mouse/rat is a devil which intended to get into you to make you refuse [to pray]'; (b) 'Janet, you are not a witch'; and (c) 'Some spirit has told you how to get possessions and money'. Now, it seems to have been James, not Janet, who identified the mouse/rat as a devil. Secondly, she had not actually refused to pray, but had knelt down with the rest, so James's identification sounds like a reassurance to her that she had escaped a demonic attempt to draw her away from prayer. Thirdly, his remark that she was not a witch needs to be read with the *but* which joins it to his final statement. 'If you have managed to resist this demon and pray along with us, I suppose this means you are not a witch in the conventional sense. *But* you do owe your money and possessions' (Janet had helped to stand caution for Thomas Leitch, remember) 'to the advice of some kind of spirit'.

With this trend of interpretation Janet seems to have agreed, for she says the spirit would appear in the form of a little man. 'Little' may be significant, because it suggests the spirit was a *sìth*, a fairy of some kind. Among other things, fairies looked like human beings but might be small of stature, and they guarded treasure hidden in the earth. Janet's alternative explanation, that the spirit was the ghost of her dead husband, is not incompatible with this, but that testimony does come from someone who was trying to remember an incident and not managing to do so in clear detail – 'John Stevenson the elder depones that, having taken pains to recollect his memory, all he can remember is...' – so it is not evidence on which we can afford to put very much weight. James Paterson, therefore, has no hesitation in connecting Janet with two spirits: one, a demon in the form of a mouse or rat, and one reminiscent of a fairy. Now, whether he put this idea in her head, or whether it was already there, and James was merely referring to it in a time of mutual stress when the earth shook and the cats yowled, the record leaves us uncertain when Janet confessed to being a witch in the traditional, expected sense. One document tells us she did this in 1650. Another suggests it was not until a year, or later, that she gave way under the persistent questioning of the laird of Fulbar. When she came into court in 1656 and 1657 she denied everything, of course, but this is no more than the 'not guilty' plea offered by a majority of accused in any modern court, regardless of their actual innocence or guilt. She was thought to be attended by a spirit, this was interpreted to mean the Devil, and from that point the inferences of criminal witchcraft were easily drawn.

Apart from Agnes Bayne who came from Banff, the other cases we have been considering fall into two groups. Catherine Cass, Agnes Robert and Janet Bruce all came from the Lothians, within the geographical, religious, and political orbit of Edinburgh. All three were pricked by John Kincaid, a self-appointed discoverer of witches, whose activities we shall discuss later in more detail, although his depositions that the marks he found on them were diabolical in origin did not have the automatic effect of persuading people to find them guilty. Janet was cleared of fourteen of the fifteen charges against her, and Agnes Roberts's case was dismissed twice, the second time because the witnesses failed to turn up in court. Catherine was indicted for theft as well as witchcraft, but we do not know the outcome of her trial. In no item of their dittays was any of them accused of making a pact with the Devil, copulating with him, attending a Sabbat, or renouncing her baptism. The charges all relate to causing illness, death, or misfortune to humans and animals, and the Devil is mentioned only twice, when the laird of Fulbar pressed Janet Tulloch and when Catherine Cass 'was heard to confess that she came in to John Young's door and window with the Devil on her back, and would have been into the house; and could not enter because John Young's wife was at her prayers'. Asked why she served the Devil, 'she was heard to answer that she had no other reason [than] to be revenged of her neighbours that did her wrong'. Catherine may indeed have said such things, of course, but the phraseology and sentiment sound rather like an attempt to get her to fit a preconceived notion of how a witch (as opposed to any other kind of magical operator, such as a charmer or diviner) might be expected to act and think.

The geographical spread of cases from the criminal courts, like those dealt with by kirk and presbytery sessions, is wide. Commissions were issued for the west, the south-east, the north-east, and East Lothian, coinciding with the principal administrative centres of justice. Bessie Carnochan, Elizabeth Maxwell, Euphame MacThynne, and Janet Tulloch all came from the West Country – the area round Kirkcudbright or Dumfries. Their cases, too, involve principally the infliction of harm and death and misfortune with the occasional lifting of disease caused by magic. Janet was pricked; the others seem to have escaped that attention; and conventional witchcraft theory enters the picture only in the prefaces to their dittays. The actual charges brought against them say nothing of a pact and, indeed, scarcely mention the Devil at all. Bessie Carnochan seems to have been given to claiming preternatural powers (but said she had got them from the fairies), while her claim that 'the king of all devils is my god' and assisted her in her malefices appears to be little more than foolish and unwise boasting, of a part perhaps with her attempts to seem more significant in the eyes of her neighbours than she actually was. The case of Agnes Bayne from Ordiquhill in Banff mirrors the general tenor of these cases, too.[15] On 15 June, she appeared before justices of the peace on charges of laying on and taking off illness, and also of refusing to treat someone when called upon to do so. The wording of this last item is interesting. George Henderson in Fordyce several miles away declared that his wife was very ill with a fever, 'and hearing that the said Agnes professed to be a *doctrix*, he went for the said Agnes to his wife'. 'Doctrix' is an unusual form of the word 'doctor' which referred to a schoolmaster, not a physician. So Agnes was probably claiming to have specialist knowledge which she could teach to other people. Agnes came with George, but asked to lie in bed with his wife that night 'and she should be well'. Both husband and wife refused the request, but not necessarily because there was anything untoward about it. People regularly slept more than one to a bed, either family members, or strangers if they were travelling and had to put up at an inn. So the reason for their refusal was more likely to be something else. Agnes, however, was offended and left, and although George tried three more times to get her to come with him again, she refused 'and shortly thereafter the said sick person died'.

Now, these cases we have been considering in detail may be taken as representative of the kind of people who were being accused (women), their clients (neighbours, and strangers drawn by their reputation for magical abilities), their accusers (both men and women, largely neighbours with whom the accused person was said to have quarrelled at some point), and the nature of their 'witchcraft'. This last principally involved the laying on of an illness which resulted in the death of the sufferer, human or animal, or the laying on and taking off an illness, or ruining someone's livelihood, and in this there is scarcely a mention of the Devil or of the accused person's making a covenant with him. When the Devil, the covenant, the mark, and so forth do appear, they are contained in the preface to the panel's [defendant's] dittay. This preface presented and read to the court therefore tends to fall into two sections. The first accuses the panel of disobeying divine law and the Scottish Witchcraft Act, of entering into service with Satan, making a pact with him, renouncing her or his baptism, and receiving the Devil's mark. (There may also be mention of carnal copulation with him and being given a new name). The second briefly summarises the type of particular offence which follows in the detailed list making up the bulk of the dittay. There tends to be little or, indeed, no correlation between the actual offences allegedly committed and those relating to Satan and his service, listed in the first part of the preface. But these initial prefaces are formulaic, repeating one another near enough word for word in many instances, and so we must take it that the allegations anent the Devil spring from something other than the offences attributed to the individual panel. They are, in fact, as we have seen, inferences drawn from the accusation of being a witch. Dittays pertaining to other criminal offences, such as murder, theft, and so forth, by contrast plunge straight into the relevant details without any similar prefatory remarks; so the need to make what amounts to a generalised censure and reprehension of the panel before the points of her or his dittay were made known to the assize represents a new, recriminatory attitude towards both the offence and the offender, which expresses – since the records were in the hands of the authorities and emanated from them – a reaction to witches more clearly informed by the reading of Continental or Europe-inspired treatises than by theories based upon direct observation and experience of what was happening in Scotland.

Fortunately, perhaps, these prefaces do not seem to have had much, if any, influence on the decisions made by the men who heard the cases. Whether kirk or presbytery sessions, or criminal assizes, these bodies appear to have taken great pains to weight the evidence presented to them and then deliver a verdict in accordance with what they believed was truth and justice. So if 1657 was not a wholly untypical year in respect of both witchcraft activity and witchcraft prosecution, why did 1658 see a gathering storm against magical operators of all kinds, and was there any significant difference between the witches prosecuted then and in the earlier years of the 1650s?

CHAPTER TWO

1658: The Initial Storm

Calculating the number of witches and their trials is fraught with difficulty. Many of the records are incomplete; surveys are usually incomplete too (including this one), because the amount of available material is immense and, of course, cases sometimes stretch over more than one year. Some of those appearing in 1657 had begun in 1656, while others lingered into 1658. Nevertheless, if we simply take figures from the Court of Justiciary in Edinburgh, the circuit courts, and those recorded elsewhere, without taking into account cases heard before ecclesiastical bodies, the number comes to about a hundred, far in advance of the nine in 1657, derived from similar sources. What is more, these hundred largely occurred at some distance from Edinburgh. East Lothian saw nine, but Alloway and Stirling together account for thirty-one and Ayr for about fifty-three, with Dumfries adding another four.[1] Overwhelmingly, therefore, the criminal records for 1658 are telling us about cases heard in the centre and west of Scotland. Now, it would be very helpful if these records were full of detail, thereby enabling us to say more about them. Unfortunately, however, most of them are merely lists of names of those appearing before a particular court on a certain date, so we are driven back on much more general considerations for any explanation of this apparent increase in number and specificity in location. We need to ask four questions. Were political or economic conditions in the west especially conducive to an increase in local suspicions of witchcraft?

Were western ministers more hostile to witches than those elsewhere in Scotland at this time? Were the relevant circuit court judges keen to suppress witches in the west? Were the charges brought against suspect witches there notably different in kind from those levelled in other courts elsewhere in the kingdom?

The answer to our first question appears to be that although there were significant changes in the way in and the extent to which Scotland was governed between autumn 1655 and autumn 1658 by the English, whose presence therein imparted a foreign tone to the conduct of the administration, it was the Highlands which occupied rather more of the government's attention than the Lowland west or east, simply because armed unrest perpetually seethed below the surface there and threatened to break out at any moment. The clans, unlike the Scots elsewhere in the kingdom, had ready and immediate access to weapons (though officially these were granted under permit), and in consequence upsurges and robberies continued to be frequent, even though permission to carry arms had been given specifically for the purpose of enabling their holders to suppress both theft and rebellion. The army – acting throughout Scotland as a police force – thus had its attention drawn northwards to deal with this constant problem and its intermittent manifestations. The south-west as a whole presented no such challenge to the authorities, and its governance was therefore not especially burdensome. Nor did the internal quarrels which wracked the Kirk during the later 1650s either spring from or affect the west more than anywhere else. Nor did the west suffer more than anywhere else from the burden of taxation imposed by General Monck's régime on behalf of Whitehall. The Scots were expected to pay for their own occupation and naturally they tended to resist paying whenever possible, especially since it was clear that by far the largest drain on the Scottish Exchequer was the occupying army. But again, the south-west suffered no greater imposition than elsewhere and so we cannot look to economies to provide a reason either for any increase in magical activity there or official attempts to suppress it.

So what of the law? Did its administration change in any significant fashion at this time? Let us bear in mind that when Scotland had initially been subjected to English rule, the intention had been to amalgamate the legal systems of both countries. But by the beginning of 1658 this notion had been quietly dropped and, as Dow explains, 'henceforth the more conservative, pragmatic aim of despatching as many legal actions in as short a time as possible would predominate. At the same time, however, the government [i.e. Whitehall] made it clear that there were limits to its willingness to hand back to the Scots control over their own judicial system. In 1658, only English judges were included on the commission to hear criminal causes'.[2] But if at first glance this suggests that English practice and theory would overbear the Scottish courts, we need to remember that the actual administration of justice was largely in the hands of the local gentry and army officers (as justices of the peace). The justices presiding over the quarter session held at Stirling in October 1657, for example, consisted of Colonel Thomas Reid, Lt Colonel John Cloburn, Major James Matloe, Sir Mungo Stirling, James Seton, Sir John Rollo, Sir William Leviston, Captain Hugh Boswell, Captain George Everard, William Stirling, and Robert Blair – five army men out of a total of eleven. Their job was to see that order was maintained, law upheld, and suspects summoned, arrested, imprisoned, and brought to justice. Communities there had a psychological problem. On the one hand, anyone who assisted the legal process in bringing a person to book was acting, in however limited a capacity, as an agent of the central, largely alien government. On the other, an occupied country is not one which sits at ease with itself, and the potential for unrest and criminal activity tends to be increased, thereby intensifying a longing for peace and order. Thus, desire for local stability may outweigh resentment at a distant, foreign authoritarianism, and the wish to co-operate with local representatives of that alien government in order to achieve the desired stability may suppress (though not remove) immediate expressions of hostility towards it – a situation which cannot fail to engender and heighten tensions within the local community itself.

Now, kirk and presbytery sessions were ideal media for the imposition of lawful behaviour, and the gentry, who provided justices of the peace, and their army partners relied to a significant extent upon the co-operation of the ministers and elders who formed what Margo Todd has called a 'vital network of local agents... well placed to undermine the old ways, profoundly reorient religious practice, and administer the new discipline systematically'.[3] Indeed, the gentry not only relied upon such people, the success of their legal functions depended on them; for until later in the seventeenth century, the system of JPs did not work with any particular effectiveness.[4] Even under English rule, Scotland could not be called a centralised country, and in consequence it was much more difficult for Edinburgh to impose its wishes with any degree of uniformity throughout the kingdom than it was for Whitehall to establish its rule in England. At first glance, then, it looks as though one possible reason for a steep rise in the numbers of those arrested and tried for magical operations in the south-west may have been due to chance – an unexpected surge in the desires of a number of communities in Dumfries, Kirkcudbright, and Ayr in particular either to root out long-standing trouble-makers from their midst, or to cleanse their parishes from Satanic influence in an effort to make the majority of their inhabitants more righteous and less embattled against the assaults of a non-human enemy.

This last will prove, on closer examination of the source-material, to be a significant consideration. Post-Covenant and then English-occupied Scotland presented her inhabitants with two frightening situations. Both tended to divide communities into groups of the Godly Few intensely conscious of their constant need to keep alert in the face of those who either might or who actually did seek to undermine them to their perpetual destruction, and this had its effect on local attitudes to the non-conformists in their midst. England/Satan was seen as constantly threatening Scottish/Presbyterian independence and, indeed, in the troubled years of the late 1650s might be said to have come close to a permanent occupation. So if, by this time, fighting Satan had become in one sense a substitute for fighting the English who by now appeared to be well entrenched in Scotland, it would not be surprising if resistance took the form of an intensified battle against Satan's army – the witches, the charmers, the diviners – who would have to be ejected and removed if the multitude of Scottish communities were to hope to regain their spiritual freedom.

What kind of battles were the ministers and people fighting, and what were the tactics employed by their Enemy? We have already discussed examples of the name-calling and charming of 1658, and it is worth noting that the latter frequently gives evidence of magical practices which have nothing to do with witchcraft (in the classical sense of sixteenth-century treatises on magic, which defined it as magic done with the assistance of spirits, usually with harmful intent), but rather reflect common exercises which drew upon presumed occult sympathies or bonds between disparate objects or entities. Thus, Margaret Imrie from Dunbarny sought to cure her daughter's illness by passing the girl three times through a circle made of blankets tied together, and throwing a stone or clod after her on each occasion.[5] During the sixteenth century this would have been treated simply as evidence of witchcraft. By the mid-seventeenth century, however, the authorities were apparently distinguishing between these two general types of magical activity. Proclamations issued in March and July 1658, for example, to enable sheriffs in Kelso and Perth and Cupar to hold courts for the trial of a very wide range of named criminal offences include 'witchcrafts and charmings' as separate, though obviously interlinked items, just as they designate 'saying or hearing of Mass' and those 'guilty of Popery' as separate though companion offences.[6] The clear implication is that the authorities were targeting aspects of popular culture which they saw as undesirable in themselves as well as dangerous because of their diabolic affinities; and the prefaces to dittays in the criminal courts, formulaic though they be, give unmistakeable evidence of an official cast of mind which recognised those affinities and drew inferences of Satanic association where none such overtly appeared in the details of the actual charges against the panel.

It was probably a similar cast of mind which led the formulators of the 1563 Witchcraft Act to include consultation of magical practitioners along with witchcraft itself as an offence worthy of the death penalty; and we can see the result of this in the case of John Milne from Inverurie in Aberdeenshire who was accused on 6 September 1658 of 'charming and abusing the country people [i.e. people in the immediate locality] these many years bygone by your sorcery and witchcraft'.[7] The charge related to an incident in Fetternear, a village belonging to the same district as Inverurie, and alleged that John had removed an ague or headache from a man and transferred it to a woman. The woman was, naturally, aggrieved and threatened to delate John to the justices unless he removed the illness from her. So John gave her some powders wrapped up in a small piece of linen cloth and told her to wear this round her neck for nine nights and then burn it. This she did, and recovered as John had promised. 'For which unlawful and devilish laying on and off-taking of the which ague and sickness by your sorcery and witchcraft, you, being convened before his Highness's justices, confessed the aforesaid charm to be of truth'. The subsequent trial, we are told, was abandoned, for what reason we do not know. But here we can see two magical cures interpreted as witchcraft, on the grounds that the illness appeared to have been transferred from one person to another – an act of malefice – while the original reference to 'charming' has been turned into one of 'devilish… sorcery and witchcraft' in relation to the simple cure with powders.

James Dalrymple, later Viscount Stair, a stiff Presbyterian and legal luminary, first appointed judge in 1657, explained why certain crimes warranted punishment even as far as the death penalty, *regardless of whether anyone had been harmed by the offence or not*, a consideration directly relevant to charmers as well as witches:

> Obediential obligations are these, which are put upon men by the will of God, not by their own will, and so are most part natural, as introduced by the law of nature, before any addition made thereto by engagement, and are such as we are bound to perform solely by our obedience to God: as conventional obligations are such, as we are bound by and through our own will, engagement or consent.
>
> Obediential obligations are either by the will of God immediately, or by the mediation of some fact of ours; such are obligations by delinquence, whereby we become bound to reparation and satisfaction to the party injured, and are liable in punishment to God, which may be exacted by those who have His warrant for that effect. Of these obediential obligations there be some which tie us to God alone; whereby there is no right constitute in man to exact the same as his own due, or any warrant or command given him by God to exact them on His behalf. And some, though they constitute not a right in man, yet man is commanded and warranted to vindicate them, as the crimes of witchcraft, blasphemy, bestiality, and the like; for which there is an express command to inflict punishment, though there be no injury done therein to man, of which there could be any reparation [*Exodus* 22.18, 19, 28]. For the command, 'Thou shalt not suffer a witch to live' [*Exodus* 22.18] takes place, though the witch have committed no malefice against the life or goods of man.[8]

That this was indeed carried into practice can be seen from illustrations provided by Sir George MacKenzie in his *Laws and Customs of Scotland in Matters Criminal* (1678):

John Burgh was convict for witchcraft, *anno* 1643, for curing beasts by casting white stones in water and sprinkling them therewith, and for curing women by washing their feet with south-running water and putting odd [spare] money in the water. Several other instances are to be seen in the processes led *anno* 1661, and the instance of Drummond is very remarkable, who was burnt for performing many miraculous cures, albeit no malefice was ever proved. (Title 10, paragraph 10).

If, then, in practice witchcraft was elided with charming, as seems often to have been the case, there could be no effective defence against the accusation of being a witch that the suspect had merely sought to cure people or animals of illness by preternatural means without the aid of Satan or of spirits. The preternatural act of itself was liable to be taken to support the notion that such non-human assistance was present or available, and that in consequence the operator had fallen within the terms of the Witchcraft Act.

The criminal courts were certainly busy from the beginning of 1658. John Nicoll noted in his diary that there were

two witches and a warlock imprisoned within the tolbooth of Edinburgh in February 1658. One of the witches died within the tolbooth of Edinburgh. The warlock was burned on the castle hill: and the third, being a young woman called Anderson, newly married within three months or thereby before, was condemned to be burned. Yet she was spared for a time, being suspect to be with child, which was the cause of the postponement and delay of her execution. Her confession was that she did marry the Devil, and had committed sundry adulteries; and after she was contracted with her present husband and going to the kirk to be married, she repented and would have turned back again; and confessed that at her marriage, Satan appeared to her in the kirk, standing behind the pulpit – with many other things to this purpose.

The reference to her committing adultery is worth noticing, especially as Nicoll takes it up again in his entry for 5 May:

This Janet Anderson, formerly recorded, who was condemned in March last for sundry adulteries and fornications, and for having copulation with

Satan, was burned on the castle hill. She made a happy [fitting] end, and
gave singular testimony of her repentance by frequent prayers and singing
of psalms before her execution.

Now, adultery was a serious offence. It might carry the death penalty, as
we learn from the case of Katharine Smith from Inverkeithing, who was
put on trial for witchcraft in 1655.[9] One point of her dittay makes the
situation quite clear:

> You are indicted and accused for that notwithstanding by the laws and
> Acts of Parliament of this nation, the committers of the crime of adultery
> is [sic] punishable with death: nevertheless, it is of verity that you, being
> married to… William Brown, your husband in his lifetime, viz. upon the
> 1, 2, 3, and remaining days of January, February, March, [etc.], the years of
> God 1632, 1633, 1634, 1635, and 1636, at least on one or other of the said
> days and months, have polluted and defiled yourself in adultery in hav-
> ing carnal copulation with John Lochtie, you own servant for the time:
> wherethrough you have incurred the punishment of death contained in
> the said Acts of Parliament.

The rest of the items in Katharine's dittay relate to maleficent magic
– laying on illness, killing people and animals magically – and in one
instance, effecting a cure, so the accusation of adultery comes as something of a surprise. The officials involved may have been trying to kill
two birds with one stone by amalgamating all her offences, thereby
doing away with the need for and the expense of two separate trials; or
the adultery may have been linked in some way with her alleged witchcraft, although nothing in the records actually suggests that this was at all
the case. It does, however, show that it was possible in some instances to
formulate a link between a woman's illegal sexual activity and her traffic
with Satan, most vividly illustrated by the accusations of carnal copulation with the Devil, which appear in many prefaces to Scottish witches'
dittays in the seventeenth century. Such copulation would automatically
be adulterous if the woman was married, and fornication if she was not.

Over in the south-west Janet Miller and Katharine Clacharty were
burned for witchcraft in April.[10] Katharine's offences all concern the
infliction of illness on people or animals, resulting in the death of most

of those so afflicted. In one case, the illness was transferred to a woman who had asked her to give back her brother his health, and then, when *her* sister begged Katharine to cure her, the illness alighted upon her and ran its course until she, too, recovered. Katharine, perhaps not surprisingly, seems to have acquired the reputation of being a witch. When Robert Pollock suddenly fell ill and remained incapacitated for thirteen weeks, his son was forced to do his job for him. This clearly proved a strain and, while he was drinking one Sabbath afternoon, he swore 'that if his father died of that disease, he should help to burn thee with his own hands'. Likewise, the goodwife of Newhall became ill, and Katharine was threatened by some of her family 'that they would cause burn thee for a witch if she should die'. Her case thus conforms to what is emerging as a common pattern, and it is not unexpected that eventually she found herself in front of the local magistrates.

Janet Miller's case, however, is particularly interesting. She came from Dundrennan, a village in Kirkcudbright, and was accused of sixteen points of witchcraft, none of which, however, has anything to do with diabolically inspired malefice. Five of the sixteen involved fairy power, and item one may be taken as a fair example of the rest. Janet Martin from Borgue, a village not far from Dundrennan, but over on the western side of the River Dee, informed the court that while her husband was threshing in a barn, he suddenly lost the power of his tongue and side. His wife went to Janet Miller to ask her advice (so obviously Janet was a well-known magical operator in the district, specialising, so to speak, in diagnosing and curing illnesses which were suspected to have a preternatural origin). Janet told her 'that the fairies had taken the power of them from him, and that it was not his tongue they were set for, but his life, were it not that there was a friend of his with them that hindered it'. Had Janet Martin's husband stayed twenty-four hours in the barn where he suffered his affliction, said Janet, he would have recovered. There was no point in his going back there now, though, because it would do no good.

Janet then gave her prescription for a cure. His wife was to 'take fox tree [foxglove] leaves (of the kind that do not shoot), and at cock crow go and fetch some south-running water'. She was to have someone with her while she did this. They were to sign themselves under their breath as they went out of the house: that is, they were to make the sign of

the cross and whisper 'In nomine Patris et Filii et Spiritus Sancti', or
perhaps the English version 'In the name of the Father, the Son, and
the Holy Spirit', after which they must remain completely silent. Only
when they took the water were they to speak and say, 'We lift this in the
name of God', and then, three times, 'Whatever thou be, either above
earth or beneath earth, that hath taken his health from him, give it him
again, for God's sake'. Janet also instructed that the water must not be
set on the ground until it arrived back in Janet Martin's house where
it was to be boiled with the fox tree leaves and then used to bathe the
patient. Notwithstanding Janet's strict enjoining upon silence, however,
Janet Martin and her companion spoke to Marion MacGimpsy when
they met in her house, so Janet Miller warned them that Janet's husband
would not recover but would shortly die – 'which fell out accordingly'.

Janet's cure, which appears in much the same form in seven of the
items against her, was extremely common, and it is not surprising
that Janet should have recommended foxglove leaves in this instance,
because the foxglove is a fairy plant in folklore tradition. South-running
water was almost always recommended, too. Belief in its efficacy was
not confined to Scotland, nor to the seventeenth century. A witchcraft
case which came before the ecclesiastical court of Durham in *c.*1570, for
example, had Catherine Fenwick testifying that 'about two years ago, her
cousin Edward Wydringham had a child sick, and Jenkin Pearson's wife
asked... how Benjamin (the child) did'. Janet Pearson (the wife) then
suggested that the child's mother come and speak to her. Catherine, for
some reason, went instead, 'and the said Pearson's wife said the child was
taken with the fairy, and bade her send two [people] for south-running
water: and these two should not speak by the way, and the child should
be washed in that water'.[11]

Janet attributed to the fairies several of the illnesses about which she
was consulted, but also claimed to recognise when one of them had
been caused by a witch. John Simpson, she said, 'would never recover,
for he was roasted as betwixt two witches', one of whom she named
as Rosina Milligan, a widow in Twynholm – a village we have already
come across: it was there that Bessie Carnochan was examined by justices of the peace – and the other as Janet MacGowan, living in Borgue.
Janet's message to John's wife was a mixture of discouragement and reassurance. On the one hand, she said, '"thou thinks he hath a light pain,

but his pain is as great as if he were roasted betwixt three fires", (pointing to the ground as if there were one here, another there, and another there)'. Asked why these witches were tormenting him, 'for he never did wrong to any of them, neither was he in way of marriage with any of their children', Janet replied that 'there were several of them who would have had him to their daughters, that never let him know of it'. What a pity, she said, John had not bestirred himself to do something about his condition. He should have

sent or gone to the houses of the women whom he suspected, and stolen from above the lintel of the door three stalks of straw and, in the morning before daylight, burned them about him [while he was] standing naked on the floor, [so] that their smoke might have blown upon him. Then the witches would have had no more power over him.

This, she added, was how she had unwitched John Kirkpatrick in Orchardtown. As it was, however, there was nothing his wife Agnes could do for him, except give him something to drink to slake his thirst. Agnes burst into tears. 'Alas, I fear he [will] be dead before I get home', she said; and Janet answered, 'He will not be dead before you get home, but he will not live long after', a prophecy the record notes came true, 'for within ten days after she went home, he died'. But Janet also offered the reassurance that 'though they have power over his body, they will have none over his soul, for' (clapping her hands together) she said, 'as sure as these ten fingers are together, his soul will be in glory'.

One further remark Janet made is very revealing:

She required that [this consultation] should be kept close, especially from their minister, of whom she said he threatened to cause burn me for a witch; but (honest man), it is a wonder how he keeps his feet among them for there are more [magical operators] about him than he realises.

The minister of Dundrennan at the time was John Duncan, a relatively young man aged only twenty-eight, who had come to the parish in 1655. He was actively hostile to the restoration and the episcopal settlement when they happened and, in consequence, was deprived of his ministry in 1662. Janet was particularly keen he should not find out what she was doing, for she asked another of her clients, too, to keep quiet for the same reason about her curing his child. Now, John Duncan was one of a group of local ministers with the same history, all belonging to the parishes whence came the witnesses against Janet Miller. Thomas Wylie in Kirkcudbright, John Wilkie in Twynholm, and Robert Ferguson in Buittle were all deprived in 1662 for refusing to accept the new political and ecclesiastical dispensations; and Adam Kae in Borgue was imprisoned that year for continuing to hold meetings of the presbytery after these had been forbidden. The likely tone of their sermons may be gauged from that of Donald Cargill who, on 26 May 1660 ascended his pulpit in the Barony Church of Glasgow, and launched into a reprehension of the restored monarchy. 'This is the first step of our going a-whoring from God', he said, 'and whoever of the Lord's people this day are rejoicing, their joy will be like the crackling of thorns under a pot; it will soon be turned into mourning. He (meaning the King) will be the woefullest sight ever the poor Church of Scotland saw. Woe, woe, woe unto him! His name shall stink while the world stands for treachery, tyranny, and lechery.'[12]

In Duncan, Wylie, and so forth, we have, then, a group of ministers actively opposed to changes to the presbyterian and covenanting system dominant during the years of English commonwealth rule. All belonged to the presbytery of Kirkcudbright, and all therefore met each other regularly. Such meetings would have provided ideal opportunities to exchange information and reinforce notions and beliefs they had in common, and it is interesting in this connection that the last four items on Janet Miller's dittay all come from residents in Buittle and appear to be additions to the list. Was this because the presbytery had asked – as presbyteries often did – for inquiries to be made from the pulpits under its jurisdiction anent any other complaints relating to Janet Miller? If so, it illustrates the possible co-operation between ministers in rooting out information about suspect offenders.

We have already seen in the introduction the effect upon Sir Archibald Johnston of Wariston of intense sermonising from clergy such as these, and it will be useful to remind ourselves of this intensity. Here is Andrew Gray, preaching in Glasgow in the early 1650s:

We would only propose this unto you: did ye never know what it was to be under the impression [pounding, stamping] of the sinfulness of sin?

Or did you ever know what it was to water your couch with tears under
the impression of it?... Certainly the day is coming when ye who never
knew what it was to crucify a lust, Christ shall crucify you upon that
cross of everlasting pain, when He shall tread you in the wine-press of
the indignation of the Most High, when He shall make the arrows of His
indignation sharp upon you.

Gray's answer to this predicament was the standard presbyterian urging
to self-examination, and he promised 'that a Christian who is much in
self-examination doth behold such spots and blemishes in himself that
he is forced to wonder that it is not worse with him, and so is constrained to glorify God in the fire'.[13]

David Stevenson has remarked that 'the proposition that one of the
central aims of a Calvinist upbringing was to induce manic-depression
has something to recommend it'.[14] Robert Wodrow recorded an incident
in 1711 which seems to illustrate this point, and although it is dated to
some fifty years after our period, the principal themes are still pertinent
to the religious psychology of at least some west Scotland communities
in the mid-seventeenth century:

I hear from good hands a very strange account of one [...] Gilmore, a
Glasgow youth, who went down and was a baker in Campbeltown. He
was a very great mocker and scoffer at religion, and a very lax man. For
a twelve month before May last he had a great many convictions, on the
Sabbath, when hearing Mr. James Bowes, minister there; and he owned
he was never almost at a Sabbath but he came away with a bosom-full of
convictions. However, he found means to stifle all and turned through the
week to his old courses. In the beginning of May last, one Sabbath night,
in the morning, he fell a-dreaming that two devils came to him; and one
of them said, 'You must go with us'; and he said he would not. The Devil
said he belonged to them! He said, 'No', he hoped to have God's mercy.
The Devil upbraided him for his sins, in particular, drinking and mocking
and scoffing, and told him that God had given him many offers and many
convictions, which raised resolutions, and he had slighted them all; and
that there was no mercy for him. He was theirs!

All this passed in sleep, and the fright and terror awaked him, and he
got up out of his bed. It was just a little after the break of day, and so light

that he could see. And when he was up on the floor, there were just two devils in the shapes he saw in sleep accosted him; and the room filled full, as he said, of devils, and had the very same converse, and he made the same answers as above. At length one of them came up and gave him a stroke on the side and said, 'If you will not go with us now, you shall go with us this days eight days!' – and they disappeared and left him in dreadful terror. It was in the time of the Assembly. Mr. Bowes was there, and there was not a minister in all that bounds to be had, though he earnestly desired them. He went to Christians and they came to him, and continued under the fearfullest terrors imaginable. He was otherwise perfectly in the use of his reason and senses, only complained of a pain in his side, where he said he had got his stroke, and otherwise was in perfect health all the week, and continued till that day eight days, at which time he died under great terror.[15]

The heightened emotionalism evident in both sermon and episode may go some way to explaining why Janet Miller and, indeed, Katharine Clacherty who was executed with her in April, found themselves targeted as witches. Three of the ministers – Duncan, Wylie, and Wilkie – took up their posts in the presbytery of Kirkcudbright in 1655. Of these, Thomas Wylie is perhaps of especial interest. He had been appointed to the parish of Borgue in 1642, transferred thence in 1646 to Mauchline in the presbytery of Ayr, and from there to Kirkcudbright in 1655. Now, eight of the sixteen charges against Janet were made by people from Borgue, and a ninth by Geillis Young described as 'now in Kirkcudbright', but relating to a suspect witch, Jean Thomson, in Borgue. Another article says that when the deponer wanted to seek a cure for a long-standing illness, 'she went to Janet Miller in the town of Kirkcudbright'. So is it possible that Thomas Wylie, with his pastoral experience of Borgue only twelve to sixteen years previously, and his present responsibility for Kirkcudbright where Janet had also been living, provided a stimulus for her arrest and subsequent trial, urged on, perhaps, by the youthful enthusiasm of John Duncan whose personal hostility Janet said on more than one occasion she feared?

Borgue certainly saw its fair share of witches. Janet MacGowan and Janet Thomson from there were accused before justices, the former in April, the latter in May, each on eleven points of witchcraft.[16] Both seem to have inflicted illness upon people and animals, but MacGowan was the more vindictive of the two, for the majority of her inflictions ended in death. By contrast, Thomson saw fit in most of her similar cases to lift the disease she had caused, and so allow the person or beast to recover. Geillis Young, who testified against Janet Miller, also offered information in relation to Janet Thomson. Thomson, she said, had brought the falling sickness upon her and refused to cure her. So Geillis 'went to Janet Miller, the witch woman who sometime dwelled at the Abbey, who first prescribed unto her the use of foxtree leaves and south-running water for the remedy; and afterwards, without any previous information from the said Geillis, or any in her name, (so far as she knows), did discover Jean Thomson to have been the on-caster of that sickness upon her'. Miller lent authenticity to this identification by telling Geillis exact details of the circumstances leading to and including her first fit, and then added, 'She [Janet Thomson] is a very devil. Many times she set upon thee before, but could not prevail against thee'. Geillis reported to the court that Miller's remedy had proved entirely effective, and that she had suffered not a single fit since taking it.

Meanwhile, across the shire border in Ayr, the presbytery of Irvine, 'having formerly, upon advice from the justices of the peace, recommended to the several ministers to try within their parishes what persons were under such presumptions of witchcraft as might be recommended to the justices of the peace for taking present course with them', had decided to ask the justices to look into accusations against Janet Steel from Kilmaurs, Isobel Henderson from Irvine, and Janet Ross 'once living in Fenwick' whose minister was willing to testify that she had confessed to being a witch.[17] There are three notable features attached to these cases. First, the impulse to investigate seems to have come from the presbytery acting upon the justices' advice. Secondly, all three women are alleged to have confessed that they had entered into a covenant with the Devil, renounced their baptism, and so forth – the usual formulae belonging to the prefaces to dittays at this time – and to have 'laid on and taken off sundry diseases, as well upon men, women, and children as on goods and animals', a set of accusations which is beginning to look very familiar and which, if the other examples we examined earlier are indicative of the kind of magic allegedly operated by such people, has nothing to do with Satan or a Sabbat.

Thirdly, a ten-year-old girl from Irvine, called 'Wallace' (her Christian name is missing from the document), 'had before the minister and several others, who are ready to depone the same, confessed that she was present at several meetings with Satan and others, and had consented to be his servant'. Young children do not often appear in Scottish witchcraft accusations, so one wonders how Wallace came to be involved here. It may be significant that Isobel, Janet Ross, and Wallace were currently resident in Irvine, and that the minister there, Alexander Nesbitt, was a comparatively young man of thirty-five in 1658. It is also worth noting that George Ramsay, minister of Kilmaurs, was deprived of his ministry in 1662, and that William Guthrie, minister of Janet Ross's former parish of Fenwick, had become a Protester in 1651, Protesters being those who were steadfastly opposed to state interference in ecclesiastical affairs and government. They were particularly strong in the west of Scotland, as the number deprived of their ministry in 1662 indicates. Ralph Rodger, one of those appointed by the presbytery to urge the local magistrates to take action against Janet Steel and the others, was also a member of the Protesting party. So it looks as though the cases in Kirkcudbright and in Irvine may have something, however slight, in common – a strong adherence to strict presbyterian government among the ministers involved, along with the possibility that this commitment meant they were living in a state of heightened emotional embattlement against the various forces, political and demonic, they saw ranged every day against them.

This is very much worth bearing in mind when we come to the death of Janet Sawyer in the town of Ayr. A letter from an English official, Colonel Sawrey, dated 26 April 1658, records what happened, and notes the prevailing public attitude towards witchcraft:

Upon Friday 23rd instant, was one Janet Saers, late an inhabitant of this town, according to a sentence passed by the judges, (the assize having found her guilty of witchcraft), strangled at a stake and, after that, her whole body burned to ashes. She did constantly deny that she knew anything of witchcraft, and at her death made a very large confession of her wicked life, and had good exhortations to the living, but remained to affirm that she knew nothing of witchcraft. And, as I was informed by those that heard her, when the minister was urging her to confess, she had these words. 'Sir, I am shortly to appear before the Judge of all the

earth, and a lie may well damn my soul to Hell. I am clear of witchcraft
for which I am presently [now] to suffer'. And so with a seeming willingness submitted herself to death. The people in this country are more set
against witchcraft than any other wickedness, and if once a person have
that name and come upon an assize, it's hard to get off with less than this
poor creature.[18]

It is a touching account, but for that very reason we need to stand at a
little distance from it. Making a good end was important for everyone
and Janet's final words (which may or may not be her *verba ipsissima*, since
they come to us second hand) are intended, if only in part, to create that
impression. Balanced against these is the verdict of 'guilty'. We have seen
already that assizes were by no means always biased against the panels
whose cases they tried, and a good proportion of Janet's assizors will have
been drawn from those who knew her or knew what her local reputation was. Since we do not know what were the charges against her, nor
the pattern of voting followed by her assize, we have no means of telling
whether she was actually innocent or guilty or a combination of the two.
When she insisted she was not guilty of witchcraft, she may have been
telling the truth. But this does not rule out the possibility that she was a
charmer or a practitioner of entirely beneficent magic, and this she could
legitimately have distinguished from witchcraft, even if her indictment
had failed to do so. Janet, therefore, may have died completely innocent,
suffering the verdict of an assize which had been prejudiced against her,
or innocent after a fashion; and it would be unwise of us, at such a distance and so ill-informed of the details attending her case, to press our
opinion of it too far in any direction. When Colonel Sawrey mentioned
that 'this country' was set against witchcraft, he was using the word in
its older sense of 'district', here referring to Ayr. Sawrey was, in effect,
deputy-governor of the shire in the absence of its appointed governor,
Colonel Cooper, and he seems to have caught the prevailing psychology
although, again, it is worth reiterating that we are not entitled thereby to
assume that Janet's assize *must* have been biased against her.

By the time Janet died, the presbytery of Irvine's efforts to uncover
the extent to which witches had penetrated the parishes under its jurisdiction bore fruit in a list of forty-two suspects, only four of whom
were men.[19] They came from the town of Ayr itself, Carbolton, Craigie,

Riccarton, Kilbride, Ardrossan, Dunlop, Largs, and Irvine, and it will not come as a surprise to learn that most of their ministers were deprived in 1662. All these villages are grouped quite close together, although the vagaries of borders mean that they belonged to three different presbyteries, Ayr, Irvine, and Greenock. Seven of these wanted people are recorded as dead at the times of the authorities' visit – two from Irvine, one each from Carbolton, Craigie, Kilbride, Ardrossan, and Dunlop. Christina Larner suggests that they may have been dead for some time, or that they may have committed suicide, or that relatives were concealing the fact that they had fled.[20] Any of these, of course, is possible. But the mention of suicide is slightly misleading in as much as we have no idea how old the individuals were, or if they had been ill of a fatal disease. It is also worth remarking that recorded suicides of suspect witches tend to take place in prison after the individual had been arrested, questioned, and spent some time in durance. Suicide is therefore not the first explanation of their deaths for which we should look, and the notion that their relatives may have been lying to the officials, while plausible, has no warrant from the record, just as there is no explanation given for the disappearance of six individuals – one from Riccarton, four from Dunlop, two from Largs – who were not to be found and in consequence could not be summoned to an investigation.

Larner's suggestions rest upon and appeal to the unspoken idea that *innocent* people were being targeted by the authorities, and that they had succumbed to justified panic when officials arrived in their neighbourhood. However reasonable this may seem, however, we must also try to bear in mind that, with the use of various kinds of charms, gestures, objects, and liturgically-based words so widespread among the people, a large number of those accused of being witches may well have been guilty of practising some of kind of magic, even if it was not necessarily maleficent in intent. Whether this made them disappear, with the connivance of relatives and neighbours, is purely guesswork and, given that the majority of accusations against individuals came from relatives and neighbours, the notion that suspects could evade arrest through some network of well-meaning lies, with no one in seven different communities stepping forward as a collaborator, is perhaps not quite as happy as it may seem at first glance. But one fact does remain. Forty-two people were targeted as witches, principally by the presbytery of Irvine, and this represents a notable escalation in official interest in magical operators. What happened in the end to twenty-five who are recorded as being prosecuted, we do not know.

In the case of two other suspect witches from Ayr, however, Elspeth Cunningham, and Janet Sloan, we know they were convicted and executed.[21] Janet Sawyer, mentioned along with them in the record, as we have seen was garrotted and burned in April 1658 but Elspeth Cunningham and Janet Sloan did not face execution until March the following year, a not infrequent occurrence, for we find letters of complaint and petition addressed to relevant authorities by members of the suspect's family, or other interested parties, asking that she or he be brought to trial or released on caution after spending many weeks or months in prison. Thus, for example, on 2 May 1650, Robert Brown and William Brown wrote to the Committee of Estates on behalf of their wives, Marjorie Durie and Katharine Smyth, and John Dickson on behalf of his mother-in-law, Beatrix Douglas, explaining that the three women 'have been retained these nine or ten months prisoners in the steeple tolbooth and other ward houses of Inverkeithing, where they have suffered the extreme rigour of a cold winter, to the undoing of their persons and their private fortune, being delated by some as guilty of the crimes of witchcraft'. There had been a thorough investigation of these alleged crimes, wrote the men, and yet insufficient evidence had been produced thereby. Consequently, the men asked the Committee 'to put them to a speedy trial, or else to set them to liberty upon caution'. The Committee listened to the request and instructed the magistrates in Inverkeithing to set the women free on caution of £1,000 (presumably Scots rather than sterling), or to send the minister or some appropriate person to Edinburgh 'upon Tuesday next, fully instructed and authorised to show a reasonable cause why the same should not be done'.[22] The minister, Walter Bruce, had already been suspended from his ministry in 1649 for giving voice to some slightly crackpot notions from his pulpit, and was deposed on 26 June 1650 for gross neglect of his pastoral duties. It is easy to see, therefore, why Marjorie, Katharine and Beatrix may have found it difficult to stir the local officials to hear and resolve their case, since one of the key officials would have been the negligent Walter Bruce himself.

April 1658 also saw the trial of Marion Lewars in the circuit court of Dumfries.[23] It may have been one of several instances which stimulated the presbytery to issue a notice to all its ministers, urging them anent suspect witches to 'make public intimation unto their several congregations to come to the session or elders, and delate the particular scandal they have to charge them with'.[24] Marion came from the parish of Urr in Kirkcudbright and, according to the record, had been well known as a witch for twenty years. There were ten items on her dittay, and most seem to have arisen as the result of bad blood between herself and a local family called MacIlduf. Seven involve the death of farm animals, losses attributed by the MacIldufs and a friend or neighbour of theirs, Andrew Thomson, to Marion's spiteful magic. If we are to believe what the MacIldufs and others alleged, Marion appears to have been what can only be called a nasty bit of work, although her principal animus against her local community was directed against animals rather than people. Their deaths, however, could easily spell financial hardship or ruin for their owners, so harmful magic employed against them would undoubtedly have been bitterly resented. But one or two curious and contradictory points come out of the recorded testimonies. About August 1657, Marion went to the minister, George Gledstanes, complaining that Robert MacBrair had called her a witch – the kind of slander which, as we have seen, often appears in kirk session records – and when she came before the session on a charge of witchcraft (perhaps the same occasion, perhaps a later) she offered the minister a bribe to befriend her. Both actions bespeak a woman who was both brazen and, perhaps, insufficiently sure of her ability to withstand close scrutiny anent magical working. It was not the first time she had attempted to bribe an official, for when a witch-pricker came into the area, she offered Robert Ferrers of Barnbarroch twenty pounds if he would deliberately pretend not to know who she was. Barnbarroch is only about eight miles or so south of Urr, so Marion was obviously trying to bribe one of the local gentry, a possible, indeed likely, justice of the peace. Why was Marion so unsure of her position? Perhaps the combined force of the MacIlduf family was bearing hard upon her and she thought they might exercise more sway than she with the local authorities. But perhaps she had legitimate doubts about her own innocence.

The final item in her dittay – added to it in a different hand – is short, but odd. 'The said Marion was seen in the night time go three times widdershins naked about Andrew Thomason's house, and thereafter all his living farm-stock grew weak and died'. Andrew Thomson claimed to be an eyewitness of this, and his daughter furnished the court with her testimony, too. The nakedness is somewhat unusual. It was associated with Eve, of course, and therefore sin, and witches both old and young are frequently portrayed in works of art as naked. But in many illustrations, and in the literature of witchcraft, witches are always seen as fully clothed while they operate their magic or fly to a Sabbat. It is possible, if we believe Andrew's evidence, that Marion was gathering herbs, since there is a little scattered evidence that this was sometimes done naked. But the evidence comes either from Classical legend, or belongs to the Middle Ages, and none of it is directly associated with Scotland. One could solve the problem, of course, by suggesting that Marion was off her head, or that Andrew and his daughter were lying, but there is no evidence to support either contention, so the problem still remains. Going widdershins (contrary to the direction of the sun) was undoubtedly associated with harmful magic. In May 1671 Janet MacMurdoch from Dumfries was described at her trial as walking three times round her neighbours' yards, barefoot, as a result of which their animals fell ill.[25] Here, I think, is an explanation of what Marion was doing, and her 'nakedness' would thus refer to her being barefoot, a much more likely circumstance than her going without clothes altogether. So was this episode genuine testimony to Marion's actually practising hostile magic? If we may interpret it so, it would explain Marion's nervousness at the arrival of a witch-pricker in the neighbourhood, and her somewhat extraordinary attempts to bribe the minister and a local landowner, for it would be evidence that she did indeed practise magic and thus fell within the terms of the Witchcraft Act.

A notice summoning witnesses to court was sent out on 5 April, and Marion was tried in Dumfries on 9 April. The assize voted to acquit her. Their verdict provides an interesting comment on the conduct of many of these trials. Acquittals were not uncommon (although it must be said that guilty verdicts were more frequent), and this suggests that assizors – at least half of whose number would have come either from the same community as the accused or from very near it, and who would therefore be likely to know the accumulated local details which had gone into making the suspect's reputation – listened to the available evidence and made their decisions on what they knew and what they had heard in court. A greater degree of fairness and concern for justice, no matter what the circumambient atmosphere or attendant local tensions, seems to have prevailed in those trials whose records contain sufficient information to allow us to come to a judgement.

This care not to convict without regard to the quality of the evidence can also be seen in those trials which were deserted before they had a chance to get under way. Agnes Nimmo, for example, was accused of several points of witchcraft in March and again in July 1658.[26] She was a married woman from Liberton, which was then a village to the south of Edinburgh, and was examined in Edinburgh Castle on 4 March 'anent several points of sorcery and witchcraft alleged practised… upon sundry persons, and upon certain goods and animals'. The evidence was very thin. Most of it relates to a series of incidents in May 1657. Her husband, James Davidson, was looking after some horses and let them stray into Robert Young's corn. Robert, naturally enough, rebuked him for it, but James was not abashed and called out some abuse as Robert walked away. When Agnes heard of this, she sought out Robert Young and, in the presence of several other people, gave him a piece of her mind. She also told two more (who later gave testimony to the court) that Robert had beaten both her and her husband – assertions which the context of the complete evidence suggests may well have been untrue. Within eight days of the incident, Robert was coming back from Edinburgh with a black horse, and happened to meet Agnes at John Dickson's house. Whereupon 'the horse fell down and was not able to rise, nor to carry his own saddle until All Hallows' Eve', and 'the said Robert fell sick, having a dimness in his eyes, and wants the power of his right side, together with an infirmity in his tongue'. One witness, however, said that the horse recovered within three days, adding the significant rider that 'he never heard Agnes Nimmo to be reputed a witch'. This is contradicted by Alexander Paterson from Liberton itself, who testified 'he has heard several people bruit her name as a witch', but is supported by another witness who deponed 'she never heard Agnes Nimmo to be reputed a witch'. The two who spoke in her favour on this point did not actually come from Liberton, so it is possible that she may have had a very local reputation or been in process of acquiring one. But four witnesses, who remembered her cursing Robert Young, failed to make any overt connection between that and the illness of his horse and his own stricken health. So the evidence relying upon *post hoc ergo propter hoc* is not very strong.

There were one or two additional attempts to blame Agnes for a number of misfortunes. James Johnston, for example, testified that she and his wife had quarrelled, and that his cow gave blood, but was honest enough to add anent the bleeding that he did not know whether it had happened before or after the women had fallen out. But he added an interesting point. 'Robert Young being sick, Agnes Nimmo came to [James Johnston] and desired him to cause Robert Young to go to Linlithgow with a letter which she would procure from Jean Crawford in Blackfriars Wynd [in Edinburgh], directed to Marion Crawford in Linlithgow, and she would cure him'. It is frustrating not to know whether this concern for Robert Young happened before their quarrel or after it, because if it were the latter, we should be entitled to ask whether Agnes was suffering from a guilty conscience, or trying to create a more favourable impression in the looming possibility that the incident was going to cause her arrest as a witch. What this testimony does tell us, however, is that Agnes was not a magical operator herself, or that she was not one who specialised in the kind of cure that would benefit Robert.

Her case was due to be heard on 1 June, but just over a month later the judges decided to abandon the trial altogether. No reason is recorded, but it is at least possible that the court decided the evidence was too weak and in places too contradictory to prove witchcraft, and so deserted the action in order to save time and cost. We may ask why it ever got as far as the criminal court in the first place. Surely this was the kind of complaint best reviewed by a kirk session? The answer seems to lie in Liberton's peculiar situation at the time. Archibald Newton, who had been minister there since 1639, died in June 1657 and the next minister, Andrew Cant, did not take up his appointment until March 1659. The hiatus is thus likely to have produced circumstances in which the usual complaints and accusations could not be heard. Hence the escalation of Agnes's case to the Court of Justiciary.

We now come to a group of cases centred upon the parish of Alloa in Clackmannan, the smallest county in Scotland, divided from Stirling by the upper reaches of the Firth of Forth.[27] They involve delations laid before John Craigengelt, minister since 1656 of Dollar, a village about six miles north-east of Alloa, by Margaret Duchill. On 23 June 1658 the presbytery of Stirling heard her written confession (she being recently dead) of witchcraft and her delation of others. Apparently she had come

before the kirk session of Alloa on 11 May on several charges laid against
her by some of the elders, and when these were read to her, she denied
them all except one which alleged she had said to one of the elders,
William Morrison, 'that if they should take and burn her, there should
better wives in Alloa than herself be burned with her' – an unpleasant
threat which we shall be obliged to evaluate later. She was arrested at
once and imprisoned. During her confinement, she received a number
of visits from the minister and some elders, 'with many good exhortations and pithy prayers with several demands concerning that sin of
witchcraft', which finally elicited some specific information.

First, she gave a detailed account of her first encounter with the Devil,
an account we shall consider, along with others, in the next chapter.
Secondly, in answer to a question about her time in the Devil's service,
she gave three examples of her activity. The record, somewhat unusually,
gives us a fairly clear indication of the questions Margaret was being
asked, so let me now give them and her answers, slightly modified into
the form of direct instead of indirect speech.

> Question: What evil have you done in that service of twenty years?
> Margaret: The first wrong that ever I did was to Bessie Verty.
> Question: What wrong did you do to her?
> Margaret: I took her life.
> Question: How did you take her life, and for what reason?
> Margaret: She and I quarrelled at the Pool of Alloa [while we were] carry-
> ing coals. I went to the Devil and sought revenge upon her. He said to me,
> 'What will you have of her?' and I said, 'Her life'. Then he said, 'Go to her
> house in the morning and take her by the hand, and she shall never thrive
> any more'. This I did, and at once she took [a] sickness and died of it.

This pattern of quarrel, resort to the Devil, and subsequent loss of life is
repeated in the other two examples of her malefices. In the one, at the
Devil's bidding, Margaret struck Janet Houston on the back and Janet
died, and in the other, she tugged the arm of a twelve-year-old girl who
thereupon bled to death. The minister clearly had his doubts and asked
her, 'how could a tug of the arm or a punch on the back or shaking of
hands be the death of anybody?' to which Margaret replied 'that after
she got the word from John, her master, [i.e. the Devil], she would have

done it to the greatest man or woman in the world'. There is, perhaps, a slight ambiguity in the phrase 'got the word' in this context. It may mean no more than 'received permission' or 'had the command', but it is also possible that it means 'was told a secret magical word of power' through which the preternatural event was enabled to happen, Words or Names of Power being a common mean whereby magical potency travelled from the non-human into the human sphere and there had its effect.

The kirk session then turned to Margaret's threat to take others with her if she were to be arrested and executed:

Question: Who are the women you said if you were burned should be burned with you?

Margaret: I have been at several meetings with the Devil, and [there were] several women with me.

Question: Who were they?

Margaret: One night at twelve o'clock at night, Elspeth Black came to my house and took me out to the Crofts of Alloa where we met the Devil…

She went on to tell the session that the Devil had sexual intercourse with both her and Elspeth that night. She also told them that one day Janet Black came to William Morrison's house to buy snuff – was this the same William Morrison, kirk elder, to whom she later made the remark about delating other women as witches? He refused to grant her credit , so that same night Bessie Paton, Margaret Taylor, Katharine Rainy and Margaret found William Morrison at the back of his house. 'We did violently draw [him] by the arms and shoulders through the ice and snow to Walter Murray's barn', said Margaret, 'where we thought to have drowned him in a hole'. But he cried out, 'God be merciful to me!' and they all fled, except for Margaret who said she turned herself into a black dog and followed him all the way back to his house. 'But he saw me not'. The record then adds, 'All [of] which the said William Morrison did divers times, long before this, declare that he was mightily afraid, but never knew till this confession'. So the assault seems to have been real enough. What William did not realise, according to his own statement, was that he had been manhandled by witches rather than simply attacked by violent women.

The final point in Margaret's confession had her meeting Janet Black, Bessie Paton, Margaret Taylor, Katharine Rainy, Margaret Demperston and Elspeth Black in the Cunninghar, a stretch of rising ground not far from Tillicoultry, where they danced together, 'with the Devil present, going up and down among them, some of them singing and some of them dancing, and Bessie Paton leading the ring'. Dancing appears in many of the classical accounts of the Sabbat, but there may have been a particular edge to this and similar Scottish anecdotes. The Kirk did not approve of dancing, largely because it feared the intermingling of the sexes and the attendant stimulus to fornication or adultery which might result therefrom. In June 1649, for example, the kirk session of Cambusnethan decreed that men and women guilty of promiscuous [mixed] dancing should stand in a public place and confess their fault; even the excuse of a wedding day did not suffice, for on 30 October 1600 the kirk session of Stirling noted that 'there has been great dancing and vanity publicly at the [Mercat] Cross used by married persons and their company on their marriage day', and therefore took measures to stop it by saying that a couple could not be married until they had handed over ten pounds as a financial surety for their party's decorous behaviour. Ecclesiastical censure was accompanied by secular disapproval, and thus we find the burgh of Lanark enacting on 5 April 1660

> the baillies and council, taking into consideration the sin before God and the abuses that have been formerly and of late committed within this burgh by people entertaining pipers in promiscuous dancing, men and women together, not only in the daytime but in the night: for remedy whereof, the baillies and council statute and ordain that no person within this burgh suffer any piper to play at their houses or yards in time coming, under the pain of forty shillings each person.[28]

So if dancing and music were frowned on, even if they were accompanying a marriage party, how much more reprehensible were they when performed at night and in company with the Devil?

The meeting which Margaret described was followed by others, the latest having taken place only ten days before her interrogation, at Andrew Erskine's brewhouse door, from which they were chased by James Morris at eleven o'clock at night. Another meeting saw the women shape-change into cats and destroy a cow belonging to Edward Turner; another had them going to Tullibody and killing a child; another to the Bow House where they killed a horse and a cow belonging to William Menteith; another to Clackmannan where they killed Thomas Bruce's child, while yet another found them killing two more children. The apparently motiveless violence, the shape-changing, and the constant presence of the Devil at these meetings follows closely the kind of picture of witches' activities, which is given by many learned treatises on the subject, and is so far removed from the majority of the detailed and individual accusations found in most Scottish witches' dittays at this time that we must ask ourselves whether Margaret (or more likely her interrogators) had been reading one of them recently. It was certainly not *A Candle in the Dark* by the English physician, Thomas Ady, recently published in 1656. Ady was dubious about several points standard in contemporary witchcraft theory, including the swimming test, the Devil's mark, and the relationship of cause and effect anent threatening and illness. More likely, perhaps, is the *Disquisitiones Magicae* by the Jesuit Martín Del Rio, which was regarded by the Scottish jurist, Sir George MacKenzie, as a valuable source of relevant information in his *Pleadings before the Supreme Courts of Scotland* (1672) and *Laws and Customs of Scotland in Matters Criminal* (1678). Del Rio's description of the Sabbat, drawn from a number of different sources, has witches borne through the air to the place of meeting where Satan or at least an evil spirit sits enthroned during the proceedings. They worship him, make offerings to him, and then sit down to dinner with an accompanying demon:

> After the feast, each evil spirit takes by the hand the disciple of whom he has charge, and so that they may do everything with the most absurd kind of ritual, each person bends over backwards, joins hands in a circle, and tosses his head as frenzied fanatics do. Then they begin to dance... They sing very obscene songs in [Satan's] honour, or jump up and down to a drum or pipe which is played by someone sitting in the fork of a tree... Then their demon-lovers copulate with them in the most repulsive fashion... (*Disquisitiones* Book 2, question 16).

There is enough material here to influence questions anent meetings with the Devil, and singing and dancing, although clearly the Devil in Margaret's account is behaving more as one might expect a laird to behave at a country wedding, rather than the monarch of a courtly feast.

What is most puzzling about Margaret's general account, however, is not so much this narrative of dancing with the Devil, which could easily have been based on her own experience of attending marriage-parties, but her claim to have turned herself into a dog and followed William Morrison all the way back to his house after she and the others had assaulted him. Witches were known to change their shapes, of course, so this piece of information by itself would have sufficient to identify her as a witch in the eyes of her interrogators. So why did she say it? We can surmise along the whole spectrum of possibilities, from the usual sugges- tion she may have been mad or simple-minded, to the over-sophisticated idea that perhaps she was being sarcastic and threw in an evident absurdity to see whether the session and justices would be stupid enough to believe her. Neither of these extremes, however, is at all satisfactory – there really are limits, for example, to the number of times one can suggest that peo- ple in earlier times were mad or hallucinating when they say things we do not agree with or find bizarre – so we must wonder, perhaps, wheth- er she said it under duress or out of spite against those she had named in her confession. We know she made this statement on 11 May, and that by 23 June she was dead (from what cause is not recorded). Identifying her- self as a witch would have added a potent dimension to her delation of others, and if she knew she was more or less on her deathbed anyway, she could be confident of not paying the ultimate penalty, while ensuring that those she named would have a difficult time cleansing themselves from the mud she had thrown at them.

Certainly the session and justices felt bound to act. On 19 May, two ministers from Stirling, George Bennett and Matthias Simson, were appointed 'to go to Alloa and confer with the persons who are there apprehended for witchcraft, and to endeavour to bring them to con- fession and conviction [acknowledgement of their error]'. Simson had spent seven years as a clergyman in England before his appointment to the West Church in Stirling in 1655. His experience of witches prior to that date (supposing he had any) would therefore have been of the English variety, with English reactions, both social and official, to them. On 3 June, Margaret Taylor, Bessie Paton, Janet Black and Katharine Rainy found themselves before the lairds of Clackmannan and Kennet, justices of the peace, John Craigengelt, and three elders from the kirk session of Alloa. Margaret Duchill now disappears from the records of their interrogations, so it is fair to assume she was either on her deathbed or had already died. Of the remainder, Margaret Taylor was examined first. Asked outright whether she was guilty of the sin of witchcraft, she answered 'Yes', and then went on to give details of how she entered Satan's service, the meetings she had attended, the people who were at them with her, and the acts of malefice she and they had performed. She had become a witch, she said, in the winter, about three years previously, during the daytime, while she was out walking with Margaret Duchill. At Bagrie burn, the Devil appeared to her and ordered her to renounce her baptism, which she agreed to do. He then marked her on her pudenda – very unusual in Scottish experience, but more common in English, which may make us wonder if Matthias Simson was not having an influence here. About three months later, the Devil had sex with her. The reason she consented to become his servant, she said, was because her mistress, Katharine Black, had 'abused her', that is, treated her badly. Margaret then describes various meetings and activities which are very similar to those described by Margaret Duchill. At one meeting, Satan copulated with her again, and there was dancing and music, the music being provided by James Kirk on a whistle – an instrument probably like the early flageolet or recorder, and thus more or less the same as the ambiguous 'pipe'. At this meeting, too, 'their language was not our ordinary language', 'their' referring to the people who were present – herself, Bessie Paton, Katharine Rainy, Margaret Duchill, Janet Black, Barbara Erskine and Elspeth Crocket.

This unusual detail about the participants' using a different language may perhaps suggest that they were engaged in some kind of ritual invocation. Magicians frequently uttered what appeared to be barbaric and meaningless Words and Names of Power, building them up into lengthy passages of foreign-sounding jargon which would have struck non-operative listeners as both exotic and bizarre. But against this is the fact that such invocations were invariably performed by learned men, not women, and that there is no evidence for rituals of this kind in Scottish witchcraft tradition. A different linguistic point, however, may have occurred to one of Margaret's questioners. One of the Latin words for 'witch' is *strix*, and, as the demonologist Sylvester Prierio noted in his *De strigimagarum daemonumque mirandis* (1521), *strix* also referred to 'a night bird deriving its name from high-pitched, shrill, grating, whistling and shrieking (*stridendo*), because it shrills and grates and whistles when it screams'. A witch can thus be perceived as essentially non-human. By entering into a pact with Satan and renouncing her baptism, she has forsaken her natural, human state and become Something Other which cannot, and therefore does not, use human language any more – a condition which the witch's well-known ability to metamorphose into animal shape will have emphasised. A witch is thus someone who inhabits the natural world only, as it were, on sufferance, her human form being merely one of several she can adopt at any moment. Thus, according to Margaret, when Margaret Duchill came to summon her to a meeting, she came 'in the likeness of a cat, and thereafter appeared in her own shape', and we have already seen that Margaret Duchill claimed she had followed William Morrison home in the shape of a black dog. It is possible, therefore, that behind Margaret's information that she and the others used a language other than their own ordinary tongue lies a question prompted by learned speculation based either upon a notion of what learned magicians did, or, more likely, upon presumptions drawn from *strix* = night bird/witch.

Margaret confessed she had attended more than one meeting with the Devil and the others she had named already, adding hearsay evidence from Janet Black – 'Janet Black, she affirms, said she was the death of a bairn in Tullibody' – from Margaret Duchill, and from Janet Miller in Tullibody. 'Janet', she said further, 'told her that the Devil had appeared to her, yet the said Janet knew not that she was a witch', an interesting observation reminiscent of the Glasgow youth we noted earlier, who saw and heard devils upbraiding him for his sins. Janet Miller from Tullibody may, then, have been suffering the after-effects of powerful and emotive sermons, just like young Gilmore, and could indeed have been shocked at the suggestion she was a witch.

One of the most significant parts of Margaret's testimony, however, concerns a masked gentlewoman 'that had [a] black bag, green waist-coat, and grey clothes'. Margaret said she herself did not know her, but that the woman was known to Bessie Paton and that she was present with the others and the Devil when they went to Thomas Mitchell's yard [garden]. This piece of information appeared to agitate Margaret's examiners:

Being again pressed and earnestly exhorted by sundry present that, without fear of favour of any, that she would be free in her confession and not concerned what [who] that woman was, she answered that she could not tell what she was, but said that she told what she heard others say concerning that woman with the bag. It was again desired that if she feared to tell out publicly her name, that she would whisper it in the laird of Clackmannan's ear, and the laird of Kennet's. She answered that she could tell nothing but what others said to her, and that she would whisper – which she did.

Margaret's insistence that she was repeating only what she had been told is an indication of how nervous she was at revealing the woman's identity.

This reluctance was shown by others, too. Bessie Paton, who was examined next by Robert Wright, the minister of Clackmannan, and others unnamed (but likely to have included the two justices), was asked first if she was a witch, to which (unlike Margaret Taylor) she answered 'No'. She did add, however, 'that she had been carried in spirit while asleep, and if so, that she knew not'. The context appears to suggest that her transvection in spirit refers to a flight to a Sabbat, but we cannot insist on this interpretation because we lack the wording of the question or questions which prompted that answer. Likewise, 'and if so, that she knew not' is not clear. Does it mean, if she really had been carried in spirit she was not aware of it? This would be odd, because if she was not aware of being carried, how was she able to say she had been? If, on the other hand, it means 'and if she actually was a witch, she did not know she was', the phrases would echo that of Janet Miller from Tullibody. Once again, however, we are without the context which would make the meaning clear. But she did deny 'all that was formerly written', that is, the entire contents of her dittay, although whether this denial was grounded in genuine innocence or represented an initial attempt to evade confessing to guilt cannot be determined with any certainty. Finally, her interrogators came to the subject of the unknown woman. Bessie denied telling anyone anything about her, 'but that some bade her say what she had said [so] that the rest might thereby be induced to confess'. The word 'some' is suitably vague for the occasion. We know, of course, that all these women would have been visited in prison by ministers, and perhaps others, who would have endeavoured to bring them to a state in which they would willingly make confession and repentance. Did one or more of these – the word 'some' suggests more – persuade her to lie? If so, it is an interesting insight into the pressures which might be exerted on suspects.

Next, they examined Janet Black. Asked if she ever did good to humans or animals by means of charms, she replied cagily that she never did them any evil, and sought to illustrate her answer by telling the session about discovering a blind puppy one day when she was out beyond the village. She brought it home, but it would not eat, only drink, and because she thought it was unlikely to survive, she buried it – perhaps after putting it down, but one cannot be sure. This anecdote may have been intended to demonstrate that she never did harm to animals, but as it does not include charms or magic of any kind, one wonders whether she told it merely as a diversion from her tacit acknowledgement that she did indeed use charms. She admitted attendance at various meetings with Margaret Taylor, Margaret Duchill, Bessie Paton, Katharine Rainy, 'a gentlewoman with a black bag', and, on one occasion, 'a gross round woman unknown to her', but made no mention of the Devil's being present, only that on three occasions they danced at night.

Finally, the session heard Katharine Rainy. Her recorded testimony mentions the usual meetings and names of those who were present, but adds further intriguing details to those the session had heard before. She saw 'a woman with a black bag and grey gown and a green waistcoat', but did not know who she was because 'she was covered with a black crêpe [veil] over her face'. There was also 'a gross woman with a white coat [skirt]', but 'she knew not what she was, except that she might guess… It was like Elspeth Black, but [she] could not say that it was she'. Thirdly:

> she saw a man in grey clothes with a blue bonnet… [He] took her by the hand and asked her if she would be fee'd [taken into service]. She said that she cared not… His hand was cold, and when she found it was cold, she was feared and took out her hand again. She thought he was not righteous. She thought it was the Devil, and she heard that she signed herself [i.e. made the sign of the cross].

It is interesting she had to be told by someone that she had made the sign of the cross. Does this indicate it was an instinctive gesture on her part?

If so, the instinctiveness further suggests she may have been a Catholic, since no one else would have made the sign of the cross without realising she had done so.

The masked or veiled woman is an intriguing figure. A young boy, Jean-Jacques Bacqué in Béarn, confined within the Bastille in summer 1671, had denounced 6,210 people from thirty communities as witches. He said he could recognise the Devil's disciples by 'a darkness like a black cloth taking the form of a kind of mask from the eyebrows to the chin' which he saw upon their faces.[29] *Masca* is a Latin word occasionally applied to a witch – Del Rio observes that it was used by the people of Lombardy in their legislation, and suggests that people wore grotesque masks during their assemblies in order to disguise themselves, or because they had dreadfully deformed faces – while others tells us that *masca* and *witch* were synonymous in French, Tuscan, and English as well.[30] Masks were also worn during masquerades which tended to represent an upside down world in which normal values and behaviour were reversed, and they were also symbolic of the metamorphosis which was an important attribute of a witch, that she or he could alter shape and appearance at will. But even if we accept Katharine's version that the woman was veiled rather than masked, her appearance and keeping company with the others raises questions. Since she was a 'gentlewoman', she may have wanted to keep her identity secret; but this ploy may not have been successful, since Margaret Taylor was able to whisper her name in the justices' ears, or at least, the name she had been told by other people. If, on the other hand, the woman was wearing a mask the intention to disguise herself may have been the same, but the effect upon others is likely to have been different, since a mask suggested, if not actual witchcraft, at least inversive behaviour, and association with the world of demons and *diableries*. Why would a normally respectable woman of good family be prepared to participate in such dangerous, improper behaviour? No surprise if the justices were keen to have that question answered.

This examination of Margaret Taylor and the others was followed by another. Some indeterminate period must have intervened between the two interrogations, because now we learn from Margaret, Katharine Rainy and Bessie Paton that they had been tortured to make them reveal the identity of the masked or veiled woman. Margaret makes the situation clear. 'She further declared that John Thomson did torture her by making her stand up high on a stool and caused Thomas and John Kidstone in Cambus put hot stones to her feet, (which was after her first confession), bidding her tell of the woman with a black bag'. Katharine suffered the same kind of maltreatment – 'she was tortured by David Verty, John Short, and Robert Archibald, by putting hot stones to her feet, and putting their feet on hers, pressing her feet to the hot stones' – and Bessie said 'that David Verty, James MacNair, and James Nicoll did torture her by putting stones on her back and feet, and burned her legs with fire, (which she says are not yet whole), and that they did it to make her confess'. There is no mention of torture in Janet Black's new statement, and we are not entitled to assume that she was subjected to any.

The five men involved were brought before the justices on 19 July and questioned about their actions. Katharine, Bessie and Margaret are named as the complainants, Janet is not, so it looks indeed as though she was not included in the torture. The men denied the allegations and were then confronted with the women – a standard practice often used to help test the veracity of accusations – but the women, perhaps not unsurprisingly, were unable to prove their own assertions. Finally, the men were called one by one before the justices and required to give their evidence on oath. Each swore no torture or burning with stones had happened. Should we believe them? Modern bias may incline us to believe the women and disbelieve the men, but a reservation of judgement might actually be more prudent, since we know so little of the parties involved – in the men's case, nothing apart from their names and the allegation against them – and a decision to credit one party rather than another will therefore be based on emotional reaction, not evidence.

If the torture did take place, it was, of course, illegal. I shall be discussing the question of torture in chapter 4, but it is worth making the point here that the reason these particular women were allegedly subjected to maltreatment was, in Margaret Taylor's case, to elicit information about the masked woman, and in Bessie's, 'to make her confess', although confess to what exactly is not recorded. In Katharine's case, no reason at all is given. Since Margaret Taylor had already whispered something into the ear of both justices at their first official investigation, it looks as though her information was either not believed or needed to be confirmed by at least one other testimony. But the name of the mysterious woman, if ever it was accurately divulged, has not been recorded.

With this set of interrogations, the authorities brought proceedings to some kind of conclusion. It was resolved that, because Margaret Taylor had confessed both witchcraft and paction with the Devil, and there was strong circumstantial evidence against the other women, the criminal court be informed, with a request that all four be brought to trial. George Bennett, minister of St Ninian, and Archibald Muschet, minister of Gargunnock, were deputed to visit the women again, 'and seriously and gravely, by prayer and exhortation, to deal with them towards confession, and endeavour to convince them of their heinous offences'. Confessions from Bessie and Katharine and Janet would shorten their trials considerably and remove all possible legal doubt from the minds of their assize. But no such specific confessions were forthcoming, and the two ministers had to report to the presbytery next day that they had managed to uncover no further information.

When it came to their trial on 3 August, all four accused pleaded not guilty, but the assize, which came entirely from Alloa and may thus have had good knowledge of many attendant circumstances unknown to us because they were not recorded, unanimously convicted Margaret and Janet and Katharine. In Margaret's case, the assize had no other choice, since she had confessed to being a witch. In Bessie's case, however, the assize was split and she was convicted by a plurality of votes. All four women were executed.

With this, 1658 seems to have brought its witch trials almost to a close. John Nicoll records that 'four women, one of them a maiden, all notable witches, were burned to death on the castle hill of Edinburgh' on 12 August[31] although what he meant by 'burned to death' needs to be questioned. Burning alive was rare in Scotland. The condemned person was tied to a stake and garrotted. It was the dead body which was burned. But without further evidence anent these four particular cases, we cannot be sure they provide exceptions to the rule. Back in Alloa, Katharine Black was imprisoned on charges of witchcraft some time in September. She clearly suffered, because a letter dated 7 December notes that the conditions of her imprisonment had made her very ill – 'want of food, coal, candle, bedding, and other necessities' are mentioned specifically – and she was still there on 18 December when, in reply to her husband's letter of protest, the justices ordered her release on caution, with the usual proviso that she be ready to stand trial on the first day of the next circuit session.

She was duly released, but by March 1659 she had been rearrested and put back in the tolbooth, apparently without official authorisation, as a second application for caution makes amply clear. This was granted on 16 March, after which she was speedily brought to trial. Elspeth Black (perhaps a relative, although one must not assume so), whom Katharine Rainy had named during her testimony, had likewise been imprisoned as suspect of witchcraft, but was quite unfit for trial.[32] A local elder and other men from Alloa testified on 28 December that she was 'for the present mightily troubled with a disease called "the bloody flux" [dysentery] which she has in the baddest sort, and by reason thereof is very unwell in her body'. Like Katharine, she too attributed her imprisonment to 'the instigation of certain evil-disposed persons', and, like Katharine, she was kept in the tolbooth a long time – eighteen weeks, says her petition for release. On 6 January, the commissioners ordered that she be set at liberty upon condition she turn up for trial on the first day of the next circuit court, and on 22 March we find that the trial of both women had been held. They had been found guilty, but had not been sentenced to death. A note in the circuit court book for 24 March says that they, and another woman, Elizabeth Crocket, were to be banished from Scotland, England, and Ireland, never to return, on pain of death, and that meanwhile they should remain in prison until they could be transported.

The sentence resulted in a further petition, this time by Katharine and Elspeth conjointly. They explain that the assize was split in its decision. 'The petitioners were fylled [found guilty] by eight of the said assize who had imprisoned and linked themselves together to ruin the petitioners, and were assoiled [found not guilty] by seven honest, judicious men unknown to the petitioners'. We must be careful not to accept these statements at face value, since they are precisely what complainants would say under such circumstances. On 7 December, it is recorded that Katharine was 'recommended to the public prayers of the parishioners of Alloa and accordingly thereto was publicly in the church prayed for', and her supplication to the justices mentions that her liberty was 'earnestly sought for by her friends'. So the malice to which she refers does not seem to have been universal in the town. But it is interesting, (if the detail be true), that Alloa men are accused of being determined to find the women guilty, whereas the non-Alloa part of the assize was persuaded of their innocence. Perhaps a case of familiarity breeding contempt, or an indication of that especial animus against witches which Colonel Sawrey had noted in a letter anent the West Country, and Janet Sawyer in particular. Katharine and Elspeth then go on to allege that the verdict should be set aside on grounds of two legal technicalities. First, the testimony of dying witches (that is, witches about to be executed) had been used as sufficient proof of itself against them, a perfectly valid point, if true, since legally this testimony should have been supported by other witness. As Del Rio pointed out, no matter how many pieces of evidence might be given by persons of ill repute, or by accomplices of the accused, a judge cannot pass sentence on the strength of these alone, and the Scottish jurist, Sir George MacKenzie, noted that 'he who was a sharer in the committing of the crime with the person accused, or *socius criminis*, cannot be received a witness'.[33] Secondly, it appears that the judges, in considering which items of the dittays were relevant – that is, carried sufficient weight to be heard by the court – and which were not and should therefore have been struck from the dittay before it was heard by the assize, had ruled against the admission of testimony by these dying witches, but had had their ruling ignored by the court in Clackmannan. 'May it therefore please your lordships', the women wrote to the commissioners, 'to delay sentence and execution against the petitioners until the first of June', in order to give time for the assize to be summoned before the commissioners and required to explain its apparent disregard for these legal points.

How did Katharine and Elspeth come to fashion their request? Neither seems to have been a wealthy woman. Indeed, the fact that Katharine languished in gaol for three months, and Elspeth for four-and-a-half, suggests that they had no one who was in a position to help them afford even the barest necessities. Thomas Mason, Katharine's husband, is described simply as an indweller of Alloa, but there is no other indication of his status or employment. Katharine was granted liberty on caution of £1,000 Scots, with her son, Robert Mason, and a John Sands standing as cautioners. Does this mean they could have afforded to pay it if necessary, in which case, why was Katharine allowed to remain unsupported in prison? Did the men offer themselves as cautioners, knowing they could not pay if Katharine failed to turn up in court, in which case, why were the justices willing to grant her liberty? It is easier, perhaps, to explain how the women probably came by their legal advice. Panels were entitled to representation in court, and by the seventeenth century this had come to mean a proloquitor for the panel [defence advocate], whose job was principally to see if he could raise sufficient legal objections to the inclusion of items on the dittay, and thus have them removed from consideration by the assize. It was therefore almost certainly Katharine's or Elspeth's proloquitor who advised them of the points they made in their joint supplication to the commissioners, and so paved the way for a possible reconsideration of their cases. But three years later they were still in prison. A supplication dated 7 November 1661 was presented in their names to the Privy Council which had already given directions that they were either to be tried (again, it seems), or put to liberty by 1 September. Since this had not happened, the Council issued another order to the same purpose, naming 1 January 1662 as the new terminal date. It is a sad indication of how even commands from the Privy Council could be circumvented or delayed, either through malice or incompetence, and how people could remain in prison for a very long time, apparently forgotten and certainly neglected.

What made 1658 different from 1657? During the most active witch-prosecuting months of 1658, April to August, while the courts were in session, neither the political nor the economic situation in Scotland underwent much change – nothing sufficient, at any rate, to trigger a sudden outburst of witchcraft cases. Given the relative slowness at which processes were often introduced into the criminal system, however, it is likely that several of those tried in 1658 began their legal journey in 1657; but the same observation applies. Nothing happened in 1657 in particular to set off a chain of complaints which would lead the accused into a criminal court. John Nicoll observed in his diary that the harvest of 1657 was very good, early, in fact, because of the hot, dry weather. 1658, on the other hand, he recorded as quite the opposite. 'The crop was very poor by reason of the Spring time which was very cold and burdensome for the space of many weeks, which produced a thin harvest and dear food. The price of this year's did double the price of the year preceding'. Wolfgang Behringer has suggested that the onset of certain waves of witchcraft prosecution in Europe may not have been unconnected with periods of unusually bad weather, and Scotland of course would not have been immune from this.[34] But the evidence is that although, in general, the conditions for agriculture in Scotland were

not as good in the seventeenth century as they had been in the early sixteenth, they were not especially bad. Moreover, witchcraft cases initiated
in 1657 would have been started during favourable weather. It is unlikely,
therefore, that Scotland's physical environment at the time had much to
do with precipitating a larger number of accusations.

The witchcraft cases we have been reviewing seem to fall into three
groups. First come those from the West Country, Ayr and Kirkcudbright in
particular, where we learned that the population was especially set against
witches; and indeed Janet Miller, Katharine Clacharty, and the others were
convicted on charges of doing harm as well as removing illness, the latter apparently not providing sufficient warrant to excuse or forgive the
former. Marion Lewars from Dumfries and Agnes Nimmo from Liberton,
however, both escaped conviction because their assizes noted grave difficulties in their cases. Marion may perhaps have worked spiteful magic,
but it was clear her main accusers, the MacIldufs and their friends, were
full of animus against her and were making a concerted effort to get her
convicted and executed. Agnes Nimmo, again a woman who may have
tried to inflict harm by magical means, had not yet alienated her community which was split in its view of her reputation. Some thought she was
a witch, others that she was not; and therefore her process was deserted.
In Alloa, the Devil finally occupies centre stage after making only a token
appearance in the prefaces to a number of dittays. For Margaret Duchill
and the others accused with her, Satan was the principal actor in most of
the scenes of their personal dramas, and although we have to bear in mind
that this survey of cases in 1658 is by no means complete, it suggests that
Ayr and Kirkcudbright were hostile to witches because of the harm they
had done, while Alloa concentrated not so much on the harm as on the
witches' submission to, meeting with, and attendance upon the Devil. It
thus begins to look as though we must look for localised explanations
of the surge in witch prosecutions at this time, rather than any over-
arching reason or general account which will apply to the whole of
Scotland; and in view of the Devil's entry into the foreground, it is time to
consider more closely contemporary views of Satan, and try to elicit what
made him, at this juncture, step forward into the limelight.

CHAPTER THREE

1659: The Devil Enters The Picture

When accused witches confessed to having met Satan and spoken to him, and copulated and danced with him, what picture do they give of their infernal Master? They had a long tradition upon which to draw. From very early times, Satan assumed an extraordinary variety of shapes and appearances, some human, some animal, many of them grotesque.[1] The Council of Toledo in 447, for example, described him as tall and black, with horns and claws, asses' ears, glittering eyes, and gnashing teeth; and in 1045-6 a Burgundian monk, Rodulfus Glaber, tells us he met the Devil three times, and saw him first in the middle of the night, standing at the bottom of his bed:

> He was, as far as I could make out, of fairly small to medium height, with a slender neck, a lean face, very black eyes, a wrinkled, pinched forehead, and downward-sloping nostrils. He had a long, thin mouth with swollen lips, a receding and very narrow chin, a beard like that of a goat, and hairy, very pointed ears. His hair stood on end and was all over the place. He had teeth like those of a dog; the back of his head tapered to a point; he had a barrel chest, a hump back, and his buttocks were always in motion. His clothes were filthy.

The traditional picture, in fact, has him veering between animal and human shape. Fra Angelico, for example, painted him as a kind of gorilla, and the

German demonologist, Johann Wier, tells us that Heinrich Agrippa used
to be accompanied everywhere by the Devil in the form of a dog. This last
is reminiscent of some Scottish evidence.[2] On 8 September 1644 Christian
Thomson told Liberton kirk session that Janet Stevenson's mother had the
Devil in a straw rope, and when she was asked whether the Devil was like
a man or a beast, answered, 'rather like a beast', and thereafter, 'that he was
like a black dog'. Satan might also appear as a ghost – when Nicole Obry
saw him first, he had taken the shape of her deceased grandfather – and
also as a woman. Male witches frequently said she looked like a woman
they knew. No wonder, then, that the people of Yorkshire saw him as a
big, black horse galloping before a storm in 1165 (*Chronica de Mailros*).
Luther remarked: *Sathanas transformat se in diversarum species personarum*
('Satan changes his shape so that he looks like different creatures'). The
word *persona* here is interesting because it refers to a theatrical mask, and
we are reminded that 'mask' was often associated in one way or another
with participants in a witches' Sabbat. 'The Devil', wrote Wier, 'is a master
of disguises'.

Since Satan is a spirit, of course, he has no body of his own and is
therefore compelled to construct one out of air, or to create an illusion
so that the human being he seeks to dupe imagines she or he sees an
actual person. Thus, Giordano da Bergamo tells us that the Devil once
disguised himself as a beautiful girl in order to seduce a hermit who lived
near Peschiera on Lake Garda (*Quaestio de strigis, c.*1470); and Chaucer's
friar tells the story of a fiend who appeared to a summoner, dressed like a
yeoman in bright colours, with a short coat of coarse green material, and
a hat with black fringes (*Canterbury Tales: Friar's Tale*, vv. 1380-83). These,
of course, are fiction. Appearances of the Devil in real life, however, are
often not reported with very much difference. Ursula Götz confessed
in 1624 that thirty years before, she had met and had sex with a demon
who was dressed like a farm servant in multicoloured clothes; in June
1656, John MacWilliam told the court that 'Satan came to him in the
likeness of a high [tall] man with a hat, and with a cloak and clothes like
himself'; and Thomas Jackson recalled a piece of oral history:

> I well remember a tradition that was old when I was young, better believed
> by such as told it than if it had been canonical Scripture. It was of a maid
> that liked well of the Devil making love to her in the habit of a gallant

young man, but could not enjoy his company, nor he hers, so long as she
had vervain and St. John's grass about her.

Most frequently, though, Satan chose to make himself known either as a
black man or as a man dressed in black clothing, a mode of appearance
common to witch-testimonies in Europe. Thus, for example, in Germany
he often wore black clothes and a black hat with a black feather in it; in
Dommartin, a village in the Jura range, evidence was given in 1498 that
witnesses saw the Devil at Sabbats like a man clothed in black, although
he also turned into a cat (once black, once grey), during the proceedings;
in Lorraine, testimony was given in 1624 that he was a tall black man
with black clothes, a dagger at his back, and a black feather in his hat;
and in 1682, in the English county of Devon, Susanna Edwards told the
court she had met the Devil two years before in a field near Biddeford,
and that he was a gentleman dressed entirely in black. No surprise, then,
that we find Elspeth Jameson in 1624 saying she saw people dancing on
the sea shore, and 'the Devil like a great black man, leading the ring', or
that Agnes Pride met the Devil in May 1656 in the form of a black man
who 'laid his cold tongue upon her brow'. This is how Margaret Gourlay
from Stirling recollected him in February 1659, and Helen Wilson and
Elspeth Fowler from Tranent in April that year. John Douglas, also from
Tranent, met him thus in March, but he had encountered him once
before when the Devil appeared to him 'in his own house, about ten of
the clock at night, and said to him, "John, will you be a piper to my servants and I shall pay you your wages?" and that the said John promised to
do; and then the Devil said he should not want'.

On this occasion, the Devil wore green clothing, and we find that this
was also the experience of Bessie Lacost and Helen Tait from Dunbar in
January and February 1659, Christian Cranston from Tranent in March, and
Janet Crooks in April. Alison Fermor, on the other hand, saw him in grey,
and so did Janet Man from Stenton in March. Sometimes the Devil changed
shape. In April 1659, Janet Thomson from Tranent said that about two years
previously, she had been taken out of her house by Janet Douglas, a witch,
to a place called the Stony Well, where 'the Devil did first appear to her in
the likeness of a black cow, and thereafter changed his shape in the form of
a man clad in green clothes', and Marion Logan, also from Tranent, had a
similar experience ten years before. She was drawing water from a well, she

said, at about seven o'clock in the morning when the Devil appeared and
struck her on the mouth with his hand which she thought was very cold.
He looked, she added, 'like a big green working man' – presumably a man
wearing green clothes as in the case of Jean Thomson – and then, 'shortly
after that, the Devil did appear to her like a black dog'.

The green aspect clearly suggests the possibility that the suspect
thought she or he was describing a fairy encounter, and that the alien
figure has become demonic under the suggestive pressure of official
questioning. The belief in fairies of one kind or another was deeply
embedded in the Scottish consciousness, and remained a long time after
the period of witch prosecutions.[3] As late as 1793, John Grant, the minister of Kirkmichael in Banff, was lamenting that his parishioners were
still given to this ancient credulity:

> Not more firmly established in this country is the belief in ghosts than
> that of fairies... About 50 years ago, a clergyman in the neighbourhood,
> whose faith was more regulated by the scepticism of philosophy than the
> credulity of superstition, could not be prevailed upon to yield his assent to
> the opinion of the times. At length, however, he felt from experience that
> he doubted what he ought to have believed. One night as he was return-
> ing home at a late hour from a presbytery, he was seized by the fairies and
> carried aloft into the air. Through fields of aether and fleecy clouds he
> journeyed many a mile, descrying, like Sancho Panza on his Clavileno,
> the earth far distant below him, and no bigger than a nutshell. Being thus
> sufficiently convinced of the reality of their existence, they let him down
> at the door of his own house, where he afterward often recited to the
> wondering circle the marvellous tale of his adventure.

Elspeth Astian from Burntisland was said to be a healer and to 'walk
with the fairies', and John Duncan told Dirleton kirk session he heard
Margaret Henderson call Margaret Kemp, 'fairy lady runt that the Devil
rode upon'; in March 1660 Jean Campbell was accused before the kirk
session of Rothesay of 'going with the fairies', an allegation the session dismissed as no more than slander, even though 'it was commonly
reported through the country [district]'; and the presbytery of Duns
heard, in February 1669, that Harry Wilson claimed to be able to reveal
secrets, and that 'some years ago he had been with the fairy folk about

the space of nineteen days where, he said, they had mirth, piping, and dancing'.⁴ He was careful, however, to maintain that he had *not* received his ability from them, although his subsequent explanation was no less suspicious. Pressed on this matter by the presbytery, 'he said about Yule last year, in the twilight, a woman came to him, who appeared here several nights; and that the third night he spoke with her, and that she bade him make use of his gifts to reveal secrets'. One notices he still had not actually told the ministers the source of his divinatory powers; but after a spell in prison, he was brought before the presbytery again and

after many shiftings and tergiversations, and after much pausing, he said he would tell freely all his mind, and confessed that the cause of all his skill was from that woman who appeared ordinarily to him, and that he could not be rid of her; and that when anybody came to him to inquire anent things lost or stolen, that he gave no perfect answer, but appointed them to come to him some other day; and in the mean time, the said woman appeared to him in the night and informed him how to answer.

She sounds somewhat similar to what one may anachronistically call a 'spirit guide', examples of which can be found elsewhere in Scottish witchcraft texts. In the 1570s, Elizabeth Dunlop from Lyne in Ayrshire had visits from Thomas Reid, a man who had died nearly thirty years earlier, who appeared to her as an elderly man dressed in grey, with a black bonnet and a white stick; and in the 1580s, Alison Pearson from Boarhill in Fife was assisted by a spirit in the form of her dead kinsman, William Simpson. Both men are presented ambiguously in the records as spirit-forms, perhaps ghosts, perhaps *sìthean* (fairies), perhaps evil spirits mimicking human beings; while Harry Wilson's auditors would not have mistaken his woman for a ghost, they might have thought of fairies as well as, or even instead of demons.

No less intimately woven into the fabric of the Scottish psyche was the expectation of seeing the Devil, quite apart from any witch or fairy context. Donald Cargill, for example, includes in his memoirs an anecdote concerning a woman from Rutherglen, not far from Glasgow. One day, she was milking her cows when 'two or three of them dropped dead at her feet, and Satan, as she conceived, appeared unto her: which cast her under sad and sore exercises and desertion, so that she was brought to question her interest in Christ and all that had formerly passed betwixt God and her soul, and was often tempted to destroy herself, and sundry times attempted it'. Similarly, the minister Robert Blair tells us of a day when he was visited by two men, one of whom was the chief constable of the parish. Business concluded, the constable asked Blair if he might have a word in private, and 'as soon as he entered within the doors, he fell a-trembling, and I a-wondering… At last his shaking ceased, and he began to speak, telling me that, for a long time, the Devil had appeared to him'. First, he bought a horse from the constable and offered him a lot of money; then, a few days later, he turned up at the constable's house:

Being thus molested with these and many other apparitions of the Devil, he said he left Scotland; but being come to Ireland, he did often also appear to him; 'and now of late he still commands me to kill and slay; and often', said he, 'my whinger hath been drawn and kept under my cloak to obey his commands; but still something holds my hand, that I cannot strike'. But then I asked him whom he was bidden kill. He answered, 'Any that comes in that way, but the better they be the better service to me, or else I shall kill thee'. When he uttered these words, he fell again a-trembling, and was stopped in his speech, looking lamentably to me designing me to be the person he aimed at. Then he fell a-crying and lamenting. I showed him the horribleness of his ignorance and drunkenness. He made many promises of reformation, which were not well kept; for within a fortnight he went to an ale-house to crave the price of his malt, and sitting there long at drink, as he was going homeward, the Devil appeared to him, and challenged him for opening to me what had passed between them secretly, and followed him to the house, pulling his cap off his head, and his band from about his neck, saying to him: 'On Hallow-night I shall have thee, soul and body, in despite of the minister and all he will do for thee'. The man, being exceedingly terrified, sent presently for me, and told me as is here presently set down. Being driven to his bed by this terror, when I came, his wife told me with what amazement he entered the house bare-headed and his band rent, saying he had hardly escaped. He entreated me for Christ's sake to be with him that night wherein Satan had threatened to carry him away. I instructed him the best I could, and, praying with him, promised to be with him that night, providing he would flee to Christ for refuge, and not to me, who was but a weak and wretched creature.

On All Hallows, just as daylight was fading, Blair went to sit with the constable, and prayed and expounded Scriptural passages to him throughout the night, at the end of which his unfortunate penitent 'took great courage to himself, defying Satan and all his works'. 'The last time I saw him', adds Blair, 'I asked at him whether Satan had ever appeared to him after that night wherein I continued with him. He answered, "Never", taking the Lord witness thereof, and shortly thereafter died'.

His conception of evil personified was not peculiar to Scotland, of course, nor even to the Calvinist experience. But it is essential to bear in mind that ministers of the reformed Kirk were accustomed, by their own accounts, to hearing and seeing angels and ghosts and demons, a trait they shared with their several congregations, and that an expectation of non-human apparitions or voices was entirely natural to them. We should also be aware that the alliance between depression or deep anxiety, and the extreme tenderness of a conscience constantly examined for sin by the individual and assaulted from without by reminders that damnation was an ever-present possibility unless one regulated every aspect of one's life according to the dictates of censure and self-disapprobation, was a particularly notable feature of the religious confession to which seventeenth-century Presbyterians were encouraged to give their adherence. Margo Todd has observed that 'the Sunday preparation sermon gathered the whole parish together in a sort of orgy of self-examination, recrimination and repentance', and that such sermons 'were designed as cathartic experiences, eliciting moaning and weeping from the whole congregation'. The self-doubt and pain and despair which often attended this kind of experience were taken to be signs of spiritual progress, and interpreted as wounds to be expected in the individual's constant struggle with Satan. We find a good example of it in the case of an English woman, Hannah Allen, who suffered from just such a period of despair, and left an account of her sufferings in the 1650s and 1660s. One bout of depression troubled her with blasphemous thoughts both day and night, which she attributed specifically to 'the enemy of my soul', and then two years later she married, but was still subject to a variety of temptations, 'wherein the Devil had the more advantage', until eight years further on her husband died, and she fell into a deep melancholy. The Devil, she says, took advantage of this to torment her further and one night, in May 1664, she heard what she thought were the voices of two young men singing in the yard behind her house, 'which I said were devils in the likeness of men, singing for joy that they had overcome me'. It was an experience which convinced Hannah that she was damned.[5]

What we may take from these accounts and observations, then, is the *normality* of an appearance by the Devil, and in Blair's case we have an interesting example of how a clergyman dealt with the problem of someone's face-to-face encounter with the Enemy. It required no torture, or even browbeating, to produce testimony that a person had met the Devil, and neither the suspect witch nor the officials listening to her would have been in the least abashed or surprised by his intervention in her life. Nor would anyone have thought that the appearance of the Devil was in any way a figment of a troubled person's imagination. When Marion Wilson was cited before the kirk session of Inveresk on 5 April 1659 for saying she saw the Devil sitting with Agnes Adamson, she may have been lying or telling the truth as she understood it; but in neither case was she saying something her listeners would have found either incredible or unlikely.

Now, 1659 was not an especially notable year for witches in the available ecclesiastical records. Indeed, the Kirk seemed to be concerning itself more with charming than with witchcraft although, as we have seen, the former could often and easily be interpreted as a manifestation of the latter.[6] In January, Margaret Henderson from Kilmadock in south Perthshire sought a cure from a woman cited under the Gaelic form of her surname, NicOstrich. It is clear from the session record that the woman was travelling in the area, for she was asked how many nights she had stayed in Margaret's house, and answered two, with six weeks in between, and by June we learn she had moved on into the parish of Kincairn (also in Perthshire). Her skill lay in divination as well as curing. On 7 February, the session was told that she actually did nothing to Margaret except 'take her by the wrist and looked at the hollows thereof, and said that she could do her no good, for she had got a blast'. A 'blast' referred to a misfortune or illness brought on by witchcraft. It could also refer specifically to a shock of paralysis, so the woman's diagnosis described both the type of illness from which Margaret was suffering, and its cause.

The case dragged on till the end of October, at which time NicOstrich denied she also divined by 'turning the riddle [sieve]', but said she had seen it done a long time ago in the house of someone long since dead.

The session, clearly grown impatient with the whole business by this time, passed her on to the civil magistrate for further trial. Shapinsay in Orkney similarly referred Margaret Wirk to the secular authorities in February. She had been delated of witchcraft by Magnus Irvine, a kirk elder, who had seen her coming from his house the first day of harvest, bow three times in different places, grope about with her fingers, and then walk three times widdershins round the town. Not long afterwards, Magnus's mother, father and brother all fell ill, and four of his beasts died. Margaret was well-known to the session for her swearing, and to the civil magistrate who had had her whipped 'for her lewd life and gross miscarriages', and she was given a sharp rebuke by the minister and then handed over to the magistrate 'for her practices tending to delude the people by what may savour of witchcraft' – an echo of the wording of the 1563 Witchcraft Act which referred to magical practitioners' deceiving people by claiming abilities they did not actually possess. There is, however, an interesting postscript to her appearance before the session. Only a week later, the clerk noted that she was

lying under such extreme sickness that she is not able to go abroad and seek alms to supply her necessity, as she used to do. For which cause, the minister is to make public intimation to the people the next Sabbath, requiring them every one, according to their ability, to extend their charity to her and send somewhat to maintain her.

People's feelings towards their local suspect witches, as also in the case of Katharine Black from Alloa, whose congregation was asked to pray for her, it seems might be ambiguous – perhaps understandable since these practitioners were capable of working beneficent as well as maleficent magic, and represented to their communities one type of immediate solution to a practical problem.

During the same month, Mary Scott fled from Linlithgow under suspicion of being a witch, and in the west, the presbytery of Dumbarton received a report that Humphrey Rankin and John Gardner had confessed to consulting 'with such as they took to be soothsayers'. In February, another Gaelic healer, Katharine NicGregor, was delated, this time to the kirk session of Dunblane. It was said that she took water from a well, which she used along with a charm, to effect her cures. The words

of her charm are recorded – rough doggerel with references to St John,
making the sign of the cross, the Virgin Mary, and a wish that the illness
may go away and never return. Her case rumbled on through various
divagations until the end of March when the presbytery of Dumfries
heard the extraordinary tale of Marion Curror from Kirkpatrick-
Irongray, a parish in the north-east of Kirkcudbright. Marion sought
to cure one of her neighbours, Janet Curror, of the falling sickness, by
burying her in a pit (it is called 'a grave' in the record, and one has the
impression Janet was covered with earth, which might be feasible provided the nose or mouth were left uncovered) and then cutting her belt
into nine pieces. Apparently Janet recovered and suffered no more fits
until the two women quarrelled, after which the disease came back to
her. Stirling, relatively fresh from its encounters with Margaret Duchill
and the others, received a request for advice anent witches and charmers from one of its ministers, Matthias Simson, who had served parishes
in England for seven years before being transferred to Stirling. As often
happened, however, the presbytery referred the question elsewhere – to
the synod, in fact, which thereupon passed it back in May.

The presbytery of Deer in Buchan had been troubled in October 1658
by an incident of animal sacrifice. James Crowden had beheaded a cow
and buried the head and the body in separate pieces of land in order to
effect a cure of certain sick beasts. James, for various reasons, had not
been brought to punishment, and perhaps it was knowledge of this that
encouraged Thomas Forbes to do something very similar, which was
reported to the session in March 1659. Apparently 'he had caused behead
a living ox upon the threshold of a door, over which the living and the
dead had gone, and had caused bury the head in another heritor's [land-
owner's] land for preventing a disease to the rest of his oxen, wherein
some had died'. He named Magnus Gourlay as his adviser, and said his
four servants had done the actual work. When summoned to the presbytery, Thomas 'alleged he did not know that there was in it any guiltiness
or matter of stumbling to God's people', a claim of ignorance which
may or may not have been genuine, and one which was not infrequently
used by suspect witches and charmers before ecclesiastical sessions.

The ministers continued in their efforts to get hold of James Crowden
at the same time as they pursued Thomas Forbes, but April passed without
action because Thomas's minister, Robert Keith, was ill. Keith had had a

colourful career already, joining the Protesters – those clergy who objected to accommodation with the state in Kirk affairs – in 1651, and was to
be deprived of his ministry in 1662 for refusing to accept episcopacy in
Scotland. He had recovered by 10 May, but then Thomas Forbes fell sick.
In June, however, James Crowden turned up and confessed to making
a sacrifice, explaining that he had done so because he had seen such a
ritual before 'for curing of sudden diseases amongst cattle'. But he denied
using any words while beheading or burying the animal and, like Thomas,
claimed he did not realise his action was sinful. The presbytery either found
or chose to find that the man was ignorant, and appointed three ministers
to 'make him sensible of the heinousness of that fact [deed]'. They managed to do their job, although he did not actually perform public penance
until near the end of November, partly, at least, because he had moved
into a different parish and there were problems in getting him back to be
humiliated in the parish in which he had committed his offence.

Thomas proved somewhat more difficult. In June the minister was
unavailable to pursue the case, and in July Thomas was absent; so it was
not until August that he and his fellow-offenders were persuaded to
confess themselves guilty, and it is notable that the presbytery had decided to interpret their sacrifice as one offered specifically to the Devil.
Thomas seems to have done his penance by late September, but the session records make it clear that actually neither he nor his companions
nor many others in the neighbourhood had the least idea they had done
anything wrong:

> The presbytery therefore appoints the several brethren to intimate from
> their pulpits that none of their congregations use such diabolical practices,
> and that they endeavour to convince them of the sinfulness of the same,
> and that they beware thereof or of any charmings, under the pain of the
> highest censures of the Church, that so henceforth none may pretend
> [claim] ignorance.

Thomas's confession, then, seems to have been made for form's sake,
and his repentance less than genuine. In view of the Kirk's constant and
continuing battle against magic of all kinds, Thomas's case appears to be
symbolic both of the Kirk's general problem all over Scotland, and of its
failure to make much of a genuine impact upon it.

Further evidence of a magical practice similar to those of Thomas and John, but this time used for maleficent purposes, comes from Duffus, a village about five miles north-west of Elgin, where James Breadhead complained to the kirk session that John Russell had slandered him 'in saying that I had taken a calf's guts and laid [them] upon his land, and thereafter his ox fell down in the plough', a complaint which was upheld after investigation. We also come across an example of the ancient use of urine for magical purposes in the case of Jean Hunter from Fetteresso in Kincardine, 'who is suspected to be a witch'. Apparently she was accustomed to come begging to Thomas Naughtie's house, and one day 'was seen to take up three or four handfuls of urine, wherewith she wet her wyliecoat [under-petticoat], folding it up after it was wet with urine'. When people from the house asked what she was doing, she replied it was for the head of a scabbed pig, in other words, a cure. Perhaps in other hands this might have been seen merely as a natural remedy. In December 1659, Abbotshall session heard that Katharine Lundie had been consulted by two women who brought her a specimen of urine and wanted to know if the 'owner' was pregnant or not. There is no overt suggestion of magic attached to this, but the fact that it came before the kirk session indicates that someone was uneasy in case the consultation turn out to be one involving a *subsequent* use of charms, or the urine be employed for maleficent rather than for diagnostic purposes. Jean's case is not altogether dissimilar, except that she was already suspect as a witch because she was blamed for having caused Thomas Naughtie loss among his goods.

Consequently, further allegations tumbled out to the minister on the following day, 3 April. 'James Donald declared upon oath that the said Jean Hunter said in his hearing, "The Devil take them out of the ground that first learned [me] to be a witch" and when she was asked who that might be, she answered, her own husband, John Middleton'. Likewise, David Watt gave evidence that his wife and Jean Hunter had quarrelled, but that Jean, in an apparent gesture of reconciliation, gave his wife some fish roe, whereupon his wife became 'distracted'. David then threatened Jean with burning – that is, to have her burned as a witch – and Jean assured him his wife would recover, as indeed she did. Jean's case is a good example of how an evil reputation could throw a lurid light on even the simplest actions. James Donald's recollection of her admission she was a witch dated back two years, and his wife produced for the session a memory even older, declaring 'that she saw her three or for years ago in Hogs Bog, as if she had been winding up of a cleat, crouching downward towards the earth. And she asking her what she was doing in that posture there, she replied that she was seeking the end of a thread which she had lost'. We must be careful not to misinterpret this, of course. It is quite possible that Jean was doing no more than she said she was doing, but we cannot be absolutely certain that she was not actually engaged in some magical action; and even if James Donald's wife had dismissed the incident at the time (always granted she was telling the truth and not making it up), something about it had obviously lodged in her memory, sufficient to bring it to the fore later on when Jean's reputation as a witch was being more firmly established.

A combination of people's very frequent resort to magic in general and the delicate balance between a woman's good or bad reputation in her community are sufficient in themselves to produce a communal outlook which genuinely saw preternatural behaviour where we see none, and we cannot brush aside these recollections of past words or actions as merely simple malice or hostile reinterpretation without foundation. They could be, of course, and we have already seen instances of it. But, as the frequent complaints of slander illustrate, the possibility that someone might be revealed as a witch by some simple words spoken in anger had always to be borne in mind. Thus, Haddington kirk session found itself in May and June 1659 dealing with the case of Margaret Argyll, who had been unwise enough to repeat Jean Kirkwood's assertion that Janet MacNab was a witch. The session was in no mood for gossip, and referred Margaret to the magistrates for confinement in the tolbooth . When she came before the session again, the minister and elders decided she was guilty of calumny and handed her over to her employer, the laird of Hermiston, to be put in the jougs, a hinged iron collar attached by a chain to a wall or post and locked around the neck of the offender. Margaret's mistake in repeating the slanderous gossip, however, had had another unfortunate result, for at the same session she was told to find caution for herself to appear before the session again, 'to answer for [the] crime of witchcraft for which she is to be challenged'. Acts of, or involvement in slander could thus always place the defendant on a knife-edge.

The second half of the year shows little difference from the first in relation to the kind and number of complaints anent magic coming before the ecclesiastical courts. In July and August, Holyrood kirk session in Stirling summoned people who had been seeking cures from charmers, 'that courses may be taken for removing their odious scandal'. The summonses produced several individuals, one of whom, James Anderson, confessed to having employed one Isobel Bennet seven years previously, so the crackdown was clearly serious and meant to be effective. Kirkliston, a few miles south of Queensferry, heard a strange tale from Isobel Thomson anent Janet Miller. According to Isobel, while she was lying in child-bed, 'she saw the said Janet Miller coming in with a number of other suspected persons at her back'. They entered through the door which blew open suddenly 'with a blast of wind', and one of them tried to take the child from her. But Isobel commended herself to God and they all fled through the door, leaving it open behind them. Eighteen months later, Isobel met Janet who was carrying a burden upon the Lord's Day. So Isobel reproved her, and Janet knelt down and cursed her and promised revenge; whereupon, some time later, Isobel was lying awake with a pain in her arm, and 'perceived her thumb shot through with that which they call an "elf-stone", and the blood of her thumb sprinkled along the floor; and then, looking to the floor, [Isobel] saw [Janet] standing upon it with another who is dead'.

What may appear to us to be a series of non-sequiturs is thus revealed as a sinister sequence, given veracity both by Janet's reputation and by her behaviour. Kneeling down to curse was not uncommon, but when something untoward happened later, it was thought the two events were bound to be connected – a natural way of thinking in a world which posited lines of sympathy between everything in creation. If the moon and the tides were connected, or red flannel with the cure of smallpox, or the predominance of Saturn in a person's horoscope with a disposition to melancholy, clearly a suspect witch's semi-ritual behaviour could have something to do with a subsequent misfortune.

In September, Janet Edmond from Slains in Buchan was delated for charming, and in November came before the kirk session and started to repeat the words of the charm she had used to cure John Symson – 'The Lord God spake it with his own mouth, and commanded me in his own name to oration for the head fevers and the heart fevers, for the livers and the light fevers' – but then noticed that the clerk was writing down what she said, and so refused to repeat any more. The year ends, so to speak, with a case from Trinity College Church in Edinburgh, which began in mid-October and lasted, on and off, until the end of December. It started with Margaret Neilson, a servant, who on the advice of Barbara Moncrieff, another servant, went to a dumb woman to ask about some money which had been stolen from her. Margaret appears to have known who the thieves were – fellow servants who shared the same bed or bedroom – and was consulting the diviner for confirmation of her suspicions. Alexander Finlay, the dumb woman's husband, came before the session on 20 October to deny his wife practised divination at all, but he was contradicted by Barbara Moncrieff who said the woman had indicated to her where she might find a spoon which was stolen from her. The case was sent to the presbytery which advised 'that they that had consulted with the dumb woman should be dealt with as those were dealt with in North Leith that consulted with an astrologer', but their public repentance was delayed because Margaret had further revelations. On 24 November, she told the session 'that William More's wife, and Margaret Fender, heard Helen Rutherford ask the dumb woman what her fortune should be, and the dumb woman said she would be married to a writer [lawyer]'. When questioned, Margaret Fender tried to dissociate herself from the consultation. Her version of events was that she came in to the principal room of a house to fetch a pint of ale, and saw the dumb woman, Helen Rutherford, and Margaret Neilson sitting together, eating porridge. Helen Rutherford said the dumb woman had promised her a lawyer as a husband, and Margaret said she had been allotted a baker. Helen then reluctantly confessed that Margaret had brought the dumb woman to her, and that 'there was something like a fortune spoken before, when she was in the main room of a house up the way', but denied that she actually consulted the dumb woman, or that she spent time in her company. By the middle of December, all those involved had been rebuked, although the experience seems to have had little or no effect on the dumb woman who continued to ply her trade, as a further case in March 1660 bears witness.

These ecclesiastical cases reveal a number of interesting points. First, they are not very many. Even if we were to add a few instances of name-calling to the number, we should not find any great surge of accusations against magical operators during 1659. So it seems likely that the majority of witchcraft cases coming before the *criminal* courts that year originated in complaints made directly to the civil authorities rather than to kirk or presbytery sessions; and this in turn suggests that people were aware of the relatively light penalties suffered by suspect charmers, diviners, and witches tried by an ecclesiastical court, and that they wanted the more vehement rigour of the criminal statute applied to them. In other words, the wave of accusations seems to have been driven by a desire to have these people purged rather than reconciled. Secondly, the ecclesiastical instances show no concentration of cases. They are scattered throughout the central belt, the east, the west, and the north. Only the south shows nothing, but that, given the limited number of samples we have chosen for discussion, may simply be due to chance, although William Hay does have one or two references to witches in Biggar and Skirling in the shire of Peebles.[7] On 26 September, he noted in his diary that nobody attended a meeting to discuss one Margaret Robison who was suspect of witchcraft. By 22 November, however, she had certainly been examined, because Hay had seen extracts of her process, prepared for the presbytery, and on 19 January 1660 he wrote that he was due to revise them before the next presbytery meeting on 2 February. On Monday 10 October he tells us he went to see the minister in Skirling and was informed 'that John Cleghorn [from] Kirklawhill did one dark night see a good many men and women dancing, and a great light with them, which immediately disappeared, and which he says were witches'. This he pursued on 22 October, by questioning 'Wilkin Shankley anent these women in Skirling, who was said to be witches, and whom he saw when they frightened him. He named one Murray, mother to John Penman, [a] smith in Skirling, and Maly Purdie, and said he durst say these two were there: and desired us also to examine the baillie's wife'. Thirdly, the kirks and presbyteries were dealing principally with charming, that is to say magic which neither the accusers nor the authorities chose to press and interpret specifically as witchcraft, although it was still a great offence for, as the English Puritan William Perkins observed, it was better to die of an illness than offend God by going to charmers, because their help was 'dangerous and cometh from the Devil, whereupon, if ye rest yourselves, ye join league with him'.[8]

Secular prosecution of witches during this year, however, was a different matter. We may care to note at this stage that the weather for 1659 was very changeable and was taken to mirror the changeability of the times. Nicoll wrote:

> It is very remarkable, considering the great changes and alterations, reelings, turnings, and overturnings that is fallen out thereuntil. For the first two months (viz. January and February), did foretell the same by horrible storms and tempests of wind, which prognosticate high treasons and alterations. The like stormy winds arose upon the 2 and 22 days of June; thereafter upon Lammas Eve [31 July], and upon the first, second, third, and fourth days of September next thereafter following: all of them exceeding ominous, leaving behind them sad effects, as the towns of Edinburgh, Leith, Musselburgh, Dalkeith, Lasswade, and other parts adjacent can declare, who had their mills, houses, and kilns, timber trees and ironwork, and dams utterly destroyed, to the admiration [astonishment] of many.[9]

One of the most common malefices of German witches in particular was to raise winds and storms with the intention of destroying crops. Can this feature be seen in Scotland in 1659? If so, it would be somewhat unusual, since Scottish witches were not especially associated with this activity; but a notable rise in prosecutions in March–April, August, and September–October might indicate a connection between witches and these notably destructive winds.

In spring this year, the civil administration was still working, but by May the Protectorate had started to collapse, and with constitutional and administrative descent into something like chaos, the courts were finding it difficult (although not impossible) to function effectively. Burgh courts continued in operation, as did sheriff courts until mid-July, and there is evidence that the criminal courts managed to go on hearing cases, although they suffered much interruption. There were, however, no circuit courts that summer, and therefore a build-up of cases from them began to happen.

Now let us see how the various situations we have noticed were reflected in the work of the criminal courts.[10] In Stirling on 13 January, Magdalene Blair confessed to striking a horse and hoping to God it died. Since the horse did indeed die the same day, the item appeared in her dittay. She also agreed she had cursed John Steill because 'he had gotten a bairn with her and would give her nothing', after which he became ill for a long time and suffered financial loss. Both allegations of witchcraft came from Helen Ker who also said that, after some heated words from Magdalene, she came home, and when she went to bed at ten o'clock, found a lump of something dead, the size of a mole-hill, between her sheets, whereupon she 'took sickness which hath continued with her ever since, the extremity of it lying upon her at that hour of night till last Saturday when she told the minister that she suspected the said Magdalene had wronged her: and since [then], her pains come not before till midnight'. Magdalene then hinted that Helen herself was not entirely blameless, so on 14 January the minister, Nicholas Sampson, Robert Russell the baillie, and others examined her on her alleged use of a charm to try to regain her health. Helen confessed that, yes, she had been charmed by Katharine Greg who had also charmed the minister at Dunblane and Kilbridge, Thomas Lindsay – a confession which, if true, is an interesting indication that ministers were not necessarily more immune than their parishioners from the attractions of magic if they thought it could solve an immediate problem. When asked if she thought Magdalene had bewitched her, 'she held up her hand in sign that she did think so', claiming that she was so ill, she had nearly died only two hours before her examination. A further session on 18 January heard from Helen Ferguson that a year previously, in March 1658, after Magdalene had reproached her for not being kind to her [Magdalene's] husband when he was ill, she had known nothing but bad luck.

On 16 March, a summons was sent out to witnesses for three cases of witchcraft, those of Magdalene Blair, Bessie Stevenson and Isobel Bennet, to attend a justice court in Stirling on 22 and 23 March. Magdalene's process was tried on 22 March, and a new, rather interesting piece of information emerged. William Luckison, a maltman, fell ill in 1653 or thereabouts, and decided to visit his sister, Katharine. He found her sitting with Magdalene in Andrew Cowan's yard, Andrew being Helen Ferguson's husband. The following conversation, which I have turned into direct speech from the indirect version of the record, then took place:

Katharine: Magdalene, what do you think is the matter with my brother?
Magdalene (to William): Is there any enmity or discord between Isobel Bennet and yourself?

William: None that I know of, except that sometimes, when her fowl are in my father's corn, I'll throw stones at them to call them out of it.

Magdalene: Go to Isobel Bennet, take a firm hold of her coat tail, drink a pint of ale with her, crave your health from her three times for the Lord's sake, and you will be well.

William, we are told, failed to do this. His version of events paints Magdalene as a woman who knows what to do to unwitch someone suffering from an illness brought on by someone else's maleficent magic. This would immediately bring her under suspicion as a possible witch or charmer herself. We may also note the name 'Isobel Bennet'. Since she was one of the three to be tried at Stirling along with Magdalene and Bessie Stevenson, it is clear the two cases have overlapped in this particular item. Magdalene, perhaps aware of the danger to herself, or perhaps simply telling the truth, replied to William's charge that Katharine had actually asked her what would do her brother good, and that she had recommended a rose cake – perhaps a cake made from the crown end of potatoes, known as the 'rose'. But she appears to have changed her story when confronted with William and Katharine. Whether this indicates she was lying at first, or that she altered her evidence out of fear or nervousness, we cannot tell. Katharine's husband also offered testimony against her, saying she predicted he would never marry anyone other than Katharine; but Magdalene replied she had merely told him he would never find anyone else as suitable. If the evidence against her strikes us as thin, it seems to have had the same effect on her assize, for we learn that it found her not guilty – although by a plurality, not a unanimity of votes – and she was released on 24 March on caution of £20 for her future good behaviour.

Isobel Bennet was tried for charming, to which she confessed, and witchcraft, to which she did not. Examples of her charms are given in the record. To preserve people from harm, she recommended taking a live mole, putting it in a box, and burying it under the outside of their threshold. For charming children who are maw-turned [nauseous], 'she declares she leads them thrice round about an oaken post, expressing these words thrice: "Oaken post, stands thou. Bairn's maw, turns thou. God and Saint Birnibane the Bright, turn the bairn's maw right"'. For treating those who were blasted [paralysed] because of bewitchment, 'she declares that she washes such persons with water brought forth from the hollows of the sea, and takes a little quantity of meal and strews it in the four corners of their bed'. To this she added a small bit of the shoe of a horse which had been ridden by the fairies, a hook, and a piece of raw meat. Then she said three times, 'The Father, the Son, and the Holy Ghost'. Since Isobel confessed her charming, the assize found her guilty. It also convicted her, by plurality, of witchcraft, the details of which do not seem to have survived. Nevertheless, in spite of her double conviction, she was simply sentenced to be whipped through the streets of Stirling the day after her trial between ten o'clock and noon, and then to return to prison until she could find caution of £20 for her good behaviour. Bessie Stevenson, on the other hand, whose charming was no different in kind from Isobel's, was convicted by unanimous vote of her assize and sentenced to be executed on 1 April. This may have been an arbitrary or prejudiced decision, of course, but in view of the care taken by most assizes, it is perhaps more likely that allegations of a much more serious nature were presented at her trial. To say so, however, is merely speculation.

In February and March, two more women from Stirling were examined by justices of the peace. Margaret Gourlay came before them on 25 February to hear Janet Miller testify to several different points against her. Six weeks earlier, she said, she had visited Margaret. Isobel Frier was there, too, and a black man, 'and a table covered with a white cloth, with some boiled beef and bread'. Margaret offered Janet some meat, which she refused, so Margaret told her to go away, and immediately thereafter, a fire broke out in Margaret's bed and was put out by Andrew Wright and George Wordie. Next morning at dawn, Janet caught sight of a woman in Andrew Wright's house where Margaret was kindling a fire. But either Margaret was remarkably careless, or a suspicious co-incidence occurred, for fire broke out again in one of the beds and had to be extinguished by Andrew and George. This was two days after a great clap of thunder at Margaret Gourlay's window, and at bed-time, a banging at her door and stones thrown at her wall. Wherever Margaret went, it seemed fires broke out. Andrew was putting his horses away the following night, and saw a fire in Margaret's house, which he and his wife put out. Then fire broke out in his own house in three different places, which required a number of people in the neighbourhood to deal with.

1 Edinburgh during the seventeenth century.

2 Edinburgh Tolbooth.

3 Perth during the seventeenth century.

4 Ayr during the seventeenth century.

5 Dundee in
the seventeenth
century.

6 *Peasant Dancers*.
Heinz Weiditz,
c.1521.

7 Witches feasting with demons. French, sixteenth century.

8 Duddingston kirk.

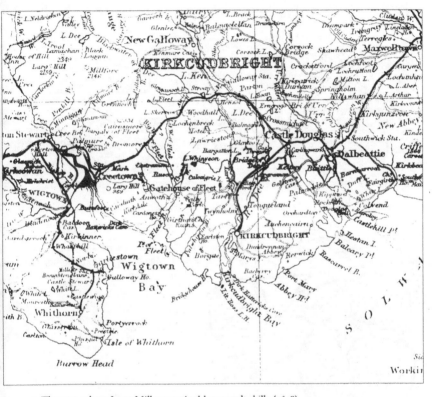

9 The area where Janet Miller practised her occult skills (1658).

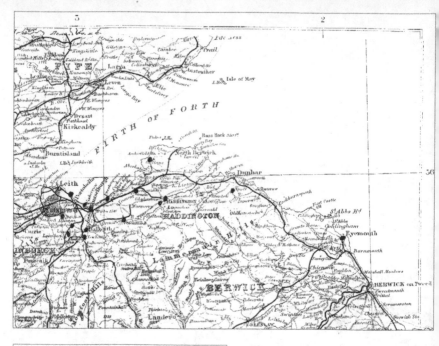

10 The principal centres of witch-prosecution in East Lothian in 1661.

11 The Devil seducing a woman. Ulrich Molitor, *De laniis et phitonicis mulieribus* (1489).

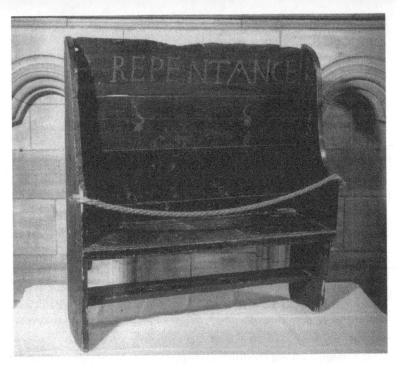

12 Penitents' stool, Holy
Trinity Church, South Street,
St Andrews.

13 The human heart taken
over by Satan and evil spirits.
German, early nineteenth-
century edition of a sixteenth-
century French original.

Two days after that, at twilight, Janet saw Margaret speaking to a female stranger who was wearing a white petticoat and a plaid, and half an hour later fire had started up in the male servants' bed in the byre. Two days later, Margaret was with Isobel Ker and Margaret Harvey. Margaret Gourlay was winding wool, and when fire was discovered in five different places in the barn yard, a black crow flew back and forth over the house. Fire broke out where Margaret was standing, yet Margaret stood still and did nothing. That same day, Janet Miller was going to visit her father at twilight, and met a black man who asked her where she was going and laid a heavy hand on her shoulder. Janet was terrified. The man tried to reassure her, and then asked if Margaret Gourlay was at home. 'He inquired if ever Margaret Gourlay desired her to go out with her awhile. She answered, no. Then said he, "She will speak to you and bid you do something", after which he left her, but looked back at her often. Two nights later, she saw him again, but committed herself to God, and the man did not speak to her'. Janet then relates one or two further instances of fires' breaking out, and her testimony was complete.

It is unusual among Scottish witch-texts in as much as most of the evidence relates to a concentrated period of fire-raising – everything seems to have happened in January 1659 – and to point to Margaret Gourlay as an arsonist. Janet's final testimony suggests this quite clearly. One Sunday morning, Margaret was tending the fire in her house and asked Janet to go and borrow a besom from John Wright. This was refused. Margaret then took a burning peat-coal and asked Janet to lay it on top of the wall next to the cows, which, for some reason, Janet did, while Margaret went to the far end of the house, where she was seen on her knees, as if in prayer. John Wright came to the byre and found the coal 'blinking' – an interesting use of the word which can mean either to glow red suddenly as a breeze or draught catches it, or to glance at someone with the evil eye, 'blinkit' being a term for 'bewitched'. 'But it had not [yet] set any of the house on fire', says the record. So John removed the coal and asked who had put it there, to which Janet confessed it was she.

What gives a sinister angle to Janet's evidence is the presence of the black man and the ill omen of the wheeling crows. All four women – Margaret Gourlay, Isobel Ker, Margaret Harvey and Janet Miller – were questioned, and Janet Miller was arrested, for she is referred to as 'prisoner' in the lists of witnesses against the others, dated 16 March. Margaret

Harvey gave evidence damaging to herself and to Isobel Ker. She confessed she had advised a woman with a sick child to seek a cure from Isobel by going to Isobel's house, taking three straws from the thatch above her lintel, and asking her for the child's health for God's sake. This was a tacit allegation that Isobel was a magical healer and a witch, because taking three straws was intended to afford protection to the client, and asking her to restore the child's health was an admission that Isobel possessed magical powers. By going to consult her, the mother too had broken the Witchcraft Act and, of course, Margaret's testimony was evidence that she had incited her to do so. Still, the assizes seem to have distinguished between the offences alleged before them. Janet Miller, in spite of her arrest, was acquitted unanimously, as was Margaret Harvey. Margaret Gourlay was acquitted on a majority verdict, but Isobel Ker was convicted and sentenced to be executed on 1 April.

It is interesting that the assizes seem to have dismissed the figure of the black man in the evidence. The phrase, certainly, is ambiguous. It can mean 'a man of very dark complexion' or 'a man dressed in black', although in the latter case the records tend to draw attention to the clothes. For a countryman to be described as 'black', his complexion – darkened by constant exposure to the weather and probably engrained with dirt – would have had to have been very dark indeed. But evidence heard by the assizes, and not surviving, or possibly their own deliberations about the behaviour of the black man, seems to have allowed them to decide against equating him with the Devil. His encounter with Janet, for example, though frightening for her, had nothing demonic about it. He did not ask her to be his servant, or promise her money, or give her his mark, or try to have sex with her; and his appearance at Margaret Gourlay's table sounds like that of a human rather than a diabolical guest. Whatever fears Janet may have had, then, neither she nor her interrogators seem to have gone as far as openly identifying him as Satan, and without that demonic content, the case for calling Margaret Gourlay and Janet Miller witches seems destined to fail, as indeed it did.

Meanwhile, over in the west, Barbara and Elspeth Cunningham from Ayr were presented for trial.[11] The main points against Barbara were that she had quarrelled with Henry Wallace who, a short while before his death, blamed his condition on her, an accusation which gained added weight from Barbara's correctly prophesying that Henry would die a beggar. Henry's wife, Grissell Black, was ill. One day, Barbara met Grissell's servant and asked after her mistress's health. 'The servant said that her mistress had suffered much, but she was growing better. Barbara replied that it was little she had suffered in respect of that she *would* suffer'. A house caught fire after Barbara had been annoyed by one of its owner's servants; John Love, the local baillie, had fined her two dollars, and because she was angry, she would not come to him when he was ill, even though, interestingly enough, he had sent for her. It was also alleged she might have bewitched James Cuthbert's horse which sweated to death. She certainly showed little sympathy. 'The said Barbara, seeing the said horse when he was dead drawn out, said, "Ay, the fellow's horse is dead, and my malt is still in the mill"; and when some said to her, "Mistress, that is not well-favoured language", she replied, "Take out candles and wake him"'. According to one witness, she also suggested they 'blew in wind at his arse'. Finally, when her own son died after quarrelling with his mother, the clear suggestion was that she had killed him by maleficent magic. Her assize, however, was not persuaded of any of it and found her not guilty on every count in her dittay. So she was set at liberty, but had to find £30 as caution for her good behaviour.

Elspeth Cunningham was not so fortunate, and it is not difficult to see why. She laid illness on people and refused to cure others when they sent for her. William Ryla gave evidence that Mary MacGreen's husband blamed Elspeth for his death and that when the sick man sent for her and asked her for his health, 'she came to him and turned the back of her hand to him', a ritual gesture of refusal. She was also accused of meeting the Devil in Irvine kirk, although according to Barbara Melling, a convicted witch, when Elspeth turned up at the church, she was prevented from coming in. In addition to these points, there was also the supportive testimony of the pricker. Thomas Gravane said 'he thrust a pin in the Devil's mark, and it went in to the head, and she was not sensible of it', a trial which was witnessed by Theophilus Rankin, who 'saw one pin go in on her side amongst her ribs, to the head', by William Blair who saw six pins in her and heard the pricker say, 'This is the Devil's marking', and by John Rodger who 'saw several marks on her, and the pin go in some of them as easily as in butter, and there was no blood or sense'. Even so, the assize acquitted her on a number of points; but it was not sufficient to save her from an overall guilty verdict, and she was sentenced to be executed on 2 April.

If March had seen a flurry of prosecutions in Stirling, it saw the cul-
mination of another in East Lothian. Helen Heriot, Alison Fermor,
Marion Angus, Jean Sydserff, Janet Wood, Janet Man, Helen Cumming
and Bessie Lacost were all fetched to Dunbar and to Stenton (which
are only about six miles or so apart), to be heard before justices of the
peace.[12] Significantly enough, in view of the increasing part played by
the military in maintaining the rule of law in Scotland, the magistrates
who examined them were both soldiers, Captain Thomas Simnell and
Captain Robert Home. Bessie Lacost first appeared on 23 January. She
confessed to several meetings with the Devil, and to having had sexual
intercourse with him. On the first occasion (about eleven years previously), he was in Agnes Angus's house 'where, before ever she knew
[realised what was happening], the Devil stood up among them all who
were in the house, and kissed them all, and lay with her'. The second
time, Bessie and the Devil nearly had a falling out, as is shown by their
first exchange:

> Devil: You are welcome to me.
> Bessie: God make me welcome to Heaven.

At this, the Devil and all those with him were very angry. Then he made
her renounce her baptism, and we are given, most unusually, the words
employed for this purpose – 'I renounce my baptism to you and take
it away from Jesus Christ' – after which the Devil wanted to give her a
new name, Jeanie. But Bessie objected that she did not want two names,
and had a name already. So the Devil said, 'Bessie be it, then', and thereafter copulated with her. His body (perhaps a euphemism for penis, but
perhaps not) was harder than a man's, and colder, said Bessie. They had
many meetings with him, she said. 'They' meant 'Marion Wilson and
Isobel Kemp who are burned, and Alison Fermor who is yet alive', and
'Jean Sydserff, Helen Heriot, Marion Angus, and Janet Wood [who] were
as great witches as she'. This naming of others, a fairly constant feature of
witch-confessions, thus lets us see why the other women were arrested
and questioned.

Their meetings were presided over by the Devil 'in sea-green clothes,
sometimes with a hat, sometimes with a bonnet', according to Bessie.
The differences between the two headgears was a matter of class

distinction, the former belonging to the wealthier sort, the latter to farmers, while the sea-green clothing in this Scottish context strongly suggests a fairy rather than the Devil. Together, he and the witches drank ale, ate wheaten bread, sang to each other, danced, and 'made gorravadge', that is, behaved without restraint by guzzling and romping. As Christina Larner points out, kirk sessions and burgh councils were keen to clamp down on parties and gatherings consisting of more than a very small number, so 'the details of witches' meetings appear to reflect most frequently a particular kind of seventeenth-century deprivation'.[13] Nothing, indeed, could be further removed from the Sabbats described by German or French witches especially. These regularly involved reversal of accepted moral or social norms, such as incest or bizarre behaviour in dancing; their feasts often turned out to consist of disgusting rather than palatable food; the Devil frequently presided in the form of an animal; and if priests attended, they offered blasphemous parodies of the Mass in worship of Satan. Such assemblies had about them the quality of nightmare and are reminiscent of the corrupt fantasies of a clerical imagination. Scottish witches by contrast seem to meet in riotous night-time versions of a peasant wedding-party, or simply a sociable gathering of friends and neighbours, a scene which, in many ways, also fits the description of fairy revels.

On 8 February, the justices met at Dunbar in order to oversee a confrontation between Bessie and the women she had delated. Faced by Janet Wood, Bessie said that Janet had attended several meetings with the Devil, and had asked him for monetary redress against George Crumbie who had refused to marry her. The Devil, however, said he could not help her because 'George has good prayer about his house'. Janet had also been a witch before Bessie knew her. Marion Angus, said Bessie, had attended several meetings and had asked the Devil for a personal revenge against someone called Abbott, a revenge which was not granted her until two years had passed, when she gripped Abbott hard 'and took the power of his tongue and side'. Marion had two sons by different men. The second was sick but recovered, and the record of Bessie's testimony hints that he got well at the expense of someone else's child who died. Jean Sydserff also had a petty favour to ask of the Devil, this time to seek revenge on the minister's wife, while Helen Heriot wanted amends of the minister himself, a revenge she got, because both of the minister's children died. Helen also seems to have had a closer relationship with the Devil than the others. 'At the Gallowhop, she took the Devil by the hand and went up the Capgate alone with the Devil', and 'the Devil called her "Bessie"'. Alison Fermor had a more serious grudge than her companions in evil. 'She desired amends of the Englishmen that took her away, and the Devil said they were out of Scotland, he could not get amends of them'. Two points may strike us about this last. Although Alison does not say so directly, her abduction – 'the English took her away to the Grange and left her there' – suggests rape rather than kidnap. Alison was clearly not a rich woman, so there would have been few pickings for anyone hoping to make money out of her release. Secondly, the power of the Devil seems strangely limited. It is as though Alison were conceiving him as a kind of Scottish laird whose authority ceased to be effective once it reached the Scottish border. It would not be surprising, of course, if such a person provided the model for Alison's conception of the Devil. What other figure in authority did she readily have to hand except for the minister and, given the highly tangible, personal, and in many ways ordinary nature of these Scottish encounters with Satan, the attribution of limited power even to the Devil seems entirely consistent with such a paradigm.

The women all denied what Bessie was saying of them – Janet Wood *in toto*, the others in part. They agreed to the allegations of their discord with someone else, and to the reasons given for it, but would not admit to being witches or to meeting Satan or to performing malefices. But, after consideration, and after receiving Bessie's confession, the justices ordered that they all be arrested and sent for criminal trial. Since Bessie had confessed, there was no need to examine her further, and Janet Wood's testimony seems to have been dismissed, for she does not appear again in the record. The others, however, were brought once more before the same justices on 21 February, again in the tolbooth of Dunbar. The intervening fortnight had served to clarify the prisoners' minds, and they produced the kind of testimony the justices may have been expecting to hear. Marion confessed to meeting the Devil, renouncing her baptism, and having sexual intercourse with him. Helen confessed the same, but also produced another cause for her willingness to attend these meetings. She wanted 'to seek amends from the Devil of an Englishman, a sutler [soldier's servant] that quartered in her house'.

Was this inspired by Alison's complaint, or was it a genuine grievance she had either not mentioned before, or which had not been recorded previously? We do not know. The Devil, she said, was wearing green clothes and a grey cap which, on another occasion, is described as a bonnet. Alison agreed to making a pact with the Devil who was dressed in grey, and to drinking and dancing with the rest, adding that 'at the said meeting of the Gallowhope, she fell in the ring when she was dancing and hurt her knee a little, and the Devil took her up by the hand' – ever the gentleman, as is consistent with the way he is portrayed. Finally, Jean said much the same as the others in general terms, but informed the justices 'that after Bessie Lacost was apprehended, she [Jean], with the forenamed persons and a man which she thinks was William Richieson met at William Manderson's barn end in Stenton; and a man clothed in grey clothes, with a round bonnet on his head, commanded them to deny that they were witches, and he would warrant [protect] them, and [said] that he would give them anything they would ask'.

All this, of course, was quite sufficient for the justices to ordain that the women be taken under escort to Edinburgh and there stand trial before the criminal court on 1 March. But why had the women confessed it? There is no indication in the record that they were tortured, and we are not entitled to assume they were. Other conditions in prison, which we shall discuss in the next chapter, may have been sufficient to make them broaden their accounts to include details such as paction with the Devil and commission of malefices, which would have been enough to warrant their criminal trial. Nevertheless, there are one or two aspects of some of the women's testimony which seem unduly reckless, given their situation. Why did Helen Heriot say she had killed the minister's children? Why did Jean Sydserff claim she wanted vengeance on the minister's wife; and why did she gratuitously drag in the name of William Manderson? Manderson was one of the baillies of Stenton, and both he and his fellow-baillie, Richard Wait, were put in charge of all five women on their journey to the Edinburgh tolbooth. It was surely unwise to point the finger at these people, even if Helen and Jean actually did bear some grudge against them. The processes were duly heard and the women found guilty. John Nicoll recorded their fate in his diary on 9 March. 'There were five women, witches, burned on the castle hill for witchcraft, all of them confessing their covenanting with Satan, some of them renouncing their baptism, and all of them oft-times dancing with the Devil. All these five were brought from Dunbar'.[14]

They were followed on 11 and 14 March by two other women from Stenton, Janet Man and Helen Cumming. Janet first met the Devil in Alison Fermor's house. She had come there to seek alms, and Alison suggested to her that there was an easier way for her to seek a living. Janet asked, 'How may I get it with more ease?' Whereupon Alison took her 'into the west chamber of her house where the Devil was sitting, like a man in grey-coloured clothes and a hat on his head, like a gentleman'. He wanted to have sex with her and did so, and then required her to renounce her baptism, which she did. He called her Bessie, 'and he touched her right hand and arm, and there was a pain left on her arm above the bough'. Later, she went to a meeting where everyone was dancing and having a riotous time. The dancing was led by Bessie Lacost, and Janet was able to recognise and name six others – the witches from Dunbar whom we have just been discussing, including Janet Wood who still seems to have escaped arrest – 'and other three which she does not remember of'. This meeting, she said, took place at about eleven o'clock at night. A visit from the minister, however, produced a wholesale transformation:

> She could not get a heart to repent, for the Devil was locked in her heart, till once, after prayer made by the minister, she got freedom to confess her other sins, and then she thought her heart was something lifted up, and now she thanks God she hath gotten a heart confess the sin of witchcraft to.

Not only witchcraft: Jean also confessed neglect of the church for the past twenty years, 'that she lived nine years in uncleanness with one Alexander Cathill, and brought forth three children to him, for which she never yet repented'. The tone is reminiscent of Robert Blair's ministry to the baillie and, *mutatis mutandis*, his recollections may give us some notion of how her minister dealt with Jean. It is also a useful reminder that these efforts by the clergy who visited imprisoned suspect witches was to get them to confess so that they might free themselves from the Devil and so reconcile themselves with God, a role perfectly in tune with his duty as a pastor, and one which Del Rio had likened to being both judge and physician at the same time.

Helen Cumming, who also named Alison Fermor, refrained from recognising 'a great number of women – she thought above forty – '[because] there was so great a mist betwixt her and them that she could not know them: likewise she saw a great number of men in another place, but there was a great mist betwixt her and them, too'. Helen first met the Devil at Carfrae burn [stream], 'where the Devil was riding on a horse and came plunging into the water, so that she was affrighted and cried, "Lord, save me!" Whereupon the Devil bent down and she saw him no more at that time'. On 2 April, both women confessed and ratified their confessions, and on 7 April they were found guilty and sent to Edinburgh for sentencing.

In May, Nicoll noted in his diary that a large number of witches from Tranent had been arrested and executed. Thirty are named in the records for April and May, twenty-seven women and three men, of whom eleven are known to have been executed. Three others escaped or died in prison; two were acquitted; the fate of the rest is not known. Many simply appear as names in others' confessions, and we do not know whether they were even brought to trial. Consequently, we have no right to add their names to the list of the executed.[15] The dittays of eleven of these suspects from Tranent have several points in common. Most record appearances of the Devil. He appeared to Christian Cranston, John Douglas, Janet Thomson, Barbara Cochran, Janet Crooks and Marion Logan in green. John Douglas also saw him as a big black man, as did Marion Guild, Helen Wilson and Elspeth Fowler, while on one occasion he appeared to Janet Thomson as a black cow, to Helen Wilson as a pot and as a man, and to Marion Logan as a black dog. Scarcely any magical activity is attributed to any of them, except for Christian Cranston who confessed that she used to cure diseases with the help of foxgloves and south-running water. Otherwise, the suspects' accounts deal principally with meeting the Devil and attending the usual assemblies at which they would dance and enjoy themselves. Indeed, John Douglas was recruited by the Devil to act as a piper on these occasions, most of which, according to the confessions, had taken place quite recently, within the last three months.

Meeting the Devil for the first time happened in a number of different places. Christian Cranston, for example, met him in the countryside, John Douglas in his own house, Marion Logan at a well while she was drawing water. Their assemblies generally took place somewhere in the country near Tranent or at the saltpans of Preston a couple of miles away, although Helen Simbeard said that one meeting took place at the old kirk; and Barbara Cochran, Janet Crooks and Marion Lynn mention the presence of people wearing masks. We have come across this before, and it is a nice point whether to regard the reference to masks as a device allowing the suspect to avoid having to name names, or whether to accept the evidence as true, in which case the individuals concerned may have been wearing masks in order to conceal their identity. The latter supposition, of course, carries with it an acknowledgement that the meetings were real and not imaginary, but, as we shall see when I come to discuss torture in the next chapter, this does not necessarily mean that the meetings consisted of witches, merely that some of the confessing suspects were perhaps drawing upon recollections of late-night parties attended by neighbours and others whom they may not have known very well.

The Devil often had sexual intercourse with the confessing suspect. In Christian's case, this produced an unpleasant experience, for 'when he went from her, he appeared to her greater and greater and uglier; at which sight she was afraid... and took sickness thereafter for the space of eight weeks'. But he also came to Christian in her own house – the previous occasion had been in the open – 'in the night time, about midnight, the door and window being shut, and lay upon her brow with his face which she found to be cold, like lead, and the rest of his body above the clothes'. Sometimes the sex was attended by violence. Janet Thomson testified that she was taken from her house by Janet Douglas to a place in the countryside called the Stony Well, where the Devil appeared to her first as a black cow and then as a man clad in green. 'The said Janet Douglas, who was sitting behind, said to the Devil, "Debone her, debone her!" and presently [immediately] thereafter the Devil in the form of a man (as said is) threw her over near to the said well and did carnally know her'.

What strikes us about these accounts of meeting and copulating with the Devil is that if we remove the preternatural elements from them, they sound like reminiscences or fantasies of purely human fornication, and it is perhaps worth bearing in mind that fornication and adultery were the offences most frequently dealt with by kirk and presbytery sessions. Indeed, not only were these sins uppermost in the consciousness of the Kirk, adultery appears more often even than murder or theft in the lists of the criminal courts, and sex with the Devil, because of the overt or tacit pact between him and the would-be witch, was regarded as a form of adultery. Lauren Martin has expressed the situation succinctly: 'The demonic pact operated along the lines of the barest requirements of a legally binding marriage; as such it was a linchpin in the legal definition of the contract of marriage. Similarly, a woman became a witch through the present or future consent to enter a demonic pact followed by sex'.[16] Once again, therefore, we have congruity between the suspect witch's confession and her examiner's expectation. Both accepted as real and genuine personal, apparently physical appearances of the Devil, and both were acutely aware of the great frequency of irregular sexual intercourse in their community. So it needed no great stretch of the imagination, or much persuasion by a committed pastor, to produce an account of sex with Satan, which was perfectly credible to both sides of the interrogation.

The other point these Tranent dittays have in common is the search for and discovery of the Devil's mark. Six of the eleven whose dittays have survived were pricked by John Kincaid, 'the common tryer of witches', who may well have known them all, and they him, for he also came from Tranent.[17] Pricking consisted of inserting a long needle into a suspect's flesh, in various places, to test for a spot which would not bleed when the needle was withdrawn, and whose insertion caused no pain to the individual being tested. This spot – or these spots, for it was common to find more than one – had been rendered insensible by the Devil's grip. Marion Guild, for example, told the justices that the Devil 'took and gripped her by the left shoulder, where the mark is', and Barbara Cochran said that after the Devil had known her carnally, 'he laid his hands about her neck, where the marks are'. In Scotland, these marks rarely appeared in a woman's pudenda because it was no part of Scottish tradition that she was nurturing a familiar, or spirit, by means of a hidden teat – although one was discovered next to Marion Guild's mark inside her left armpit. A late description (1705) describes such a mark as 'sometimes like a blue spot, or a little lump, or red spots, like flea biting'. Kincaid, the man who certainly pricked Christian Cranston, Helen Simbeard, Janet Thomson and Barbara Cochran, and probably John Douglas and Marion Guild as well, first enters the record in Dirleton in June 1649, and from then on we find his name cropping up in East and Midlothian, with one visit over the water to Dunfermline in Fife. The needles he used were long. When he pricked Janet Bruce in Tranent in June 1657, he used one which was over two inches long, so one can readily understand that if a pricker did not or chose not to know what he was doing and had to thrust his needle into a suspect time and time again, the pain he would cause might be considerable. Even so, it should be noted that suspect witches often asked for a pricker to be summoned, so that they might be tested and so proved innocent.

Kincaid was paid for his services, of course. For pricking Bessie Masterson in Dunfermline, he received twenty merks which is roughly the equivalent of the cost of forty fourteen-ounce baps [bread rolls] in 1638. The possibilities of fraud in this exercise, in spite of the fact that pricking was always done in front of witnesses, must be obvious; but as always, we should be careful before we attribute chicanery to the proceedings as a matter of course. Pricking was a well-known and widespread practice elsewhere in Europe, so Kincaid was not inventing some novel procedure. Evidence of fraud in one case – such as that of George Cathie in Haddington, who colluded with one suspect witch in 1650 to identify others whom he might then be called on to test – is not evidence that all cases were necessarily fraudulent; moreover, because the test itself may strike us as bizarrely suspicious does not indicate that it must have been so regarded at the time, in spite of available evidence that it could be used fraudulently. A suggestive modern parallel can be found in the Cleveland child sexual abuse scandal of 1987. Huge numbers of such cases were referred to the local social services – 505 in the first six months of that year alone – with medical professionals using a simple anal reflex dilatation (essentially parting the buttocks and examining the anus to see if it opens by reflex action) as a common means to ascertain whether or not abuse had taken place. Public opinion initially supported the social workers and paediatricians involved, largely, one suspects, because the crime was seen to be particularly dreadful, and those involved in diagnosing it were accepted as experts. Out of such incidents, careers can be made or forwarded, and there are other recent examples akin to the Cleveland case, which could be cited. It is in the light of such experiences, and with the acknowledgement of modern fallibility, that the activities of Kincaid and the authorities in Tranent should perhaps be examined and gauged; and if Tranent represents a 'hunt', so does Cleveland.

The result of all these inquiries and Kincaid's expert testimony was that ten of these people came to trial. Elspeth Fowler would have done so, but a note dated 28 April tells us that she died of a flux in prison that morning. Marion Guild and Janet Thomson were found not guilty by their assizes. The rest were executed. Why had this particular outbreak occurred? There is no mention anywhere in the surviving records that any of these witches had been raising tempestuous winds, so it is unlikely that the dreadful storms of January and February were attributed directly to their maleficence, although it is always possible, of course, that the bad weather had had a painful effect on people's moods, and it is this latter possibility which may prove to be significant. An obvious parallel with Kincaid's activities in the Lothians is that of Matthew Hopkins and John Stearne in East Anglia during the mid-1640s. The scale of the English episode is much greater than that involving Kincaid. Over 200 people were tried or investigated by the local English authorities between July and December 1645, so the English experience was much closer to a genuine 'hunt'. But James Sharpe has made a few salient observations which illuminate what was going on fifteen years later in the east of Scotland:

> The problems caused by the erosion of traditional authority were made heavier, in Puritan East Anglia, by the populace's previous exposure to sermons and other forms of religious consciousness-raising in which the devil and his works figured prominently... It was, perhaps, not the formal Protestantism of the educated clergy which helped fuel the East Anglian witch-hunt, but rather a popular Puritanism which was being reinforced by the war.[18]

Scotland was under the firm control of George Monck, assisted by an army from which most overt signs of dissidence had been purged, and although Quakers and Anabaptists were active in Edinburgh and Leith, they posed no real or particular threat to the régime. It was therefore not the civil but the religious atmosphere which provided circumstances in which Kincaid and other prickers could flourish, although it is worth noting that some, at least, of these cases may have come to light first at the end of 1658. But, even though the death of Oliver Cromwell in September and the assumption of power by his son, Richard, could have proved the signal for unrest and dissent, Monck quickly moved to suppress it and the régime was politically secure. So one looks to the religious climate of the Lothians, and of Tranent in particular, for some kind of guide to account for the apparent ease with which Kincaid was able to operate. The minister of Tranent, Thomas Kirkcaldie, had recently been transferred thither from Carnwath in Lanarkshire where he had had ample opportunity during his twelve-year tenure there to observe and exchange views on witches during the meetings of the presbytery. That he was a man wedded to Presbyterian government of the Kirk is indicated by his being deprived of his ministry in 1662. He may have had psychological support from John MacGhie in Dirleton and Robert Ker from Haddington, neither of whom conformed to episcopacy, either. On the other hand, Patrick Cook from Prestonpans did, so there was not uniformity of opinion within the presbytery. But it may be relevant that Thomas's predecessor at Tranent had been a man of unusually lax behaviour, so much so that a complaint was laid before the presbytery in March 1657 about his 'frequent tippling and tavern haunting'. He was gradually eased out of his post and had departed just over a year later, and we may perhaps legitimately speculate that the presbytery would have sought to replace him with a man more strict in his own behaviour, and thus more inclined to root out non-conformity in his new parishioners.

If we now turn to the west, we see that during March and April and May there was another flurry of witch-prosecutions coming before the Dumfries circuit court.[19] Eleven women, six from the south and east of Kirkcudbrightshire, two from Monkland well to the north of the others, in Lanarkshire, and three whose precise habitations are not given, but who were tried with the rest at the circuit court of Dumfries, came before the justices on a variety of charges. Agnes Cairns came from Kirkcudbright and her confession is different from those of the others, because it entirely concerns her relations with Satan. He had engaged with her in childhood, she said, and then two or three years later appeared again, at which time she renounced her baptism and the two of them pledged each other in a bitter drink; but she received her mark at noon on a different occasion, 'when there was none in the house nor about it but some young bairns'. At some point Agnes and Satan had sex. They also met one Sabbath afternoon, at which time there was much dancing and merriment, in Helen Hare's house –'who, being apprehended and incarcerate within the tolbooth of Kirkcudbright as a witch, did strangle herself in prison.' The company was mixed: humans (including Margaret Clerk from Kirkcudbright and Janet Carsan from Rerrick, both soon to be tried for witchcraft) and non-humans who were described by Agnes as 'fairer [than earthly folk], and better dressed', adding, 'that they spoke with an eldritch voice'. This last suggests they may have been ghosts or fairies rather than demons, but we have no record of how the court interpreted it. Agnes also said that Satan came to her while she was in prison, held in a room just above Helen Hare, on the night Helen committed suicide, and told her he had just strangled Helen and would do the same for her, if she wished. The magistrates then asked her 'what condition it was that the Devil had said to you you would be in after death', to which she replied, 'that he said [she] would ride up and down with him' – there is a sexual implication in that phrase – 'would eat and drink and dance and be merry and not troubled any more'. We should note, once more, the readiness with which Satan takes physical form in the psychology of this period, and we should also hesitate before assuming that Agnes (or any other witch in her or his confession) was merely using a form of speech or metaphor when she spoke of appearances by the Devil in her life. The manner in which he is constantly described, and the near-universal acceptance that the spiritual and material worlds were capable of interpenetration so frequent as to be almost constant, mean that people who said they saw and heard and touched the Devil were experiencing certain moments in their lives in a way quite different from any which might occur to us. It also means that these experiences of theirs were real in their terms and in their understanding of those terms, and that, in turn, has implications we shall explore later.

Agnes, along with Margaret and Agnes Clerk (the latter from Lochrutton in east Kirkcudbrightshire), was summoned on 15 March to appear at the next circuit court at the beginning of April. Margaret and Agnes Clerk were accused of the usual range of magical activities, and Satan played no direct part at all in their confessions. Margaret was alleged to have inflicted illness, sometimes lifting it, sometimes not. In one case, we catch a glimpse of the way people might act when their health failed for some reason. Margaret cursed Alexander Kingan who fell ill. Instead of blaming her for it, however, he sent for someone to bleed him – a tacit assumption on his part that his illness was rooted in natural, not preternatural causes – and it was not until this had failed and Margaret turned up, sat down on his bed, and 'spoke some words, he knew not what', and he began to recover, that suspicion of her original involvement must have been roused. So people did not automatically see magic in every untoward or unpleasant incident, as the decisions made by assizes often make clear. Indeed, Margaret's assize unanimously acquitted her on this particular point. On another, however, they were equally unanimous in finding her guilty. In c.1657, John Shennan from Kirkchrist in the south of Kirkcudbrightshire quarrelled with Margaret (who seems to have been his servant) after she had been rude to his wife. 'The said John called you "witch-thief", and caught a stool, and threatened to cast [it] at you'; whereupon John's business began to go through a bad patch. This eventually proved too much for his wife's temper and she took the opportunity one day to assault Margaret, who cursed her and then went to the stall where the family kept its cow. 'You said to her [the wife], "Thief, thy cow has a better bed than I have at home"; and after speaking of these words, you stamped with your foot, and immediately thereafter the cow took sickness and wasted away to death'.

The following Sabbath, John gave Margaret the key of his chest so that she could get him a drink, which Margaret did, locking the chest afterwards:

> And about midnight, there came a cold hand and lifted the said John up in the bed, and laying the hand upon his hand which was then under his cheekblade. Whereat the said John being greatly afraid, upon Monday morning as he was able, he arose and found his own chest laid open with the lid upward; and all the rest of the chests of the house open.

Which of these two experiences – the apparent malefice or the ghostly hand – impressed the assize more? It is extremely difficult even to hazard a guess, and the final item in Margaret's dittay presents a similar problem. Margaret cursed Robert Callendar, 'and shortly thereafter, the said baillie's bairn being sitting upon the midwife's knee, within the baillie's chamber, and a cat having leaped upon the said midwife's knee where the bairn was, the bairn cried and soon thereafter died'. So far then, we have a parallel with Margaret's curse and the death of a cow. But we are also told, 'Janet Miller, who was burned for a witch at the last circuit court, affirmed that you, Margaret, was the cause of the said bairn's death'. Delation by a confessed witch was not necessarily sufficient in itself to provide proof of another's being a witch, so perhaps it was the combination of the two incidents which provided one item considered significant enough to be entered on the dittay. Even so, Margaret's assize convicted her of this last point only by a plurality of votes.

The name of Janet Miller appears several times in these West Country dittays. She delated Helen Tait from Buittle and Janet Neilson, both of whom came to trial on 5 April, and she was consulted by more than one individual anent sickness and its cause. Margaret Thomson, for example, fell ill and sent to Janet for remedy; whereupon Janet declared that Janet MacKnight had inflicted the disease and advised Margaret to send for Janet MacKnight, ask her to restore her health, touch her clothes – an interesting reminiscence of Jesus's cure of the woman with an issue of blood, *Matthew* 9.20-21 – take three pieces of straw from above the lintel of her own door and burn them. Janet also told Janet Black that Janet Carsan had made her brother, Andrew, ill, and John Kirkpatrick consulted her to find out who had laid a sickness on him, and was told it came from Janet Callan. Clearly, then, Janet Miller was acting principally as an unwitcher, someone who advises others on how to lift bewitchment, or performs the necessary ritual her or himself, which may or may not have meant that she herself practised maleficent magic and was therefore also a witch. Jeanne Favret-Saada, however, who investigated witchcraft in the Bocage during the 1950s, found that the witch and unwitcher tended to be separate and maintain their individual functions, and it may be that this distinction obtained in earlier times as well.[20]

Agnes Clerk inflicted and cured illness in humans and animals. So did Janet MacKnight, Helen Tait, Janet Neilson, Janet Carsan, Janet Callan and Marion Kermont. Janet Carsan also met Satan in company with several other women whom she named. She did not actually call him 'the Devil', but described him as 'a tall, black, ugly, gruesome man', which, along with the naming of witches in the company, would have been sufficient to identify him, although it is worth noting that Janet's assize unanimously declared her not guilty of this particular point. Marion Kermont's dittay illustrates one of the sore points of the period, that of having English soldiers quartered in one's house. One of them, lodged with Marion, missed some money which Marion's servant, Janet Brown, told him Marion or her husband had taken. Forced to repay the sum, Marion then cursed Janet who fell sick, languished, and died. The same trooper was invited by another, quartered in Alexander Cowman's house, to help him slaughter a sheep brought to him by Marion. Together the soldiers cut its throat and removed its feet and skin, but the sheep suddenly jumped up on to its stumps, 'whereupon the Englishman said, "If ever there was a devil in a sheep, it [is] that sheep"'.

We are told that Agnes Cairns, Margaret Clerk, Janet MacKnight, Agnes Clerk, Janet Carsan and Janet Callan were all convicted and executed, but it is worth noting the variations in the verdicts on separate points reached by their assizes. Margaret Clerk was cleared of five of her eight items, four of them unanimously. These consisted of accusations of inflicting and lifting illness. Agnes Clerk was convicted of four of twelve points by plurality, and acquitted of the rest. Janet MacKnight was found guilty by plurality of causing a child's death through magic, and of making a cow give blood and refuse to be milked, but acquitted of causing one illness and lifting it, and of magically killing a man who had called her a witch. Janet Callan was convicted by plurality of three of eight points and acquitted of the rest, and one point relating to illness followed by death was crossed out as irrelevant – that is to say, the examining magistrates thought the evidence supporting it was too weak to stand up in court, and therefore refused to let it go forward. Janet Carsan, too, had an item relating to Janet Black removed from her dittay: 'After thou was first apprehended and examined before the justices of the peace, thou sent thy daughter, Elspeth Tait, to the said Janet Black, appointing her in thy name to entreat the said Janet to inform no more against thee, and thou shouldest give her a boll [measure] of corn, and a ewe-hog for every one of her children'. Attempted bribery of a witness does not constitute witchcraft. Hence it was accounted irrelevant.

Helen Tait, on the other hand, escaped execution. She was acquitted by a plurality of votes of the eight items on her dittay, and required to pay a caution of £50 before being set at liberty. This is an interesting verdict, since most of the accusations against her concerned laying on and taking off illness, with humans or animals dying in four of the instances. Helen also seems to have fallen foul of both the minister and his wife. In about

1654 she had been lodging in a house which belonged to the minister and was told to leave it in order to make way for his sister. Whereupon the sister 'contracted a heavy sickness under which she continued until her going into the said house, which was found swept and a stone upon the hearth. No sooner did the minister's sister enter the house, but her pain became most vehement, and under that intolerable pain continued till within a quarter of an hour before her death'. The only witness to testify to this point was the minister himself, Robert Ferguson, and it is a pity the votes of the assize on this item have not been recorded, so that we might have a notion of how persuasive the minister's testimony was. But Helen must have been cleared of it by plurality at least, which may indicate either that the assize found Ferguson's testimony unconvincing (perhaps because they knew attendant circumstances which have not come down to us) or that they disliked the minister and took this opportunity to make their dislike felt. In view of Helen's acquittal on all points, however, the former is perhaps more likely.

One detail from another item on her dittay is also worth noting. In about 1654, Helen came into Alexander Kirkhoe's house and his wife gave her a bannock [round, flat cake, usually of oatmeal]. But when Helen received it, she said, 'I must also have something for my supper'. So Alexander's wife went to get her some meal, but then thought to herself, 'They say if a witch get more than one thing at once, she will have power over the giver'. So she refused to give Helen anything else and Helen left. Within two days, Alexander's wife had contracted an illness, and suffered for nearly four months before sending for Helen and begging her health again. Note that the woman clearly regarded Helen as a witch, since this is what she calls her in her silent thought, and because she sent for her (eventually) to remove her sickness. Yet, once again, the assize must have acquitted Helen at least by plurality. The woman's silent rumination, too, helps to explain why, at least on some occasions, people were reluctant to give anything to suspect witches. Objects of any kind have a relationship with their owner by the fact of being owned, and this sympathy may be exploited for magical purposes by a third party who gets hold of the object. Think in modern terms. If we touch something, we immediately transfer to it a part of ourselves in the form of a fingerprint or our DNA. A third party can then use that object to uncover our relationship with it, and so, perhaps, place us at the scene of a crime, or convict us of a felony. The logic of Alexander Kirkhoe's wife is thus entirely comprehensible.[21]

From April 1659 we have a supplication delivered to the commissioners in criminal causes by one John Short on behalf of his father, Robert from Kirkcudbright, who was being held prisoner in the tolbooth of Galloway. 'One Margaret Ireland', it says, 'and certain other ill-disposed persons, who carry your petitioner's father at great malice and envy, have slandered him as guilty of witchcraft... it being of verity he is most innocent of the said crime'. Robert had already asked the local justices to put him to trial or liberate him on caution, but they had refused to do so without higher authorisation – hence John's petition to the commissioners. John's main concern seems to have been his father's age, 'about four score and ten', a consideration which may have weighed with the commissioners, since on 21 April they ordered the local magistrates either to send Robert to Edinburgh at their own expense to stand trial, or to set him free upon caution of five hundred merks to appear there on 7 June. What became of this man and his case, we do not know. 'Great malice and envy' could have been at the root of this accusation and arrest – we should not underestimate the possibility of doing harm to an unpopular neighbour or relative offered by the prevalence of magic in society and the seriousness with which an allegation of witchcraft was invariably taken. But nor should we dismiss out of hand the equal possibility that Robert Short had indeed been practising or using magic in such a way or followed by such a concatenation of circumstances as to render the accusation both plausible and valid. Given the widespread and common resort to magic or magical practitioners, there is no reason to assume that Robert *must* have been innocent.

The Dumfries circuit court heard several other cases, too, at about this time. Janet MacGowan was accused of twelve points of witchcraft – the usual laying on of illness and infliction of pecuniary loss through damage to property. Her assize found her guilty of ten – three by plurality of votes – including one item which featured the Devil. Janet had a quarrel with Thomas Taggart, but never managed to find him at home when she came to have further words. On the third occasion, she asked Thomas's wife, Elspeth Robison, to help her pound barley and water together in a mortar, and while Elspeth was doing this, says the record, 'you gripped her behind by the middle, spanning her with your two hands. At which, she being afraid, asked why you did so, and you answered, "Thou art a small thing. Thou and I both would not make a woman betwixt us'". Elspeth replied that any woman was big enough if she was a good woman, 'and so went away from you in fear and terror because she was then with child, and you under an evil report for witchcraft'. Her fears seem to have been realised, for within two or three days 'a son of hers was chased with a devil which appeared to him in the likeness of a grievous black man', whereupon the lad became frantic and behaved as though he were mad. There is no point in our asking whether he actually did see something or someone he took to be a demon, or whether he was suffering from some kind of hallucination. Modern commentators are sometimes too quick to reach for hallucinations as an answer to past experiences they do not understand. The question is, in fact, irrelevant. What matters is what Elspeth's son said he saw, and the effect this had on himself, on his parents, and the immediate community, and on Janet herself; and we have had sufficient evidence already to make us aware that people generally in the early modern period, and in Calvinist Scotland in particular, were liable to interpret certain critical experiences in their lives in terms of encounters with physically visible demons. This item in Janet's dittay, therefore, would have been understood by her assize – and they voted upon it unanimously – in the same way Elspeth and her son had understood it. Janet had a long-standing reputation for witchcraft (a number of items go back to 1648 and 1649) and her involvement with Satan and his demons was thus taken for granted. Janet's measurement of Elspeth's waist, which to us may seem merely playful, under these circumstances was perhaps more readily interpreted as sinister; for measuring could be significant. Mediaeval prayer-girdles, for examples, were often deliberately designed to be as long as the exact (traditional) height of Christ; sick people were measured with a thread and the thread was then left in the form of a candle at a saint's shrine, and magical healers measured the belts of those they undertook to cure.[22] Given Janet's reputation, the measuring gesture was likely to provoke the reaction it did – fear and flight – and when Elspeth's son was terrified by an experience only two or three days later, his (or his mother's) interpretation of its cause as a physical demon is almost to be expected.

What caused the outbreak of these and one or two other cases in the spring of 1659? Administration of civil and judicial affairs was running fairly smoothly, so we cannot look there for a reason. But on 18 May, Robert Baillie, Principal of Glasgow University, wrote to Robert Douglas, minister of St Giles in Edinburgh: 'I do conceive our Church and land was never in so great hazard to be hurt by the Sectaries and Remonstrators as this hour', a lament for the fissiparousness of the Kirk he had made to Douglas at length the previous year, as well.[23] Religious tensions were thus likely to have been more prominent, in official minds at any rate, than civil and it may be that these, added to the particular character of the clergymen most directly involved in the initial examination of the witches, helped to precipitate a tendency to prosecute via the criminal court rather than deal with their cases entirely 'in house'. For it is notable, and may be significant, that the ministers of the principal parishes from which the suspects came – Monkland, Kirkpatrick-Irongray, Lochrutton, Buittle and Kirkennan, Kirkcudbright and Rerrick – were all deprived of their ministries in 1662 for refusing to countenance the re-establishment of episcopacy, and while strong adherence to the Presbyterian form of Church government does not necessarily argue deep commitment to the Calvinist confession, it does suggest it. Thus we are entitled to raise the question of whether these particular ministers exercised a greater than usual pressure to have the Devil's servants eradicated from their midst.

Mention of the Devil, of course, raises another question. He was prominent in the cases from Tranent in the east, but scarcely features in those from the west in Kirkcudbright. This suggests a significant difference in emphasis. Tranent and its neighbourhood saw the activity of John Kincaid, the pricker, and a pricker's job was to find corporeal evidence of the Devil's grip on the suspect he was examining. Revelation of one mark or more thus brought the physical proof of Satan's reality into sharp focus, and we may therefore expect to find this point pursued by the subject's interrogators. How did you receive such a mark? What did the Devil look like? How many times did you meet him? On what occasions and who else was there? – questions we do indeed find being asked of suspects. Now, while it is true there were also prickers in the West Country – George Cathie, for example, operated in Lanarkshire in 1649 and 1650 – they do not seem to have played a part in identifying Helen Tait and the others, and so the emphasis of the interrogations was thrown elsewhere. This is not to say, of course, that everyone involved in the Kirkcudbright episodes would not have been acutely aware of the Devil's presence in all the suspects' alleged operations: merely that, in the absence of physical examination for overt evidence of his involvement, the examiners' interest in the cases channelled itself in somewhat different directions.

These two episodes in Tranent and Kirkcudbright seem to have been the largest concentration of witch-prosecutions during the year. There were other instances, of course, but these were isolated and scattered, and constitute more or less the expected number of such cases in *any* given year. The offences listed in all these prosecutions involve a relatively small number of malefices – laying on and taking off illness sometimes causing death thereby to humans or farm animals, sometimes not; interfering with the production of milk or ale, sometimes resulting in the victim's descent into poverty; and attending what can only be described as late-night parties, with dancing, music, food, and drink, sometimes under the leadership of the Devil, sometimes in company with fairies. There is no suggestion anywhere that the destructive winds of January and February, or June, or the beginning of September, owed anything at all to preternatural machination. Indeed, on 7 September 1659, the presbytery of Stirling ordained a fast to be kept because of the excessive rains which were threatening to ruin the crops, but made no mention of local witches, even though the cases of Margaret Taylor, Katharine Rainie and others had been occupying its attention the previous year. We must presume, therefore, that it is more likely that *very* local conditions within the high nervous tension of Scotland as a whole were responsible for that limited interest in witchcraft, and it seems probable that the activities of Kincaid in the east, and the widespread fear of witches in the west, perhaps fed by the religious intensity of several clergymen, may have been responsible either for raising popular animus to a particularly high level, or doing nothing to reduce or contain it once it was rising.

CHAPTER FOUR

1660–61: The Devil Continues His Work

In view of the fever which infected the body politic in England between the collapse of Richard Cromwell's Parliament in April 1659 and the restoration of the monarchy there in May 1660, Scotland remained remarkably quiet. This was due in large part to George Monck and the army of occupation which kept a firm grip on order, suppressing, for example, between May and October, several instances of cattle-rustling and large-scale robberies (many of them armed) in the West Country and in Perthshire, not to mention roving bands of thieves in various parts of the Highlands. Such incidents could have turned serious, for if these armed groups had been able to get away without arrest and subsequent trial, political dissidents could have taken heart and joined together to pose a serious threat to continued stability. Armed crime was thus viewed as a potential political threat, and dealt with accordingly. The working of the criminal courts, however, was intermittent, although perceptions at the time that justice had ceased to function altogether were somewhat exaggerated. Some sheriffs certainly heard criminal cases and justices in Dumfriesshire and Galloway were active in keeping the peace and trying arrested malefactors. But there were no circuit courts that summer, and this meant that a number of serious offences could not be tried for the time being. Consequently, the army's role in detection and arrest proved essential to the maintenance of political control. In this, it was successful. As Dow has observed:

By the early autumn of 1659 Monck and his officers had given proof of
their ability to maintain law and order and to perform, in harness with
the civilian population, the basic functions of government at a time when
the machinery of civil administration, in the form of the Council, the
Judges, and the Commission of the Exchequer, had not prevented the
enforcement of law, or, indeed, the raising of revenue, from taking place at
grass-roots level.[1]

By the beginning of 1660, the situation had not changed all that much. The
cohesion of the army in Scotland had been achieved by Monck's remod-
elling the regiments in order to excise any elements which might have
proved dissident, a policy whose benefits were inherited by his successor,
Major General Sir Thomas Morgan. But the army was undermanned, and
the foot regiments in particular recruited among the Scots – a feature one
should bear in mind when assessing the extent to which English attitudes,
towards witches and witchcraft, for example, affected the administration of
justice. Monck left for England on 1 January 1660, leaving Scotland in a
state of uncertainty over the future. Evidence of political and social unrest
points to potential uproar, and yet Scotland remained for the most part
quiescent, awaiting, it seemed, the outcome of events in London. In March,
steps were taken to revive the efficient administration of justice by naming five military men as Commissioners, and ten judges, six Scots and four
English, although the Commissioners were hamstrung by a lack of written
confirmation of their authority, and in July the judges were forbidden to
exercise their functions and recalled to England. In July, too, government
in Scotland was given to a new Privy Council, and from that point we can
begin to see the administration of justice restored more or less in full and
acting, as far as we can tell, according to the laws and customs of Scotland,
which were in force before the English invasion. As far as the Kirk was
concerned, however, fissiparousness continued to be its watchword. But
what the Kirk did not realise was that Charles II had plans, concealed until
March 1661, to dismantle the Presbyterian form of Church government
and restore episcopacy; and this continued squabbling and the major blow
of the restoration of bishops would affect large numbers of individual clergy, and thereby their reactions to the spiritual lives of their parishioners
who would be subject in greater or lesser degree to the fervency or otherwise of their ministers' political and ecclesiastical beliefs.

What the ecclesiastical records for 1660 reveal is a very familiar pattern.[2] Witches are scarcely more frequent therein than other occult phenomena such as divination, charming, spirits and fairies. Canisbay in both January and August saw similar cases of name-calling, which contained details clearly designating something more specific and more serious than the usual angry slander. Alison Murrary called Janet Spavine a witch and a whore, and in February was told by the session to apologise; but she refused to do so, 'alleging openly that the said Janet and [an]other four with her came into her house at midnight, (there being none in the house but her husband and children, the doors being closed), and took hold of her arm and nipped the same… [Alison] also declared that the said Janet lent money to a man in Painstone, and that he never thrived thereafter'. The session was disturbed enough by this evidence to hand Janet over to the civil magistrate to be imprisoned until she fund sufficient caution to ensure she would appear before them again – clearly they thought she might try to run away in the face of such testimony. Perhaps emboldened by this result, Alison continued to call Janet a witch, a piece of triumphalism or conviction which must have tired the session, because it ordered her incarceration, too, 'until she came to acknowledgement of her fault'. On 18 March, Alison told the session that Janet had visited her again during the night ('the doors being locked') and offered to prove the truth of her assertion that Janet was a witch. But by 23 September the business had still not been resolved, and for whatever reason disappears from the session records.

On 2 September, however, Margaret Walker faced an equally serious charge. The session heard that her name was not actually Margaret Walker, but Christian Summer, and that she had been named as a witch by Robert Dewar 'who was burned for witchcraft in Winton', although at his death he had taken that back. The session ordered her to appear before them again – even if the warlock had retracted his accusation, it needed further investigation – but Christian failed to turn up on the next two occasions the session met, and although the record does not say she had decided to flee, the possibility remains that this would account for her disappearance. Her case, at any rate, does not seem to have been resolved. The only other instance of witchcraft comes from Lasswade near Edinburgh, where, on 13 May, Margaret Pringle alleged that whenever she or her husband or child fell sick, it was because Agnes Ross had laid the illness on them.

Accusations of consulting magical practitioners are just as common. On 2 April, the presbytery of Linlithgow heard nine points of complaint against Isobel Ker, one of which said that 'all these persons in the congregation that were at Jean Tweedie, seeking their fortunes, (or the most part of them), do affirm that [Isobel] persuaded and incited them to go to her', and in reply to James Ramsay's request for advice anent the censure of people who went to consult charmers, postponed any comment until the ministers had had a chance to look at the acts of the General Assembly and discuss the matter during the next meeting of the synod. In August, Janet Hall from Roxburgh denied before the kirk session of Kelso that she was a *consultrix*; in November, Elspeth Gordon from Fetteresso was found guilty of slandering James Naughtie by saying he had consulted a witch with a view to making her cow unable to yield milk; and in March, Margaret Nicoll was referred from Dron to the presbytery of Perth to explain why she had used a charm – wafting smoke from a peat fire round a sick woman – to find out whether she would die or not.

During the same month, Trinity College Church in Edinburgh resumed its investigations of the dumb woman who had been at the centre of complaints the previous autumn. Her particular gift seems to have been that of finding lost or stolen objects, and on 29 March Thomas Harper was delated for consulting her anent a gold ring, a cloak, and other missing property. The business dragged on for months, largely because Alexander Stuart who had delated Thomas constantly failed to turn up to his own kirk session to answer questions about it. He had still not appeared by the end of November, when the session's patience finally wore out and he was remitted to the presbytery – not that that had much effect, either, because he failed to appear there and had to be persuaded, under the threat of public denunciation from the pulpit, to do as he was told. Finally, on 31 January 1661 he came to Trinity and acknowledged he had slandered Thomas by suggesting he had consulted the dumb woman. But although Thomas shook hands and forgave him, we cannot be certain that the truth had been uncovered. Alexander had pushed the ecclesiastical authorities very hard, and it would have been in his interest to go through the motions of a reconciliation, embarrassing though that may have been, rather than run the risk of insisting he was right, and perhaps having the affair sent on to the civil magistrate. On the other hand, of course, we must ask ourselves why he tried to evade the issue for ten months. There is no indication in the record that he was away on business or that he had gone to live elsewhere, so we are entitled to wonder whether he was indeed guilty of slander and, conscious of the fact, was staying away from the various sessions in the hope the affair would blow over in time and thus allow him to escape public humiliation. The whole incident, however, is a good illustration both of the Kirk's frequent patience in dealing with refractory or unco-operative individuals, and of its dogged determination not to let anything pass. For every case which disappears from the records apparently undetermined, there is another such as this which shows how unrelenting could be the Kirk's grip once it had fixed its teeth upon a sinner.

In July, the Canongate kirk session heard that its minister was seeking advice from the presbytery anent three people who had consulted a diviner about stolen goods, while in September and October, the presbytery of Dalkeith considered a letter, received from the presbytery of Kelso, 'concerning Mr Silvanus, one of the parish of Newbattle, his abusing the people by giving them responses'. Mr Silvanus is an interesting combination:'Mr' suggests he had a university degree and 'Silvanus' sounds like a professional pseudonym. He was questioned by a minister and 'acknowledged that he had discovered some secret things by his skill in astrology, which he could make appear [explain] to any that would attend it [listen carefully]'. He denied, however, many of the particulars alleged against him in the letter from Kelso. He also offered to let the presbytery's representatives examine his books, which one of them did 'and found there was nothing in them but groundless vanities'. So Mr Silvanus was merely required to agree to give no more responses. Specific mention of astrology in Scottish ecclesiastical records is most uncommon, so one may guess that Master Silvanus's practice is likely to have been subordinate to another, more respectable profession. It is also noteworthy that his astrology was dismissed by the ministers as frivolous rather than diabolically inspired, a conclusion which may account for his not being punished at all.

Now, there was an Englishman living in Newbattle, whose surname is recorded as 'Seal'. In April 1669, James Hog and his servant, John Wood, had some corn and clothes stolen from them, and went to this Seal in Newbattle to find out who had stolen them. Seal, however, 'answered that he was under a promise to the presbytery of Dalkeith not to meddle with anything in that kind'. It looks, therefore, as though 'Seal' and 'Mr Silvanus' were one and the same. If he refused to help them directly, however, he did write them a letter of introduction to one David Ewart, living in Edinburgh, who could tell them what they wanted to know. James did not go himself but sent John with some money, and was rewarded with a paper from David Ewart, 'giving the marks [indications] of the person who had stolen these things'. This paper was produced and read at the kirk session of Humbie. In it, says the record, 'the said David Ewart pretended [claimed] that by astrology he knew the person who was the thief dwelt southward from the place; that he was of sandy-coloured hair, blue watering eyes with a big brow, having a star on his head on which there is no hair; and that he was an old soldier or smith'. Both James and John were then sharply rebuked 'for their sin in going to consult with one whom they supposed a magician or wizard', although the details of what their full censure should be were left to the presbytery to decide. Eventually, on 30 May, they were both rebuked in public. It is interesting that, nine years after his brush with the presbytery, Mr Seal should be keeping his word not to use astrology for the purposes of divination, but one notes he had no hesitation in referring potential clients elsewhere – it is worth observing, too, that after nine years he still had his reputation as a diviner – and that his contact was also an astrologer. Perhaps these practitioners were not quite as uncommon as their infrequent appearances in the records may suggest.

All these cases remind us of the constant presence of magic and divination in the social fabric of the period. Turning to them may have earned the Kirk's disapproval, but no amount of public humiliation, it seems, was sufficient to do more than put a temporary stop to those who practised and consulted the occult arts. Nor did it have any greater effect on belief in fairies.[3] On 8 March 1660, Rothesay kirk session was told that the whole district was talking about Jean Campbell because she was going with the fairies. The elders were instructed to investigate, and a fortnight later the session heard her father say he wanted his daughter either found guilty or cleared of the scandalous gossip. Investigation suggested that perhaps it was Jean's husband, Robert MacConochie, who was responsible for starting the rumour; but when he came before the session on 5 April, he declared that, on the contrary, he would be glad to see the taint of scandal removed. (One may note at this point that the family seemed to be the focus of ill-natured gossip, for Robert was also being examined by the session at this time on a charge of adultery with his servant, Mary Campbell – perhaps a relation of his wife, perhaps not – and was found not guilty of it).

When Jean herself was questioned, she said she had heard the gossip and was grieved thereat. It arose, she said, about three years before, when she had been ill with smallpox in her father's house. Once she was able to get out of bed, she could not keep down her food and was too weak either to speak or open her eyes for two or three days. She was also pitifully tormented with an open sore on her head, so her father sent for Janet Morrison who came to her, bandaged her head, and gave her some salve to rub on her breast. This sounds at first as though Janet may have been a magical healer, but in fact the session, having heard testimony from three of Jean's father's servants, drew no such conclusion and declared that the gossip about her was nothing more than slander; and in order to quash any attempt to prolong or renew the slander, Jean's name was to be cleared from the pulpit, with a warning 'that whosoever shall hereafter cast up the same [rumour about] the said Jean without sufficient ground and presumptions shall be repute and punished as slanderers'. The odd feature of this episode is the apparent lack of connection between Jean's illness and the gossip that she went with the fairies. Smallpox was a common disease, and there is no general suggestion it was inflicted by non-human entities. *Gruagach*, for example, were fairy-like creatures who were capable of inflicting harm if they were offended, but their punishments consisted of untying cows or spilling milk, and while so-called 'elf' arrowheads were certainly credited with doing harm to human beings, there is no evidence of their being found anywhere near Jean. One also wonders why Jean and her family should have allowed the gossip to persist for as long as three years before doing something about it. Clearly there is much more to this episode than has been recorded.

What this survey tells us is that in 1660 the Kirk was not being faced by a noticeable upsurge in the number of witches, and while it is true that the survey does not include every parish on Scotland – a very large number, if not most of the records do not begin until the end of the century or have gaps at this crucial juncture – it is most unlikely that additional anecdotes would substantially alter this observation. Those trials which do occur therefore probably originated with hearings before the civil magistrates rather than in kirk and presbytery sessions which tend to note when they hand over an individual to the secular authority, and we should ask ourselves why the state rather than the Kirk now notably busied itself with what should have been a purely spiritual matter. The answer may lie in part with the results of a witch's actions. She or he may have been inspired by the Devil, but the subsequent harm frequently involved damage to person or property. It is also worth remembering that the basis of the witch's presumed power lay in her or his contract with the Devil. That relationship was therefore grounded in the understanding of civil law, and the English writer, John Cotta, whose *Triall of Witch-Craft* first appeared in 1616, succinctly expressed the implications of that relationship.

> The first kind [of malefice] is of such supernatural works as are done by the Devil solely and simply to his own ends or use, without any reference or respect to any contract or covenant with Man. The second kind is of such transcendent works as are done with a respect or reference unto some contract or covenant with Man. In the first, the Devil is solely an agent for himself, without the knowledge or consent of Man. In the second, the supernatural and transcendent works are truly, essentially, and immediately from the Devil's; also (because out of the reach or power of any command of Man simply) yet therein Man hath a property and interest by covenant and contract, and derivation thereof from the Devil, which is truly and solely sorcery and witchcraft: for since supernatural works are only proper to a spirit, and above the nature and power of Man, they cannot truly and properly be esteemed his; and therefore it is not the supernatural work itself, but Man's contract and combination therein with the Devil his consent and allowance thereof, that doth make it his, and him a witch, a sorcerer, which is a contracter with the Devil.[4]

It is this contract which lies at the heart of witchcraft. Charming, divination, and other forms of the occult sciences may be open to diabolical interference, since they can easily tempt the practitioner to seek more-than-human help. But maleficent magic was regarded as resting entirely upon such assistance, and in consequence it was the free and willing agreement to enter into a covenant with the Devil, which made an occult practitioner specifically a witch. The making of this contract often took place in private when no one but the would-be witch and the Devil was present. In this case, proof that such a contract had been made rested entirely upon the witch's confession. On other occasions, the individual was taken by one witch or more to a meeting and there agreed to the contract in the presence of witnesses. When it came to proving this in court, however, probation rested upon the already proven guilt of the other arrested witches whose testimony or delation then formed an *indicium gravissimum*, or very strong circumstantial evidence. Even so, such evidence was not, in itself, proof and the court therefore relied on the accused's confession almost as much as though there had been no eyewitnesses at all.

Unless the accused confessed voluntarily, and made a *full* confession, the court would have been at a loss how to proceed further. Scottish law, however, followed the practice of Roman law in permitting the use of torture under clearly defined conditions in order to obtain the necessary confession, or confirmation or amplification of a confession. Now, the introduction of torture into a discussion of legal procedure runs several risks. First, it rouses emotive antipathy and, if the discussion is not careful, tempts one to suggest or imply that the individual undergoing torture must have been innocent. There is, of course, no *must* about it. Secondly, it can induce an unfortunate voyeurism in both parties to the discussion, in as much as the writer spends his or her time in recording details of applied torture which, because no evidence exists that the instruments described were actually used therein, may or may not be irrelevant to the case or cases under review. Mention is thus made merely as a dramatic device to heighten the reader's emotions, in a manner akin to the techniques of eighteenth-century Gothic fiction. Thirdly, unless the writer is careful, he or she will run the risk of implying that torture was used in all cases of witchcraft, simply because he can show it was used in some. Fourthly, the knowledge or the implication that torture was used may be allowed to seduce the reader into thinking that any resulting confession must have been fantasy, the assumption being that torture cannot or does not produce the truth. Once again, there is no *must* about it. Fifthly, it is too frequently the case that details of what happened during the excesses of witch-interrogation in some German states, such as those which form the basis of Friedrich Spee's condemnation of witch-trials in his *Cautio Criminalis*, are described as though they applied equally well to the situation in Scotland. Sixthly, and perhaps most important, the word 'torture' is not defined for the discussion, and is allowed to stand for any species of maltreatment the writer cares to mention.

The legal position in Scotland was that torture, meaning officially authorised application of instruments to inflict pain on the individual being questioned, and therefore best called judicial torture, could be administered in any criminal case only with warrant from the Privy Council or Parliament. It is a legal distinction which must be borne in mind, because the word 'torture' can be used loosely to refer to a whole range of brutal maltreatment which is, by definition, not judicial torture and therefore always illegal. Thus, when Lord Royston observed of arrested witches that 'most of the poor creatures are tortured by their keepers', he was referring to maltreatment and not to legal torture. This is also what the Council meant in 1678 when it declared that inferior judges 'might not use any torture, by pricking, or by withholding them from sleep'.[5] The distinction may appear to be nit-picking, but if we are to discuss a legal situation where exact or close definition of words is extremely important, and if we are to understand the motives and behaviour of those people involved in the process, it is perhaps better to be over-nice than to run the risk of being cavalier. (Consequently, when the Scottish jurist, Sir George MacKenzie, wrote that 'torture is seldom used among us', he was not being disingenuous but, legally speaking, accurate,[6] and Stuart MacDonald has drawn attention to the importance of these distinctions, especially if any comparison is to be made – as it frequently is – between legal practice in Scotland and other European countries).[7]

By 1661, the secular authorities were certainly aware of the various possible meanings of the word, and in many cases which came before the Court of Justiciary in July and August that year one frequently finds the records saying that no torture has been used, or no torture or violence, or no torturing or threatening. 'Torture' here seems to be distinguished from other forms of coercion, so the likelihood is that the documents which were, after all, cast in legal form and therefore intended to be precise in their expression, referred to the use of judicial torture i.e. torture with instruments legally applied under warrant. Other references from the same months indicate that judicial torture was used. A marginal note in the case of Janet Ker (10 August) says that she is to go to trial, 'but to call again for the torture', which not only implies that torture had been used already, but also – because the note was made by a clerk – that judicial torture was meant. In the case of David Johnston (28 July), he was asked whether he was guilty of the sin of witchcraft and replied that 'he knows nothing of witchcraft more than the child in the mother's womb', adding that, when he was arrested, he was put in a hair cloth which made him confess he was in company with an accused witch and with others. This sounds easy to interpret as maltreatment, but we have to bear in mind that the sackcloth which many penitents were obliged to wear as part of their ecclesiastical punishment by the Kirk was often a 'haircloth', and although this was probably worn over the clothes, it is difficult to see that simply wearing it next to the skin would be sufficient of itself to induce a confession of being a witch. It is perhaps more likely that additional maltreatment not mentioned here – such as dipping the cloth in vinegar to fetch off the skin, as mentioned by Chambers in his *Domestic Annals* – or the shame of being so dressed, played a more significant part in the process. Even so, the haircloth did not constitute torture in the legal sense, and it is not so described in the document. Consequently, when we read a marginal note in the case of Margaret Porteous (7 August), that she 'denies all and says her former confession was through torture', are we to understand that 'torture' here is being used in the judicial sense, or that Margaret, to whom the words are attributed, was using 'torture' to mean maltreatment? Similarly, when Margaret Shewingston (29 July) denied everything and said she had been tortured, and that all the confession she had made was false, was she using the word 'tortured' in its strictly legal sense, or in reference to harsh maltreatment? It is difficulties in coming to a precise understanding of what the records are telling us which makes a very careful scrutiny of the term 'torture' very important.

Maltreatment, of course, must not be underplayed. We have already come across the cases of Margaret Taylor, Katharine Rainy and Bessie Paton, where they describe their treatment as 'torture', which it amounts to in effect if not in definition. Chambers also draws attention to one incident from 1652, in which six suspected witches were subjected to being hung up by the thumbs, and being burned in various places with lighted candles, to such effect that four of them died. Needless to say, if this did indeed happen, it was entirely illegal.[8] The reason one hesitates is the source which Chambers used – the political broadsheet, *Mercurius Politicus*, an English publication which, by 1652, was overtly taking a nationalistic line with respect to subjugating Scotland to the common-wealth of England.[9] The picture it draws here of Scottish superstition and barbarity thus contributed to the political message that Scotland *needed* to be subjugated. Brutality there certainly was, however, in a number of witchcraft cases. But 'a number of' does not mean 'all', even by implication, and we are not entitled to assume its presence without good warrant.

Being pricked could also amount to a form of maltreatment in practice, although one should note that it was not employed to produce or confirm a confession, but to test whether or not a mark on the suspect's body had been caused by nature or by Satan's grip. If the latter, it would provide strong circumstantial evidence that the suspect might be a witch, but would not, of itself, furnish proof thereof. One must also bear in mind that a genuine witch's mark was supposed to be insensible, and that its discovery would therefore (in theory) cause the suspect no pain. Searching for it, of course, would undoubtedly do so.

Likewise, conditions in prison could be extremely harsh. On 8 February 1656, Isobel Monro from Forres sent a petition to the Commissioners for Criminal Justice.[10] She may have been a Gaelic speaker, because the petition says she had no English or, at any rate, so poor a command of it that they would not be able to understand her. She had been in prison for five years – although she had once managed to escape and had to be re-arrested – and for three of these 'did lie in stocks without any clothes but a salt sack which salt had been kept in, to cover her nakedness. Her entertainment [maintenance] was half a peck of beer meal in a fortnight, with a drink of cold water once in two days or three; being without either coal or candle or daylight to shine in upon [her], till she was many times constrained to drink her piss; and not so much as skin was left either upon her legs or thighs with [because of] the stocks and sitting upon [the] hard floor'. This Isobel refers to, understandably enough, as 'torturing'. But we must not be misled by the misery Isobel describes into taking her particular case and turning it into a general description. Her petition alleges that the laird and lady of Grant who had caused her to be imprisoned 'intend by her long imprisonment to be her death, as it has been the death of her husband'. If the allegation was true, it would help to account for her long and special unhappiness, since malice on the part of the landowners against a woman with no apparent means of redress would have been extremely difficult to counter or circumvent; but it would also mean that we are dealing with a very particular set of circumstances, not a form of treatment which was customarily used against suspect witches.

Close investigation of the records shows that actually the application of judicial torture may not have been used all that often in Scotland – indeed, MacDonald has argued that in Fife, for example, it may not have been used at all – so the role of judicial torture in producing confessions and thus providing a stimulus for widespread prosecution of witches must therefore to a large extent be discounted, however much this conclusion runs against the grain of conventional wisdom. As MacDonald says, 'simple answers will not work'. Instead, we must examine the various types and instances of maltreatment to see whether and how far these may have been responsible for producing the confessions which condemned many of those accused.

But here, too, care needs to be exercised. Consider the following:

(a) When we were all assembled, the Mystic rose from his seat, and taking one of the swords from the side of the brazier, held it pointing towards the altar while he intoned an invocation in a language with which I was not familiar.

(b) Anna Kemp having desired you to go with her to Haddington, where you being come, did meet with the Devil in likeness of a man in black clothes, with a bonnet on his head, and other notorious witches all dancing together: who, coming from among them, gave you a kiss, took you by the hand, and desired you to be his servant, promising you that you should never want, which you condescended [agreed] to. At which time also you renounced your baptism by putting your one hand to the crown of your head, and thereafter to the sole of your foot, and giving all betwixt to him; and received a new name from him, called 'Jenny'; and have taken his marks upon several parts of your body, viz. one on your shoulder and another on your thigh.

(c) There were about fifty people present. There was a small altar... A young cockerel was killed and the blood poured into a glass to be given to those to be initiated... The first initiate drank the blood of the sacrificed chicken, and was informed she had drunk the blood of the Devil. Twisted prayers were said. She signed a pact bearing blood, giving her soul to the Devil in return for power.[11]

The first is a statement by Betty May who lived at Aleister Crowley's Abbey of Thelema in Sicily between 1922 and 1923; the second comes from the dittay of Margaret Allan, tried for witchcraft on 16 November 1661 at the Court of Justiciary in Edinburgh; and the third is a recollection by a Birmingham housewife, Sarah Jackson, given to a Sunday newspaper in 1955. It will be noticed that the seventeenth-century Scottish confession is by far the least lurid. None of these was obtained through judicial torture. The first is an accurate recollection of a genuine experience, since ritual magic was indeed practised in Crowley's Abbey; the second is full of ambiguities, since portions of it may be true (although not in the form in which it is given here), derived from genuine experiences of a kind we shall discuss in a moment; and the third is fantasy of some kind, although it would be best not to run to the usual 'hallucination' to explain it. Mrs Jackson was 'confessing' to a newspaper, so simple fiction could be enough to account for her anecdote. It is interesting, however, that the newspaper was happy to print it, and a good deal more in the same vein, and present it to the public as fact. Collusion between client and proprietor – or penitent and confessor – whether deliberate or tacit must always be borne in mind when one reads witches' confessions, although in this latter case it must also be remembered that such collusion does not necessarily render the confession untrue or invalid.

Extraordinary details in a confession therefore do not provide evidence that judicial torture or even maltreatment *must* have been used to secure them, and we must be prepared to accept that if a suspect confessed to appearances of and traffic with Satan, she or he may have believed them to be real experiences, in which case the confession, whether obtained voluntarily or after maltreatment or under torture was true as far as both the suspect and the interrogator were concerned.

Let us now consider the practice of watching prisoners, a practice not infrequently referred to in the records, but one which is often conflated with sleep-deprivation as though the two were one and the same.[12] 'Watching' was exactly that – keeping close watch over a prisoner to make sure she or he did not escape. We have already seen that Isobel Monro managed to escape from prison (perhaps this accounts for her being confined in stocks) and the records contain several references to this possibility. A warlock imprisoned in Douglas escaped from the prison house in March 1650; a fugitive adulteress was brought to bed of a child in Christian Douglas's house in Haddington, and the kirk session 'desired the magistrates to set men to watch her, (upon her own expenses), that she escape not before that the ministers of Hamilton [whence she had fled] be acquainted of her'. Friends might mount an assault to carry off an imprisoned friend or relative. On 16 June 1681:

> the baillies and council, considering that a company of lewd and irregular persons did last night make an infall upon this burgh and by force carried away Thomas Lachlan who was a prisoner within the tolbooth of Lanark... and baited, abused, and threatened Baillie Inglis and wounded John Sherrilaw, their officer, in the head, and committed several other abuses, therefore enacted that in time coming there shall be a nightly guard kept within the said tolbooth.

It is clear, then, that escapes could be effected and that watching was not an invariable practice, but was instituted where the authorities considered it necessary. It is also clear that offenders other than witches could be subject to watching, and that watching was done to prevent escapes, not to deprive prisoners of sleep in order to obtain a confession.

When it came to witches, of course, there were particular reasons for wanting to keep an alert eye on them. Witches could change shape and might therefore escape in the form of an animal or bird or insect, an ability which had caused them to be kept under surveillance as far back as the Middle Ages. Johann Nider, for example, informs us that he was told that for about sixty years in the region of Berne, many people were practising harmful magic, the principal being a man called Scavius ['Scabby']. He boasted he could turn himself into a mouse any time he wanted and so escape from his enemies. But he was watched closely by his enemies while he was sitting near a window in the chimney. Here he felt himself safe from attack, but he was killed through the window by swords and spears. Witches could be visited by the Devil himself who might try to aid them escape. He came to Agnes Cairns in prison and offered to strangle her as he had another imprisoned witch, Helen Hare, the previous night; and in September 1661 the Devil visited Helen Guthrie in prison and tried to carry her away. He lifted her three or four feet in the air until her head was among the joists of the prison house, while those who were watching her struck out with their swords and thus prevented her escape. But it was not always necessary to guard against preternatural intervention. Trinity College kirk session in Edinburgh, for example, heard in 17 March 1664 that Elizabeth Philp had called Isobel Ross a murdering whore. The principal reason was that Elizabeth's aunt had been imprisoned in the tolbooth of Dunbar as a suspected witch, and Isobel had visited her with a drink which had poisoned her. Whether this was deliberate or accidental makes no difference. It illustrates how easy it could be for prisoners to evade further imprisonment and possible execution by escape or suicide or murder.

Still, if watching was not the same as sleep-deprivation and was not intended principally to extort a confession from the suspect, how are we to interpret a recommendation by the kirk session of Dunfermline on 6 May 1649? 'This day it is reported by the magistrates that John Murdoch, the witch, was watched; as also the ministers declared that he had come to a confession. It is thought fit that he be still as yet watched, that more confession and trial may be had out of him'. It is important not to take these statements and argue *post hoc ergo propter hoc*. John's confession certainly happened after a period of watching, but it could have been produced by a number of different circumstances of which we know nothing – conditions in prison, brutal maltreatment, constant hectoring interrogation, isolating from the comfort and encouragement of family or neighbours, intense and lengthy spiritual exhortation from the clergy upon a weak or susceptible conscience. Any or all of these could have combined to elicit the partial confession which the magistrates and session found unsatisfactory. Hence their intention to have the process prolonged.

This, then, brings us to sleep-deprivation. It is an extremely effective method of reducing someone to a state where he or she will be willing to make a confession of alleged offences, and it will also induce hallucinations which can be incorporated into the confession as factual details.

Nevertheless, we must be prepared to look at the technique through seventeenth-century rather than modern eyes, since the earlier motives for depriving a prisoner of sleep may well not be the same as ours, or at least have a dimension alien to our way of thinking, which was central, not tangential, to theirs. A very good illustration is provided by the English witch-finder, Matthew Hopkins. In his *Discovery of Witches* (1645), he gave answers to queries supposedly objecting to his methods of interrogation, and two are worth quoting in full.

Query 8. When these paps are fully discovered [on a suspect witch], yet that will not serve sufficiently to convict them, but they must be tortured and kept from sleep two or three nights, to distract them and make them say any thing; which is a way to tame a wild colt or hawk etc.

Answer. In the infancy of this discovery it was not only thought fitting, but enjoined in Essex and Suffolk by the magistrates with this intention only because they being kept awake would be more the active to call their imps in open view the sooner to their help, which oftentimes have so happened; and never or seldom did any witch ever complain in the time of their keeping for want of rest, but after they had beat their heads together in the gaol; and after this use was not allowed of by the judges and other magistrates, it was never since used, which is a year and a half since, neither were any kept from sleep by any order or direction since; but peradventure their own stubborn wills did not let them sleep, though tendered and offered to them.

Query 9. Beside that unreasonable watching, they were extraordinarily walked, till their feet were blistered, and so forced through that cruelty to confess, etc.

Answer. It was in the same beginning of this discovery, and the meaning of walking of them at the highest extent of cruelty, was the only they to walk about themselves the night they were watched, only to keep them waking: and the reason was this, when they did lie or sit in a chair, if they did offer to couch down, then the watchers were only to desire them to sit up and walk about, for indeed when they were suffered so to couch, immediately comes their familiars into the room and scareth the watchers, and heartneth on the witch; though contrary to the true meaning of the same instructions, divers have been by rustical people, (they hearing them confess to be witches), misused, spoiled, and abused, divers whereof

have suffered for the same, but could never be proved against this discoverer to have a hand in it, or consent to it; and hath likewise been unused
by him and others, ever since the time they were kept from sleep.

Here Hopkins makes it clear – and it makes no difference whether we
choose not to believe him – that suspect witches were kept awake in
order to make it easier (and more imperative) for them to call upon their
attendant-demons for aid, the appearance of whom would confirm that
the prisoner was indeed a witch. But, as was also known, witches were
capable of travelling to a Sabbat in spirit only, leaving their bodies apparently in a state of sleep, which is why, when children in the German
town of Calw confessed, during an episode of witch-prosecution in
1683, that they attended Sabbats while they were asleep, their parents
started keeping them awake at night, to prevent the Devil from coming
to carry them off.[13]

Now, it would be more than foolish to maintain that this range of
harshness we have been discussing had no effect in reducing those
arrested and those imprisoned to a state in which they were ready to
co-operate with their interrogators and produce the kind of detailed
confession they thought the officials wanted to hear. Of course it did.
Nevertheless, we must be careful not to push the available evidence
beyond its natural bounds. If torture (meaning judicial torture) is not
mentioned in any particular case, we are not entitled to assume it *must*
have been used. If the use of torture is specifically denied, we are not
entitled to assume the record is lying. Because various forms of maltreatment were undoubtedly used in many cases, we are not entitled
to assume it was used in all, any more than evidence of brutality by the
police in a number of modern instances entitles us to say that police
interrogations are always brutal. Nor are we entitled to lump together all
kinds of maltreatment and harsh prison conditions and call them 'torture', as though they were the same as judicial torture.

The temptation to do so seems to be driven by a series of tacit assumptions which, taken together, amount to an agendum, reducing witchcraft
studies to 'a psychoanalytical exploration of the killing of women'.[14] The
argument runs: witches were women; witchcraft is an impossible offence
and therefore women accused of it were innocent; therefore their confessions were extorted from them by torture; there (again) the women

were innocent; and if the women were innocent, the men who tried and executed them must have been guilty of murder. It needs to be stressed that this kind of approach explains little or nothing. It ignores the fact that perhaps a quarter of those accused of witchcraft were men. Magic of all kinds was accepted as a valid phenomenon by virtually everyone in the early modern period. Statutes existed all over Europe, condemning witchcraft in particular as a capital offence because of the harm it did. It was thus a crime like any other capital offence of the statutebook. Proving it had been committed was more difficult than proving the others, but that does not render it any less of an offence. Anyone who practised any kind of magic was liable to fall foul of a local statute, depending on how the statute was worded. Those who committed the crime were therefore breaking the law, and if they were then brought to trial and found guilty of this capital offence, their execution was perfectly legal. Substitute 'murder' or 'theft' or infanticide' for 'witchcraft', and no one would think twice about accepting the validity of the legal process. It is only because modern people have difficulties in coming to terms with the notion of witchcraft as a real crime that they try to treat it as though it were exceptional. Male judges and male juries tried, condemned, and executed other men by the thousand all over Europe for a wide variety of capital offences, of which witchcraft was one. But no one calls for 'a psychoanalytical exploration of the killing of men'.

The one feature of witchcraft which made it different from murder or theft or infanticide in their eyes was its preternatural dimension. Murder and so forth were purely human crimes. Witchcraft and other forms of magic by definition drew the spirit-world into the realm of matter, and this made them potentially much more dangerous to society; and therefore, seen from this point of view, ecclesiastical and secular authorities would have been failing in their most basic duty to protect their parishioners and citizens had they *not* sought to prosecute and eradicate from society those individuals who deliberately allied themselves with evil in order to wreak upon their fellows and neighbours a kind of harm which crossed the boundary between matter and spirit, and thus threatened genuine innocents not only in their goods and persons, but even as far as their souls.

It is also worth bearing in mind that Scottish men and women were accustomed to appearing before figures of authority, since they were often summoned to come to sessions of the kirk and presbytery, and not infrequently demonstrated that they were not overawed by the experience.[15] Margaret Robertson and Agnes Hately, for example, were called before the session of Inchture and Rossie on 29 June 1651 for quarrelling. Margaret had, in effect, said that Agnes was a witch. After due examination of both parties and witnesses, the session ordered Margaret and Agnes to be reconciled, but the two women failed to turn up between 20 July and 4 October, and when at last they did come, they refused to be reconciled and told the session they would not turn up again. There is no record of their having done so. In September 1655, Agnes was in trouble again for drying woven cloth on a Sunday, and again she did not come to the session for punishment. On 21 October, she was to be summoned for quarrelling once more with Margaret but, just as before, neither woman put in an appearance until 25 November, when Agnes came and said she was willing to be punished, but Margaret maintained her absence. On 2 December, both women attended and neither showed signs of repentance, and it was not until 13 January 1656 that the session got its way and effected a reconciliation between them.

But Margaret was not the only person to call Agnes a witch. In May 1657, Agnes complained to the session that Elspeth Milner and Elspeth Moncur had said she was a witch, and from that point until 29 September a familiar pattern resurrected itself, with Elspeth Milner failing to turn up to the session until 31 May the following year, when she flatly refused to obey the minister and elders, and then absented herself again until 9 August when she offered a compromise. She would repent any sin she may have committed against God, she said, but not one against her neighbour. Naturally this offer was refused, and she was finally reconciled and punished at the end of the following month. Similarly, Elspeth Carlisle appeared before the presbytery of Dumfries on 14 September 1658, 'being charged with many gross scandals which are proven before the session of Traquair, especially her calling of her mother-in-law a witch', and of having told the session, after invoking the Devil, that she hoped her soul might go to Hell if ever she went to the presbytery. It is not so much that she caved in which is significant, as her forthright tone to her minister and elders. We have also noted the case of Margaret Wirk in Shapinsay (Orkney), who was whipped on more than one occasion by order of the civil magistrate, apparently to no effect. Such people could be broken by judicial torture and various forms of maltreatment, of course, but they show that neither ecclesiastical nor secular authority could take for granted that enforcing obedience would necessarily be straightforward.

We now come to the various confessions freely made or elicited from men and women arrested on suspicion of being a witch. As we have seen, the great bulk of magical practices attributed to these individuals consisted of laying on and taking off illness, ruining someone's livelihood, curing illness, and identifying the cause of an illness or the whereabouts of lost or stolen articles. Only in a smaller number of cases does the Devil come into the narrative, and when he does, he almost always appears as a human being dressed in black or grey or green, behaves like a gentleman, and dances and has sexual intercourse with the woman making the confession. He requires her to renounce her baptism, gives her his mark by nipping or gripping part of her body, and changes her name to one which is perfectly ordinary. The meetings attended by witches involve eating, drinking and dancing, and sometimes the participants go on, with or without the Devil's being present, to do harm to one or other of their neighbours or acquaintances. But this last is not an invariable concomitant of their assembly which has the characteristics of a peasant party rather than the classical Sabbat. In other words, there is very little contained in these confessions which smacks of the extraordinary or of the Gothic or bizarre, for let us remember how relatively commonplace were appearances of the Devil in human form at the time in non-witchcraft as well as witchcraft contexts. The Devil looks and behaves like a human, not a demon, and his meetings are jolly rather than lurid or sinister. Why, then, we should ask, would it have been considered necessary to use judicial torture or maltreatment to elicit these details, and what may have been the experiential sources on which the accused could draw to put together their confessed narrative? Is it *our* expectation that events and appearances so alien from those we habitually experience were also alien to early modern people, and that therefore they *must* have been obtained through force and pressure?

Let us note, for example, a difference in sleep-patterns between the present day and an earlier period.[16] Roger Ekirch has pointed out that sleep used to be fragmented. 'Until the close of the early modern era, Western Europeans on most evenings experienced two major intervals of sleep bridged by up to an hour or more of quiet wakefulness', and during the wakeful interval, people often got up and attended to a variety of tasks both in and out of doors. James Brown came into Helen Barton's house to light a candle; Janet Spavin and four others came into Alison Murray's house at midnight; Margaret Tait was combing her hair on her master's fore-stair at ten or eleven o'clock at night soon after Christmas (when it would have been dark for several hours) and was joined there by Bessie Melrose and Hugh Black; the Old Kirk session in Peebles heard that various people had been moving round the town at night on Peace (i.e. *Pace* = Easter) Monday and that Helen Jenkinson's door would be open at three in the morning; Jean Bocle spent all night drinking with another woman and did not get home until four o'clock in the morning; and in Haddington, James Drew complained to the kirk session that John Veitch's wife came to his door at midnight to call his wife 'witch-begotten'. So when we are told that witches met one another 'at midnight', or were seen out of doors during darkness, as in the case of Christian Wilson who was accused in 1661 of laying on and taking off illness from Alexander Dickson, and then continuing to hang around the close where he lived 'in the very dead hour of night', we should not regard this as especially unusual behaviour, nor dismiss it as unlikely.

Meetings of women and men during the interval between the two sleeps, then, were perfectly possible. So when a witch confessed to such a meeting, she may have been telling simple fact in as far as the reality of the meeting was concerned, and in as far as the people she named as being present, too. It is the preternatural element in these gatherings, which removes them from ordinary, everyday experience. Whence, then, did that preternatural element arise? There are several aspects of the potential experience to bear in mind, and Ekirch draws our attention to one of the most interesting:

For every active intellect following first sleep, there were two others initially neither asleep nor awake. The French called this ambiguous interval of semi-consciousness 'dorveille'... Events depicted in visions occasionally appeared genuine long afterwards. An Aberdeen minister, after viewing an unusual spectacle outside his window, days later could not remember whether he dreamed it or seemed to see it in reality.[17]

Pitch-darkness intensifies untoward or unrecognised noises; candle- or lamplight causes shifts in light and shadow. The identity of objects or creatures heard or seen under such circumstances requires interpretation, and that may well depend on mood and state of wakefulness. Bear in mind, too, that early modern people almost expected to see the Devil in physical form, and that they expressed certain experiences in terms of just such an encounter. Thus, on 18 July 1661, John Scott from Duddingston confessed that he had met Satan more than once, and that the second time he appeared 'in the likeness of a man with black clothes, *after his first sleep*' (my italics).[18] So it is possible that a genuine meeting with one or two neighbours during the night could coincide with an expectation or fear of seeing Satan, followed by an ambiguous memory of perhaps having done so on that occasion; or an apparition of Satan, experienced and subsequently reported as real, merged into genuine memory of meeting with neighbours.

It should also be recollected that darkness or half-light could provide cover for adultery or fornication. On 3 August 1661, Janet Blaikie from Dalkeith gave evidence which mingles preternatural with natural events. 'The man that met with her', she said, 'lay with [her]... He was cold the first and second time, but the third time he was like another man... The Devil never desired [her] to be his servant, [and] she knew him not to be the Devil, but to be only Henry Beat'.[19] In either case, any subsequent interrogation concerning these things would elicit a narrative consisting of elements both natural and preternatural, the details of which would be reported as true, and believed to be true by the person saying them as well as by the examining officials. I am not, of course, offering this as an explanation of what did happen, merely of what could and may have happened from time to time; and if this is possible, confessions of meeting Satan at assemblies of women and men known to the suspect witch needed no torture or maltreatment to produce them, which would help to account for the frequent references to free confession and lack of torture appearing in the records.

But why would anyone voluntarily confess to being a witch when the penalty for such a crime was well-known to be death? The first and most obvious reason, which we should do well not to forget, is because she (usually 'she') was indeed a magical practitioner. The evidence that individuals used magic in the form of charms is overwhelming, and these individuals were not a minority, but constituted a majority of any given population. Those who did not use magic themselves were prepared to consult and use people who did, and even kirk elders were not immune; for in January 1651, the presbytery of Turriff directed that John Davidson be deprived of his eldership in the parish of Alva because he had advised Andrew Burgie to send for a magical healer to cure his fever.[20] The chance that someone accused of using magic was actually guilty of it was, therefore, very high, and in consequence her or his confession would be a confession of the truth.

Secondly, a person designated or considered to be a witch by her community might come to believe it herself. An English Jacobean play, *The Witch of Edmonton* (*c*. 1621), has Elizabeth Sawyer suggesting this very point.

> And why on me? Why should the envious world
> Throw all their scandalous malice upon me?
> 'Cause I am poor, deformed, and ignorant,
> And like a bow buckled and bent together
> By some more strong in mischiefs than myself,
> Must I for that be made a common sink
> For all the filth and rubbish of men's tongues
> To fall and run into? Some call me witch,
> And, being ignorant of myself, they go
> About to teach me how to be one, urging
> That my bad tongue, by their bad usage made so,
> Forspeaks their cattle, doth bewitch their corn,
> Themselves, their servants and their babes at nurse.
> This they enforce upon me, and in part
> Make me to credit it.

In addition to neighbours' convincing a person she or he was indeed a witch, the minister and elders might play a leading role in this process. Again and again the records tell us that suspects were visited by one minister or more, and sometimes by elders, too, and the intense spiritual pressure which these people could bring to bear, quite probably from the best of motives, would have taken great counter-conviction to resist. As the Englishman, Richard Bernard, advised in his *Guide to Grand-Jury*

Men (1629), 'Have a godly and learned divine, and somewhat well read in the discourses of witchcraft and impieties thereof, to be instructing the suspected of the points of salvation, of the damnable cursedness of witchcraft, and his or her fearful state of death eternal, if guilty and not repentant'. Interpretation of seemingly harmless or even beneficent actions, such as the use of a charm to cure illness, as fraught with spiritual danger and inspired by demonic prompting might easily lead someone who was not aware of the peril therein – and we have seen a number of people explaining to the kirk or presbytery session that they did not realise there was any sin involved – to acknowledge a fault grievous enough to require repentance and punishment. How much more persuasive, therefore, might a clergyman be, faced by a suspect who had had, and perhaps expressed, malicious thoughts against a neighbour, in convincing her or him that a subsequent misfortune or concatenation of unhappy events had been caused by the Devil's taking advantage of those same thoughts or words or actions?

This brings us to the much-debated point of how far the accused person was author of her or his confession, or a re-writer of conventional demonological assumptions possibly held by her or his interrogators. Much of the discussion has been conducted upon the premise that the accused was female – a reasonable presumption in most but not all cases – and Marion Gibson has offered four models, all deliberately based on English material and practice, for such confessions: (a) the key figure is the victim of the alleged witchcraft, and her or his version of events is accepted and repeated by the accused (as we can see Elizabeth Sawyer doing); (b) the key figure is the questioner, whose version is then accepted by the witch; (c) the clerk weaves disparate and not necessarily coherent elements of a confession into a coherent narrative; (d) the suspect witch recounts the narrative as a kind of fragment of autobiography.[21]

Scottish narratives, of course, were not collected in the same way as English. As we have seen, many began with complaints brought forward to a kirk session, and many ended there. Others, however, were either forwarded to the local justices of the peace, or came straight to the justices without any ecclesiastical hearing. In the first case, preliminary questioning, perhaps over several weeks or even months, had produced a file of documents, each of which more or less summarised the evidence of the accused and the various witnesses. Already, therefore, a degree of editing had taken place. The accused was then re-questioned before the secular magistrates, and further documentation compiled, after which the case might be sent forward for trial in a criminal court. This further documentation was, in some measure, also edited, and we may expect that the justices' questions were designed to test the consistency of the evidence from accused and witnesses, and to elicit further details should these be thought necessary and relevant. If the process had come straight to the magistrates, of course, their task was to produce as full and accurate a set of statements as possible without the benefit of the kirk's initial interrogations. From these, a full dittay was drawn up and it, along with all other relevant documentation, went forward to a criminal court.

Once the trial began, the accused's proloquitor [defence advocate] sought to have items struck from the dittay on the legal ground of irrelevance. It was not part of his job to argue that any charge was impossible or unlikely, or that the accusation had been brought out of malice, or that the details of any given point could be open to question or disproof. The Scottish law-court was not an adversarial theatre, and so defence of his client largely consisted of trying to reduce the number of points on which she or he would be tried. The assize whose job it was actually to try the case consisted of fifteen men chosen from an available list. The lists we have sometimes show that certain individuals could not attend a court, so the choice rested more upon chance than deliberation. In other words, the assizes were not fixed for any particular case. Occasionally, indeed, it was difficult to muster an assize. An order from the Commissioners of Justice, dated 17 July 1658, draws attention to a difficulty being experienced in Inverness anent a criminal court to be held there in September. Court officials, witnesses, and members of the assize were apparently reluctant to appear there 'except they have freedom from personal execution for civil debts' – an indication of the continuing problem caused in May 1655 by the expiry of an ordinance for the relief of debtors – and so the Commissioners ordered that no one take any action of any kind against them with a view to recovering debt, 'during the whole time of the sitting of the court, and three days thereafter, to the effect they may in safety repair to their several houses'.[22] To judge by the composition of many assizes, perhaps half the number came from the same town or neighbourhood as the accused, and perhaps half from further afield. At least some assizors, therefore, were likely either to know the accused, or the social and religious circumstances obtaining in her or his community for some period before the arrest and interrogation.

During the trial, the judge's task was to hear the proloquitor, keep order in the court, and hear the final version of the dittay read aloud. To each point on the dittay the panel [accused] pleaded guilty or not guilty, and then the witnesses repeated their accusations to the assize. Here the narrative has passed largely into the hands of the victims, although by pleading guilty to one or more of the charges, the accused took command of that part of the whole and asserted her or his ownership of it. Once all the charges had been read and the witnesses heard, the assize retired to a separate room and elected a spokesman, called the 'chancellor'. This done, they considered each item on the dittay, voted 'guilty' or 'not guilty', and then a tally of 'guiltys' and 'not guiltys' was made. A majority either way determined the final verdict.[23] The assize came back into the court-room and the chancellor delivered this verdict. If it was 'guilty', the death sentence automatically followed, since witchcraft was a capital offence, and a court officer known as the *dempster* pronounced the details – strangulation, burning of the dead body, and confiscation of all moveable goods. If the verdict was 'not guilty', the panel through her or his proloquitor 'asked instruments', that is to say, papers which would indicate that she or he had stood trial for such and such an offence and been found not guilty of it. Release from custody, however, was not necessarily immediate. Caution was required as an element of the panel's future good behaviour, and until this was paid or guaranteed, the panel was sent back to prison.

Verdicts of 'not guilty' were by no means uncommon. Christina Larner suggested that about half the cases coming before the Court of Justiciary in Edinburgh, whose outcome was known, produced a 'not guilty' verdict, and to these we must add a number of cases which were deserted, that is, which for some reason or another never completed the trial process. A part-explanation for these failures to condemn has been attributed to English influence in the Scottish judicial system at the time; but this is unwarrantedly anglocentric, and while it may owe something to the remark by Robert Baillie (1602–62), 'there is much witchery up and down our land: the English are but too sparing to try it, but some they execute', it is clear that Baillie was actually being critical of 'the English' (presumably English military justices of the peace), and was likely to have been referring to the practice of some English individuals in the west of Scotland rather than to general English legal policy in Scotland as a whole. It is true, of course, that the principal officials of the legal system tended to be balanced between Scots and Englishmen during the 1650s, and that some of the JPs might well be English army officers. But it was the assize which tried the panel, and for the most part assizes consisted of Scotsmen, and even if there were some English on some of them, they were all endeavouring to apply the principles of Scots law to the case they were hearing. Moreover, while it is true that the narrative of that case may have been shaped to a greater or lesser extent by the processes of interrogation through which the various parties concerned had passed, it also seems reasonable to suggest that, in a majority of cases at least, the opportunities for English influence (whatever that is meant to be in practice) would have been much reduced in the face of the assizors' private deliberations which, as the remaining evidence shows, were far from being crude.

In view of the general lack of bizarre or fantastic details in Scottish witchcraft confessions, the likelihood that a confession could generally be obtained without resort to judicial torture or maltreatment, the relatively good possibility that an assize might have sufficient doubts about the quality of the evidence it heard to bring in a verdict of 'not guilty', and the obvious discrepancy between ecclesiastical and criminal courts which made it preferable to get a hearing in front of the former: why were judicial torture and maltreatment used against any suspect? Human nature must account for a large degree of this. Accounts of torture, as we have seen, are often clearly those of illegal brutality, and we have to bear in mind the immense variety of individual reactions to a suspect witch. Fear and disgust could inevitably play their part and easily break out into violence, as modern instances of reactions to suspect paedophiles, for example, bear witness. What we lack in our attempts to understand what was going on in any instance are the details which would be motivating all those concerned. A survey of the large number of maleficent actions attributed to suspect witches shows that we cannot isolate one type of offence – killing a child magically, for example – and assume that this would have been sufficient to trigger an adverse reaction either in the interrogating official or the assizors. It is, in fact, almost impossible for us to know what caused an assize to vote 'guilty' or 'not guilty' with respect to any given item on a witch's dittay. So the use, and lack of use, of illegal torture and maltreatment could depend more or less entirely on the local and individual emotional currents of the moment. Judicial torture, however, was rather different. There were rules governing its application, and written warrant had to be obtained form the Privy Council before it could be used. Consequently, there are relatively few instances of its employment.

Nevertheless, even if we take into account the bureaucratic difficulties of obtaining such a warrant, and the vagaries of human nature which might react with or without restraint in the face of a witch's possible reluctance to make a confession, we are still left with the problem of understanding why brutality, legal or illegal, was considered necessary or desirable during the interrogation of a number of suspects. The answer (or perhaps part of the answer) may lie in the nature of the offence, and here modern experience of terrorism could be helpful. It seems to have induced two reactions in western governments: a genuine fear that certain individuals have tried or may try to employ methods of terror to advance their cause within their own or host community, with the result that arrests have been made and the individuals imprisoned either contrary to law or according to new laws designed to deprive them of liberties afforded to other types of prisoner; and a political calculation that the governments must be seen to be taking strong measures to protect their own citizens against a perceived threat from within. Witchcraft was conceived in terms not dissimilar to those of terrorism and dragged other forms of magic in its wake. It sought, so the authorities and their learned experts were convinced, to extend the kingdom of Satan by subverting and harming the righteous, and even the least of its successes had effects which stretched beyond the material world into the spiritual. In consequence, methods which would normally be seen as illegal might be tolerated in view of the peculiar climate of fear generated by certain episodes of terrorism/witchcraft. The feature most worth noting in this Scottish episode of 1658–62 is, therefore, not the brutality which often comes through the records, but the apparently more common restraint shown by officials and witnesses when faced by a terrorist/witch who refused to admit her or his guilt, or confess it in full.

But if 1660 saw relatively little activity anent witches in the ecclesiastical courts, it saw even less in the criminal.[24] Katharine Manson in

Orkney and Jean Campbell from Bute were put on trial, and several people in Rothesay were tried but suffered non-capital punishment, as also happened to Marion Yool from Tranent. In 1661, however, the records suddenly explode with references, and one question we need to ask is whether many of these were, in effect, cases left over from 1660 but left untried.[25] Perhaps the first thing worth noting is that kirk and presbytery sessions dealt with a remarkable number of cases specifically of witchcraft from the very beginning of the year. In January, the presbytery of Dalkeith heard the confession of a witch, Margaret Hay, and sent her back to her parish to be dealt with there; on one and the same day in March, Elgin not only had to deal with John Rhind, a charmer, who was accused of laying on and taking off illness, but also with the allegation that when a woman from the town used to go 'from her husband to her randibows [boisterous frolics] in the night, she leaves a besom in the bed in her place, and hangs a piece [of] meat on the back of the door' – a clear imputation that she was a witch who was in the habit of attending Sabbats, and with the delation of Magdalen Watson, Walter Chalmer, and others against Margaret Murray, saying that she was a witch who had killed people by her magic. In June, ministers were appointed by the presbytery of Dalkeith to examine a witch and to go to Musselburgh and Ormiston to assist in the 'trial' (that is, the testing) of witches; the presbytery of Dunfermline heard that Janet Anderson, recently executed as a witch in Kinross, had said that Christian Gray was present at a Sabbat, but had then retracted this statement, leaving Christian in a kind of limbo, since she had been debarred ever since from communion; while on 25 June the Canongate kirk session heard that Janet Allan had asked James Thomson to ride to Tranent and bring back the pricker (presumably John Kincaid) 'to try her if she was a witch, and she would pay his charges – which the said Janet did desire [again] in presence of the session, that the said man that tries the witches might be brought to her'.

A similar bravado was exhibited by Isobel Ferguson from Newbattle the following month. Having been delated as a witch and questioned by the minister, she denied the charge and was asked 'if she desired to be tried by the pricker if she had the witch marks or not. She answered that she did desire, and that John Kincaid, pricker, should be sent for to that effect'. Marks must have been found and the charges against her taken seriously enough to cause her to be imprisoned, for a week later, on 10 July, we find she had delated Geillis Charters as a witch, and the record tells us that 'after she [was] put forth for a witch by Isobel Ferguson, a confessing witch incarcerate, the said Geillis, desiring to be cleared of the aspersion, desires to be tried if she had the witch marks: who, being searched and pricked, the marks were found and she incarcerated'. These events clearly formed a topic of conversation in the village and gave rise to a number of other incidents in July and August. Steven Dickson was speaking to Janet Hargreave about witches when she told him she would not be afraid of being called a witch until Steven's mother had been garrotted for that offence. Margaret Liddell was delated for charming, and Thomas Watson told the session that she 'was seen to turn over and over the stones of a certain field, whereupon there was little or no corn grew there upon the said field thereafter'. Meanwhile, Janet Liddell (perhaps Margaret's sister) appeared before them to explain why she had said that every man and woman had marks on them, similar to those designated 'witch marks' – an interesting piece of apparent scepticism perhaps aimed at defending Margaret if she were to be pricked – and Janet Wilson and Janet Watt were accused of witchcraft, in as much as 'the one of them had laid on a disease on a beast and the other took it off again'. These various complaints and delations were pursued during August. Janet Liddell was let off with a rebuke, but Margaret Liddell and Janet Hargreave were imprisoned because they had been delated as witches by John MacMillan, a confessing warlock, and witch's marks had been found on them by the pricker. John also delated Janet Wilson and Janet Watt, saying he had seen them both at a meeting with the Devil, whereupon both women asked to be tried by the pricker. The test was done, marks were found, and so both were imprisoned until further examination. Unfortunately no more mention is made of them that year, and there is a gap in the record between 1662 and 1664, so the outcome of these cases remains a mystery.

Meanwhile, Dalkeith kirk session was told that John Dobbie had wagered John Hume 500 merks that Hume's wife, Agnes Hill, would be found to be a witch if she were tested, so Dobbie explained to the session that he had indeed said this, for two reasons: (i) Agnes Hill had been very friendly with Agnes Lasson before Lasson had been imprisoned as a witch, and (ii) because the prison-keeper and two other men had heard

Agnes Lasson ask for Agnes Hill two or three times not long before she died in prison, 'which was yet more to be noticed because the said Agnes Lasson was a confessing dying witch'. The session decided to refer the matter to the civil magistrate, and John Hume said he was content his wife should undergo the test for witchcraft. What his wife said about it is not recorded. This is similar to the case of Catharine Young, a servant in Haddington, who was delated to the kirk session in March as a witch, because she had been 'speaking secretly with Agnes Williamson and Christian Deans imprisoned for the sin of witchcraft and sorcery'. Catharine escaped with a rebuke, however, since she explained she had gone to ask Agnes for the back wages she was owed. Had Agnes been tried, found guilty, and executed, her money would have been escheat [confiscated] and Catharine would not have been paid. Witchcraft was in the air in Haddington at this time. Again and again throughout the year, the records note name-calling – women slandering women, and women slandering men – along with the occasional reference to more serious matters. Thus, on 5 May the baillie, George Brown, was told to take Bessie Kennedy to Samuelston to be confronted by Helen Deans who had delated her as a witch; on 23 June, Helen Nicholson confessed she had asked God to forgive those who had taken *her* to Samuelston 'amongst warlocks and witches', and denied she had called her husband a warlock. (She was found guilty of the slander and of being drunk when she said it, and sentenced to be rebuked, with the warning she would be subject to corporal punishment – i.e. whipping – if she offended again). Session business in Dalkeith was then suspended at the beginning of August 'because of the execution of witches in the afternoon'. We do not know how many were involved or who they were.

In Shapinsay, during August, Margaret Gune accused Margaret Gray of casting sickness on her cow, and the session heard evidence from various women in support of this. But on 25 August, John Michael stood up and took the session to task

for admitting women witnesses in that business of slandering Margaret Gray. Whereunto the minister replied he [John] knew very well that women might be admitted witness in such cases of slander, and he [the minister] would be answerable to the presbytery for what [had] been done in that particular.

He then asked John to leave the room, but John refused and continued to complain in terms the session found unacceptable, adding, 'I know better than you what women's witness-bearing is. I will not give a bubble [snot] for any woman's witness-bearing'. The minister retorted that John should stand before the pulpit for such disrespectful speeches. John answered he would make some of them split in pieces before he would do so, and the session as a whole then insisted he do public penance. John calmed down eventually. Even so, he did not perform his penance until the end of November. The minister's opinion was correct. Sir George MacKenzie recorded the legal position regarding women as witnesses. As a regular matter, he said, they were not witnesses in either civil or criminal cases, but there were several exceptions to this, such as treason or domestic violence, and witchcraft.

The presbytery of Dunfermline heard the confessions of three women imprisoned in Aberdour, who said they had made a pact with Satan, renounced their baptism, and attended several meetings with the Devil; the minister of Dunbar reported to his kirk session that he had been present at a confrontation between three people, an unnamed confessing warlock, George Boyd, and Alison Shiel; and the kirk session of North Berwick appointed Andrew Stuart to speak to the tutors of the Marquess of Douglas anent one Marion Paterson who had confessed to witchcraft. 'Tutors' here does not mean 'teachers', but people appointed under Scots law to be the guardians of someone under age, and to administer his or her estate. Presumably, therefore, these tutors were being informed in their capacity as administrators of the law in the Marquess's bounds. In September, the kirk session of Carrington, not far from Edinburgh, heard that Andrew Lindsay had called Janet Hall 'witch-begotten', and when he was asked why he had had done so, he answered that others had so accused her. Janet was then pricked, a mark was found on her, and she confessed she was indeed a witch. Up north in Arbroath, the presbytery was asked its advice anent Elspeth Eliot. James Fraser, the minister, produced a paper containing the evidence against her, and when they had heard it, the presbyters decided she should be imprisoned and sent for trial. Unfortunately, the prison-house of Arbroath was inadequate for this purpose – perhaps it would have been easy for her to effect an escape, perhaps the available space for prisoners was already full – and the town could not provide the requisite number of watchers. So it was ordained she be sent to Forfar under guard, accompanied by the minister, who was ' to cause all allowed means to bring her to a full confession'.

In October, Isobel Durward was brought before the presbytery, having been delated 'by confessing witches', and was due to be sent to be imprisoned in the kirk of Carmylie (presumably in the steeple, as was customary), where she would be watched. There were, however, difficulties in persuading the sheriff to give the requisite authority, so whether she was actually arrested remains unclear. In Innerwick, a village about four miles east of Dunbar, 'public intimation was made that if any person had or knew anything to say against William Cowan, touching the sin of witchcraft, for which he was now in ward, they should declare it in time and place convenient'. No one, however, turned up and one asks oneself what was going on in this case; for at the end of July 1659, William had petitioned the kirk session to be re-admitted to communion and had had his petition temporarily refused on the grounds that some time ago he had been processed by the presbytery on a charge of witchcraft, and written proof that he had been cleared therefrom seemed to be lacking. Was his arrest in 1661 a continuation of this original indictment, or had lingering smoke suggested to someone that there must be fire, and William was imprisoned on fresh charges? We do not know.

At the end of the year, South Leith sent forward Jean Duncan to the baillie of Restalrig, satisfied that accusations against her as a witch had enough substance to warrant her being taken to trial. Stow kirk session challenged Margaret Cooper for employing Janet Scott (designated a witch) to cure her when she was sick, and Richard Lees and his wife for using sorcery. In Peebles on 14 November, the local magistrates asked the presbytery to send ministers 'to deal with two witches imprisoned at Peebles, for bringing them to a confession', and then asked them to come to Traquair on 20 November 'to prepare them for death'. This sounds either like confidence the ministers could effect their task almost immediately, or like self-assurance that a verdict of guilty could be obtained without any problem, a somewhat chilling prospect in either case. In Inveresk near Musselburgh, too, the session and baillies were keen to get a suspect witch off their hands. The minister was asked 'to make intimation out of the pulpit about Janet Stoddart who was imprisoned upon the suspicion of witchcraft', that if anyone had any serious accusation to bring against her, he or she should do so within the next ten or twelve days, otherwise they would release her because keeping her in prison was very expensive. Finally, in December, the presbytery of Duns heard that Beatrix Ford from Langton was being examined as a suspect witch, and recommended that the relevant papers be forwarded to the sheriff, obviously with a view to her criminal prosecution. What makes this noteworthy is the remark that these papers consisted of a commission for taking her to trial, her husband's bond of caution, and the dittays against her, dated 1 June 1650. A delay of ten-and-a-half years in implementing a commission for trials seems quite extraordinary, well beyond the mixture of delay, evasion, and incompetence which might, and did often attend the bureaucratic process in Scotland. The kirk record is dated 31 December and brings to a curious end a year in which the Kirk clearly found itself dealing with an unusual upsurge of witchcraft accusations.

Granted this survey of parishes and presbyteries is not complete. It does, however, encompass much the same range we have examined for the years prior to 1661, so the difference in emphasis is notable. Moreover, it is fairly clear that a majority of these cases did not originate in 1660, but sprang up during the pressures of 1661. Something in the air, then, appears to have triggered people's fear and set it off at this particular juncture. The survey also shows a distinct concentration of witchcraft cases in East and Midlothian, and so one is bound to look for a cause perhaps emanating from the capital, perhaps from the local ministers, and to ask whether both this upsurge and apparent concentration are mirrored in the various criminal courts.

If we use the Larner-Lee-McLachlan *Source Book* as a guide (bearing in mind its faults and inadequacies), we find listed there about 250 names of suspect witches for 1661. Of these, forty-four were executed, fourteen acquitted, and three died in prison or escaped, leaving about four-fifths of the total – the overwhelming majority – as names whose ultimate fate, or even whether they got further than appearing as names in someone else's accusation, we do not know. Geographically, the names come almost entirely from East and Midlothian – over 200 – leaving twenty-six from places north of there, four south and three west; and well over half these 200 come from (a) 'East Lothian' as a general designation (twenty-eight) (b) Liberton, a village just over two miles south-east of the centre of Edinburgh (thirty-two) (c) Samuelston, a village not far to the south of Haddington (twenty-eight) (d) Dalkeith, between Edinburgh and Musselburgh, about four to six miles south of each (twenty-six) and (e) Ormiston, a village about three miles south-east of Tranent (fifteen). The first appearance of these names in the records comes between April and September: 'East Lothian' and Samuelston largely between April and June, Liberton in June and August, and Dalkeith and Ormiston in July and September. The principal clergy involved do not seem to have been especially opposed to the Church settlement worked out in Whitehall for Scotland, with the exception of John Sinclair in Ormiston, who refused to accept episcopacy in 1662 and left Scotland altogether for the Netherlands. He was the brother of George Sinclair, author of *Satan's Invisible World Discovered* (1685), a work which purports to illustrate the reality of witches, ghosts and other apparitions by means of anecdotes drawn from both Scotland and England. It is possible the brothers exchanged views on the subject, although what effect, if any, such a conversation may have had on John is open to speculation. John Primrose from Queensferry was removed from his ministry in *c.*1660 for nonconformity, and while John MacGhie from Gullane-Dirleton was also a non-conformist, he was allowed to stay in his post. James Cunningham from Pentland-Lasswade was deprived in 1662, and Gideon Penman from Crichton, who seems to have survived the restoration settlement well enough, was deposed for adultery in 1675 and imprisoned for witchcraft in 1678. By and large, therefore, the East Lothian clergy seem to have accommodated themselves to the new political and religious settlement introduced by the restoration – unlike the ministers over in the west, many of whom, as we have seen, were not so pliable and were deprived of their ministries in 1662, and this accommodation, I shall suggest later, is perhaps significant in helping to explain why there should have been such an outbreak of witch-prosecutions in this area.

With so many names and cases in a single year, it would obviously be impossible to discuss them all in any kind of detail, but in any case, as I said, large numbers are simply names in a document. The *Acts of the Privy Council of Scotland* and the *Registers of the Privy Council of Scotland*, for example, frequently record commissions issued for the trial of persons for whom this is the only mention.[26] Thus, on 9 May 1661, the *Acts* records:

commission to George Seton of Barns, Patrick Brown the younger of Colstane, Francis Hepburn of Benston, Mr. John Butler of Kirkland, Mr.

John Douglas of Nunland, Thomas Haliburton of Egliscarno, Mr. Richard Cairns of Pilmore, Patrick Young, baillie in Haddington, Alexander Borthwick in Johnstounburn, and Archibald Eliot in Drem, or any five of them, for judging of Nichol and Isobel Steill, Elspeth Baillie, Isobel Richardson, Elspeth Lawson, and Isobel Cairns, delated [as] guilty and apprehended for the abominable sin of witchcraft.

Sometimes only places are mentioned, as in *Registers* for 25 July:

Forasmuch as it is informed by petitions from heritors [landowners] and others within the parishes of Musselburgh, Dalkeith, Newbattle, Newton, and Duddingston that there are a great many persons, both men and women, within the said bounds, who are imprisoned as having confessed, or [having] witnesses led against them for the abominable sin of witchcraft: and being most desirous that the land my be purged of that horrid sin…

The Lords granted a commission to have them tried.

But the *Registers* more often do give some indication of the particular offence or offences committed by a named individual.[27] On 25 July, a commission was issued to try Isobel Johnston from Gullane in East Lothian, who had confessed to making a pact with the Devil; likewise, six women and men from Spott, seven from Ormiston, and Margaret Barton and Isobel Bathgate from Queensferry on 6 September, two female vagabonds on 3 October, a man and a woman from Innerleithen, east of Peebles, and Margaret Liddell and Katharine Key from Newburgh in Fife on 19 November. Since entering into such a pact and renouncing one's baptism were two of the standard accusations commonly contained, as we have seen, in prefaces to many witches' dittays, we cannot be sure whether these were the only offences on which Isobel Johnston and the rest were tried, or whether there were others not mentioned in the *Register*. The Privy Council also received supplications from people who asked the Lords to direct that they be put to trial or released on caution. Thus, on 18 September, they heard from Isobel Henderson, 'spouse to William Purdie, indweller in the Canongate', and ordered 'the baillies of the Canongate to proceed presently [at once] against the supplicant according to law without using any torture or indirect ways, and if she shall not be found guilty after using all lawful measures, forthwith to set her to liberty'.[28]

This emphasis upon no 'torture or indirect ways' is repeated in a number of Commissions and replies from the Council, and seems to be connected with an awareness that improper and illegal methods had been too common, at least during the past frenetic months. Hence, presumably, their insistence that John Ramsay, a pricker, answer to the Council for his actions which had been closely followed by the death of Margaret Tait, one of the women he had tested.[29] Why did she die? An illustration purporting to be of prickers' bodkins, which is often used in modern books on witchcraft, coming from *The Discoverie of Witchcraft* (1584) by the Englishman, Reginald Scot, is actually nothing of the kind. It shows an illusionist's props, nothing more. The usual word for a pricker's instrument is 'pin', a word implying a thin rather than a thick blade. Had pins as thick as bodkins been thrust into people's flesh, it would have been virtually impossible for them not to cause immense pain and not to spill noticeable quantities of blood when retracted – and the whole aim of pricking, it will be remembered, was to discover places insensitive to pain and free of blood when the pin was withdrawn. Pricking with thin pins or needles, even if long, while likely to be painful, was less likely to cause serious damage by (let us say) hitting an artery. We do not know what prompted Margaret Tait's death – it may or may not have been contingent upon her being pricked – but it was certainly unusual, and it was this unexpectedness which drew the authorities' attention to Ramsay's activities.

Sometimes we find details of the charges recorded.[30] We learn, for example, on 28 May, that Bessie Todrig from Bolton in East Lothian had voluntarily and without being pricked confessed to meeting the Devil the previous November – he had come to her, she said, in her own house, 'like a man, having brown clothes and his cloak different in colour from his clothes' – and going to a meeting in Samuelston, just southeast of Haddington, on 24 April last, the day three or four witches were executed. On 29 May, Bessie Dawson, Bessie Todrig's servant or friend, confessed that she too had met the Devil 'like a man, in black-coloured clothes', and had attended a meeting near Pilmore along with several others, whom she named, and 'a large woman with a red coat and a green apron', and another where, among others, she saw 'a small white woman whom she knew not'. (Does 'white' mean she was wearing white clothing, or simply that she was very clean?) On 30 May, Margaret Ker, too, confessed to meeting the Devil in about March 1661, who appeared first as a dog, then as a man; on 31 May Isobel Smith, who had met the Devil the previous October, described him as a black man in green clothes, and Anna Kemp on 2 June said he appeared first as a greyhound, then as a man clad in black. All these women delated others – mostly the same, since they were all clearly known to each other.

Most meetings with the Devil happened out of doors, and several happened at night. Janet Bagbie said that Bessie Todrig came three times at night to her window and called her out, and on the third occasion she went out and found the Devil standing next to Bessie by the sticks at her door. The woman usually copulated with the Devil, too. In Isobel Smith's case, this happened in the house of a friend, Elizabeth Dawson. Elizabeth had asked Isobel to come to her house and meet a gentleman, and when she arrived there, the usual renunciation and pact took place, after which they had sex. Isobel says it was not until this was over that she began to suspect she had done something wrong – a piece of disingenuousness which may have been true, or concocted in an effort to lessen her guilt in the eyes of her interrogators – 'and then there was in company with the Devil, beside the said Elizabeth Lawson and herself, Margaret Dewar and Katharine Coupland'. Are we to understand that the other women were present in the house while the gentleman and Isobel were having sex? If so – and this is not the only instance of a similar arrangement – do we here catch a glimpse of irregular fornication or adultery marshalled by women for each other's benefit, and here interpreted in terms of the Devil recruiting witches? Compare Janet Hewitt from Forfar, who in September 1661 said that:

> she saw the Devil have carnal copulation with her mother, and that the Devil having done, rode away on a black horse; and that she followed him a little way until he directed her to return to her mother; and that when she was returned to her mother, her mother forbade her to tell her father of what she had seen that night.

Likewise, a number of witches from the area of Musselburgh and Dalkeith had encounters with Satan. On 29 July 1661, David Johnston said that eleven years previously he had entered the Devil's service and received his mark, and knew him to be the Devil because he was a 'large,

grim man in black clothes'. Agnes Loch met him while she was coming from Dalkeith, 'in the likeness of a man with green clothes, who
promised her money', and to Margaret Ramage he appeared as a black
man. On 3 August, Elspeth Graham confessed he came to her eighteen
months before in her own house, 'clothed in green clothes'; Christian
Paterson confessed she was coming down the outside stairs from Geillis
Charteris's house when she tumbled over him 'in the likeness of a beast',
and that within four or five nights thereafter, the Devil came to her
bed and had carnal dealing with her in the likeness of a man; Isobel
Ferguson had one meeting with him, when he appeared 'in the likeness
of a woman in a black gown', and when a girl who was present called
out the name of Christ, the Devil 'did run out at the hole of the door
like a black cat'. Marjorie Wilson saw him as a man in black clothes and
a black hat; Beatrix Leslie, however, met him 'in the likeness of a big
brown dog' which spoke to her as she was going to fetch coal from the
local heap. It is the same kind of story in the confession of Thomas Black
and Agnes Pogavie, while Bessie Wilson actually met the Devil in her
own bed in the likeness of her own husband.

All these people came from the key areas we have noted, between
Dalkeith and Haddington, and yet this part of the country was not alone
in such an outbreak. Eight people, seven women and one man, were
imprisoned in Forfar and questioned there during September anent various points of witchcraft.[31] Each one had seen and kept company with
the Devil. Helen Guthrie, for example, told of meetings at which the
Devil was present, once 'in the shape of a black, iron-hued man'. She had
last seen him on 15 September while she was in prison. He came to her
in the middle of the night 'and laboured to carry her away... She was
carried up from the earth three or four feet high at least, her head being
among the joists of the house, and... she [would have] been carried
away by the Devil were not the watchmen, being stout [resolute, brave],
did oppose and strike at her with their swords, and did prevent it. The
truth of this last confession was testified by three men which were on
watch that night'. Here, then, if we needed a reminder, is the principal
reason suspect witches were kept under watch.

Janet Howitt met the Devil more than once. She was taken to him
first by Isobel Syrie, her mistress, and the Devil said, 'What shall I do
with such a little bairn as this?' Their encounter took place at a meeting

of witches, and they all danced together, the Devil wearing black. About a month later, Isobel took Janet to another meeting at which they all danced and ate and drank, with Janet acting as a waitress, and at this time the Devil kissed her 'and nipped her upon one of her shoulders, so as she had great pain for some time thereafter'. It was cured six weeks later, when he came to her 'being all in green', and stroked her shoulder, after which the pain eased. Isobel Syrie met him several times, of course, as did Elspeth Alexander and Janet Stout, although Janet said she avoided kissing the Devil by hiding behind others' backs. Even Katharine Porter saw him, though she had been blind for many years – he had a black plaid about him, she said, and he took her by the hand; his hand was cold and she ran away from him – and Agnes Spark complained that the Devil rode upon her as though she were his horse.

The Devil, then, was making more physical appearances than had been his custom hitherto, and was by no means restricting himself to a single area in Lowland Scotland. Still, we must not exaggerate his range. In Fife, for example, as Stuart MacDonald has pointed out, 'the Devil was almost exclusively a concern of Dunfermline presbytery and even here his name is generally confined to those records which originated from or pertained to the central government'.[32] Moreover, this resurgence of the Devil in the presbytery can be dated principally to 1649 and 1650, so during the period 1658–62, he scarcely makes an appearance even there.

Much of the witches' activity in East Lothian and Forfar concerns, as one might expect from the Devil's prominent role, attendance at meetings to eat and drink and dance. Helen Guthrie boasted that when she cursed anyone, it usually worked, and said that she was in possession of three papers with blood on them, which enabled her to recognise witches. She also confessed to murdering her half-sister, but the terms in which this is expressed – 'she struck her said sister at that time till she bled, which stroke was afterwards her death' – has nothing of magic about it. Elspeth Bruce, she said, had had some cloth stolen from her, and used the sieve and shears to discover the name of the thief. Her divination, however, 'raised the Devil who, being very hard to be laid again, there was a meeting of witches for laying of him', their number including herself, Elspeth, and Janet Stout. Raising the Devil by means of the sieve and shears is extremely unusual. It sounds like the kind of thing alleged of using a ouija board. But it may have been assumed that an evil spirit would seize the opportunity to pervert the practice for evil ends, an assumption which probably lies behind the Hungarian custom of putting a holy picture in the sieve before divination, or invoking the saints – 'Saint Peter, Saint Paul, turn this sieve and tell me who has stolen my chicken'.[33] Helen also mentioned one or two malefices, such as rendering ale undrinkable, raising a wind with the Devil's help to damage the bridge of Cortachie, and sinking a ship.

Perhaps the most extraordinary item in her confession is the one in which she said that she and several others went to the kirk in Forfar, where Andrew Watson dug up the body of an unbaptised infant and dismembered it. Whereupon, 'they made a pie thereof, that they might eat of it, that by this means they might never make a confession (as they thought) of their witchcraft'. Christina Larner suggested that this and other features of their Sabbats provided elements closer to the Continental type of confession than was usual in Scotland, but I wonder whether the source may not be nearer home. The most notorious set of Scottish witchcraft confessions before these were perhaps those connected with the treasonous magical conspiracy against James VI in 1589. On All Hallows' Eve that year, several witches allegedly met in the kirk of North Berwick and, among other things, dug up four bodies, two within and two outwith the kirk, and dismembered them in order to be able to use the parts for magic. Helen's item ends with the non-sequitur 'and she knows that Elspeth Bruce and Marie Rhind and several other witches went to see the King's coronation'. Agnes Sampson, the 1589 witch whose dittay contains the information about the corpses in North Berwick, also remarked that she had travelled to Scandinavia while King James was there, and had overheard a private conversation between him and Queen Anne in their bedchamber. The details about the Forfar witches going on board a ship by means of a cable is also reminiscent of a similar episode from the 1590–91 confessions. Was one of Helen Guthrie's examiners familiar with some of those earlier details, and did he use them as a basis for questions which produced her extraordinary and most unusual claims? One cannot press the suggestion very far, but it is at least worth consideration.

For the most part, then, both in Forfar and East Lothian, witches' activities centred upon the physical presence of the Devil, who usually appeared in human, but sometimes in animal form. One or two instances are given of a witch's malefices which do not directly depend on this.[34]

Beatrix Leslie from Dalkeith or nearby, for example, sent cats to frighten William Young and then injured his daughters by making the roof of a coal-pit fall in upon them. She also killed two other girls in the same way, and used charms in her role as a midwife – sticking a knife-blade between the bed and the straw mattress, and sprinkling it with salt. Isobel Ramsay killed Christian Porteous by magic. Margaret Hutcheson frightened David Bell with cats, killed one of his sons, and made his wife ill. She also inflicted illness on Harry Balfour and James Ker. Janet Miller killed several of James Wilkie's animals, and Christian Wilson not only spoiled William Tatchell's brewing in Dalkeith but, much more seriously, visited Susanna Bailey in June 1661, just before she herself was arrested, and tried to strangle her. There seems here to be an increase in violent malevolence. The dittays we reviewed earlier, dating from the late 1650s, certainly contain similar offences, but there appear to be fewer of them at that time, and it is as though the increased physical presence of Satan in 1661 generated an upsurge in confession to very vindictive behaviour, and as though a long-suppressed anger were suddenly being released.

But another feature of this particular set of dittays from the Dalkeith area involves the ancient belief that a corpse will bleed when faced by the person who killed it.[35] When Beatrix killed the two girls, for example, 'after you came and touched them, they did both gush out in blood, and so by your sorcery and witchcraft you have cruelly murdered the two said damsels'. The case which most clearly illustrates this, however, is that of Christian Wilson. She had been arrested in June and was put on trial in Edinburgh on 3 August along with Elspeth Graham, Christian Paterson, Isobel Ferguson, Marjorie Wilson and Beatrix Leslie, all from the same general area, Newbattle and Dalkeith. Christian's dittay alleged she had become the Devil's servant sixteen years previously and that she bore evidence of his marks. Among other violent malefices, she confessed to killing her brother in December 1660. Eight witnesses gave evidence to the fratricide. The sum of what they said is that Christian and Alexander had been at loggerheads over some property – George Erskine alleged it was about borrowing a spade – and that on the day of his death, Alexander had been in good health and was seen walking about at three in the afternoon. By five o'clock, however, he was dead, 'lying in his own house, naked as he was born, with his face torn and rent without any appearance of a spot of blood [edited in the record from simply 'blood'] either upon his body or nigh to it'. Neighbours crowded in to see the sight, but Christian never offered to come, even though she lived next door. Neither did she show any grief for her brother's death. Such insouciance was regarded as suspicious, so the minister and baillies ordered her to view the corpse, something Christian was reluctant to do, and when she did come to the house, she refused to come near the body or to touch it. But the minister, the baillies, and her brother's friends persuaded her to do so. (Clearly they all subscribed to the belief in this test for discovering a murderer). The sun was shining, and Christian gave voice to a wish – 'that, as the Lord made the sun to shine and give light into that house, that also He would give light in discovering of that murder'. This said, she gently touched the wound on her brother's face; whereupon immediately 'the blood gushed out of it, to the great admiration [astonishment] of all the beholders who took it for a discovery of the murder, according to her own prayer'. The wound, says the record, was quite clean before she did this, and it did not bleed when anyone else touched it. People stayed in the house all night, watching over the corpse – a common practice. Alexander, as has been said, was naked, and although people searched for his shirt, they could not find it. Yet in the morning it appeared, 'tied fast about his neck as a brecham [a bulky kind of wrap]'.

Not surprisingly, Christian set about shifting all her moveable goods from her own house into her daughter's, in preparation for flight. But she was arrested and imprisoned before she could get away. While she was in the tolbooth, according to William Mitchell, one of the watchers, she confessed to killing her brother, but said there were ten others involved although she did not give any names. She also denied being a witch, but this was unlikely to be believed if only because she had been delated by a confessing witch, and had also been accused thirty-four years earlier. Why she survived that earlier accusation we do not know, but it would have left a taint on her reputation to be remembered later. One other notable item appears in the evidence:

In the year 1650, when the English entered Scotland, the said Christian Wilson being then in prison at that time, did at her releasement give bond that if ever she should be found guilty thereafter of any kind of presumption or public scandal, she obliged herself to be burned without any of the least opposition [to] the contrary.

It was a legal undertaking which would weigh very heavily against her during her trial. Even so – and it is a remarkable feature of her assize's verdict – she was found guilty by *plurality* of votes, and that means that some assizors had acquitted her of some of the points against her. Perhaps this helps to explain how she escaped with her life on the earlier occasion.

By 5 November, an enormous amount of paperwork was threatening to swamp the Privy Council.[36] Consequently, it appointed a small committee 'to consider the petitions, delations, and depositions given in for commissions for judging and trial of witches, and to report [to] the next meeting'. Some of the cases which were being considered by the Lords were, or may have been, long-standing. Katharine and Elizabeth Black and Isobel Crockett had been in Stirling tolbooth since March 1659, and Jean Gyllor had been held in the Canongate tolbooth a long time (although 'a long time' would not necessarily date her imprisonment to earlier than 1661, since her supplication came before the Council on 3 October). Such evidence we have regarding the dates at which others were arrested, however, indicates that their cases belong entirely to 1661, and of course the nearer the end of the year the date of their supplication or dittay or trial, the more likely that is to be probable. Large numbers were executed. The circuit court rolls for 1661 make that clear. A typical entry (for 29 July) runs:

> David Johnston, Agnes Loch spouse to Patrick Robertson in Sunnyside, Margaret Ramage, Janet Lyle in Edmiston, and Janet Dale spouse to George Bell, collier, being found guilty of the crime of sorcery and witchcraft, were by his Majesty's justice deputes ordained to be burnt at Musselburgh, and their moveable goods escheat [confiscated] to his Majesty's use.

The same kind of list appears in August, September and November, the total amounting to twenty-one persons altogether. So 1661 stands out as peculiar. It is as though some kind of plague sore had swollen to the point where surgery was considered necessary for the wellbeing of the body politic and ecclesiastic, and in this year and the next, the poison began to flow.

CHAPTER FIVE

1662: Aftermath

If 1661 had been bad, 1662 was in many ways worse. The *Registers of the Privy Council* show that in January and February there were still many cases to be heard, cases which had clearly begun their process the previous year. Marion Grinlaw and Jean Howison, for example, had been imprisoned as long ago as the previous April, but in spite of their having applied to be set at liberty before, nothing had been done; and Agnes Williamson from Samuelston had confessed on 20 May to copulating with the Devil and receiving his mark, but did not come to trial until January 1662.[1] Requests for commissions to try named persons as witches, however, continued to pour into Edinburgh – twenty-six on 23 January alone – and as winter turned into spring, the demand scarcely diminished, requests and supplications coming in from all over the country. The witchcraft phenomenon which in 1661 had seemed limited to a relatively few small areas was now apparently manifesting itself all over Scotland, from as far south as Jedburgh to Ross and Cromarty in the north, Eyemouth in the east, and Largs in the west; and although there are local concentrations within this geographical spread – Fife, Forfar, Perth and Berwick being the most notable – the apparent eagerness of such a wide range of places to apply to Edinburgh is particularly striking. It is as though the network of presbyteries had woken up during 1661, with one presbytery alerting another to the burgeoning of Satan's power in its midst, realised that the problem had expanded well beyond the power of local kirks to deal with, and turned to the secular arm for more potent aid.

Noteworthy, too, are the indications that many of those arrested had suffered illegally in one way or another.[2] On 9 January, for example, the Council issued a commission to try Margaret Dron, from the parish of Rhynd in Perthshire, who had confessed to making a pact with the Devil, and so forth. On 1 April, however, the Lords had received information that the minister, James Gillespie, and sixteen others including local landowners and their servants, had without warrant arrested and imprisoned not only Margaret but three other women, too, 'and by pricking, watching, keeping of them from sleep, and other torture have extorted from the said persons a confession of their guilt of the crime of witchcraft'. The commission granted in January had been used to dire effect and all four women had been executed. What is more, emboldened by their success, the minister and the others had arrested four more individuals and subjected them to the same maltreatment, trying, as the record says, to 'make them lie upon themselves to be free of their cruelty and consequently to be guilty of self murder'. To 'lie on' means to draw a salmon-net against the current of a river, and is also the name of one of the ropes used for that purpose. It sounds, therefore, as though the suspects were being encouraged to hang themselves. The Lords, having noted these illegalities, ordered the men involved to appear before them to answer questions and, since the women had not yet been driven to the point of death, gave instructions that they be brought to Edinburgh and imprisoned there to await trial.

On 2 April, Adam Robertson, a maltster in Eyemouth, complained to the Council that he had been imprisoned in the tolbooth of Duns on a false charge of witchcraft, and had been let free on caution, with the usual condition that he was to hold himself ready for trial if required. Two or three days later, he was arrested again on exactly the same charges without any legal warrant or commission. Caution was found for him in the sum of two thousand merks – quite a sum – by his son, another local man, and two Edinburgh burgesses, and he was granted a warrant for his release. This may or may not have been executed. Even the Privy Council sometimes experienced difficulties in getting its orders obeyed. On 16 September, Margaret and Elizabeth Guthrie, indwellers in Montrose, petitioned the Lords for their release on caution. They had been arrested on 10 January on a false charge of witchcraft, and imprisoned separately. On 12 June, their brother, a legal clerk in Dundee, wrote to the Council on their behalf, explaining that they had been transferred from Montrose to Forfar 'where they were imprisoned, put in stocks, and a guard set to [each] one of them to their great expenses, all which while they could have scarce so much clean straw as to rest upon'. From there, they were taken back to Montrose, and on 22 May the Council ordered the Sheriff of Forfar to bring them to trial 'without any torture, pricking, or other indirect means' by the next 12 July. The order was ignored. On 12 July the Council reiterated its instruction. This, too, was disregarded. On 8 August the sheriff and his deputes were ordered to arrange the women's trial before 1 September, but again nothing was done. So this petition of 16 September was the fourth such attempt both parties were making to get the Montrose authorities to do as they were told, and in spite of the Lords' renewing their command to the sheriff, the provost, and baillies to set the women free on caution within twenty-four hours, there is no proof they actually did so. In such a climate of mingled resistance to authority and incompetence, it is not surprising to find that injustices and illegalities were able to flourish.

On 16 September, the Lords also heard from Elspeth Burnett that she had been arrested by one of the baillies of Lauder in Berwickshire, who was keeping her there in spite of the fact that several burgesses of the town were willing to stand caution for her. The Lords ordered her immediate release in the sum of 2,000 merks but, given the Guthries' experience, it would not be wise to suppose their order was obeyed. But already by 10 April a sufficient number of cases which either involved downright illegality or imprisonment of suspect persons had now been seen by the Council to warrant the Lords' issuing a proclamation.

We, Lords of his Majesty's Secret Council, being certainly informed that a great many persons in several parts of the kingdom have been apprehended and hurried to prisons, pricked, tortured, and abused, as being suspect of the horrid crime of witchcraft: and that by persons as have no warrant or authority so to do, by occasion whereof many innocents may suffer, nor can they promise themselves immunity from these who either carry envy towards them or are covetous after their means: for remedy whereof the said Lords do hereby discharge all persons whatsoever to take, seize upon, or apprehend any man or woman as being suspect or delate guilty of the said abominable crime, unless they have special warrant for that effect from the Lords of his Majesty's Privy Council, the Justice General or his deputes, [and other named authorities] within whose bounds they do reside respective, and being apprehended by warrant and order, ordains them to be carried to prison and proceeded against conform to the known laws of the kingdom without any pricking or torture, but by order, and that no other unlawful means be used for bringing them to a confession: and hereto all the lieges are to give obedience at their utmost peril: and ordains these presents to be printed and published at the mercat crosses of the head burghs of the several sheriffdoms of the kingdom, that none may pretend ignorance.[3]

One aspect of this newly-roused suspicion in the minds of the Council can be seen in the commission it granted on 7 May to try Isobel Elder and Isobel Simson in Dyke, a village in the north-west of the shire of Elgin. Permission was granted to try them under certain provisos: their confessions must be voluntary and not induced by torture or any indirect means; their malefices must be proven legally; and at the time of their confessions, they must be fully aware of what they were confessing, not out of their minds or wishing to die. It was a formula repeated on 12 June in the case of Margaret MacKenzie in Greenock, who had confessed herself guilty of witchcraft, but not of paction with the Devil or renunciation of her baptism.[4] The Lords therefore instructed that she be put to trial, but said that she could be executed only if she voluntarily confessed to renouncing her baptism, covenanting with the Devil, or committing acts of harmful magic, and that this confession must not be obtained by torture or any indirect means, that 'she was of complete [mature] age, sound judgement, noways distracted, or under any earnest desire to die', that her former confession of witchcraft must be repeated judicially – that is, before legal officers properly authorised, exactly the same instructions which had been issued in Germany between 1605 and 1613 by the ruling *Fürstprobst* of Ellwangen – and that each item of her confession must be made separately, so that there would be no vague generalisation about what she was admitting she had done, and that each item must be 'relevant', that is, specifically interpretable as witchcraft rather than any other offence. So not only was the Council much concerned to have the niceties of legal form observed, it also placed particular emphasis on the pact with the Devil and the use of harmful (as opposed to beneficent) forms of magic. It was a double emphasis which chimed with the mood of the time. The Devil, it seemed, was rampant, but the Lords, concerned for justice, wanted him defeated in the persons of his agents by lawful, not irregular and therefore potentially sinful means.

An additional revelation to the Council, which must have affected its attitude towards the legality of pre-trial interrogation of witches, was that prickers had been acting without any kind of warrant, and in such a way as to give rise to suspicion that some innocent persons might have suffered at their hands. The Lords had already come across John Ramsay on 2 August 1661, whose ministrations were said to have resulted in the death of Margaret Tait. But on 2 January 1662 John Kincaid came to their attention, and a warrant was issued for his arrest. As so often, it took weeks for the Council's order to be implemented, and it was not until 1 April that authority was given to imprison him in the tolbooth of Edinburgh. Conditions there, so he alleged, diminished his health to such an extent that on 19 May he sent a petition to the Council, asking to be released on caution, a petition the Lords may have ignored at first, because he had to renew it on 12 June. On this occasion, however, it was granted on two conditions: first, that he find caution of £1,000 Scots, and secondly, that he 'forbear the practice of pricking in future without a special warrant'. Caution was duly provided by John Somerville, a burgess of Edinburgh, and Kincaid was released on 13 June.[5]

The role of the pricker in any given witch-process is not altogether clear. Certainly Kincaid must have had an effect on the various outbreaks in East and Midlothian, but his activities did not, by themselves, initiate the original accusations, although clearly they may have assisted growth in the number of suspects as people delated or named by one individual were questioned and then perhaps tested for the Devil's mark. On 26 June the Privy Council granted a commission to try twelve people from the area round Buntoit, a small village on the western shore of Loch Ness, within the parish of Convinth.[6] These individuals, eleven women and one man, had 'confessed themselves to be guilty of the horrid crime of witchcraft'. Now, on 19 May, the Lords had issued a warrant for the arrest of John Dick[son], a pricker whose practice ranged round Inverness, Tain, Dornoch and further afield. Most of this, certainly, centred upon the Black Isle, but it is possible he operated somewhat further south, so the question of whether he could have been involved here remains open. Dickson was, in fact, arrested and turned out to be a woman, Christian Cadell. She was examined in the tolbooth of Edinburgh on 30 August 1662 and there confessed a number of interesting things: (i) she would guess if a woman were a witch; (ii) she had seen a woman in a kirkyard and pointed her out to Sir George More as a witch, and when the woman was examined later, the Devil's mark was found on her shoulder; (iii) she recognised witches by their eyes which were cloudy rather than clear, and she could see a curse in them; (iv) she learned how to test witches by seeing John Kincaid pricking them at Newburgh. All this was serious, although curiously enough, Christian was tried under an Act of James IV concerning 'common oppressors', which prescribed the death penalty, and since she had confessed to the crimes, it is difficult to see how she would have avoided execution.

Other factors, however, sometimes clearly played an important role in identifying a witch, and corruption was one of them. That some people were taking advantage of the times to prosecute a vendetta or pursue a personal advantage, for example, was made plain to the Council on 3 July in a petition received from Sir Ruaraidh MacLean of Duart, (whose seat was on the island of Mull), writing on behalf of a number of kinsfolk and friends, both men and women, sixteen altogether.[7] Sir Ruaraidh alleged that Alexander Chisholm and his brother and two of his cousins had 'conceived an inveterate hatred against the supplicants because he could not get them removed from their lands and possessions in a legal way', and so he had had them arrested and, expressly against the orders of the Privy Council, imprisoned the women in his own house and one of the men, Hector MacLean, in the tolbooth of Inverness. Donald MacLean, Hector's brother, had been forced to flee and was now on the run. Accusing the women of witchcraft, the Chisholms had been subjecting the women to gross maltreatment, with the result that 'one of them hath become distracted, another by their cruelty is departed this life, and all of them have confessed whatever they were pleased to demand of them'. Attempts to use accusations of witchcraft as a mean of removing inconvenient or unwanted holders of property were scarcely unknown before this, of course. Louise Yeoman has drawn attention to various examples between 1590 and 1650,[8] and a letter from the daughters of Janet Cock, a condemned witch from

Dalkeith, executed in November 1661, alerts the Lords to an alleged mercenary impulse which had their mother accused by the local baillie.[9] But if such cases did exist, they were by no means the norm. One needs to have property in the first place if one is to tempt property hunters, and when we can tell the status of the accused persons, the majority turns out to have had too little to make them worth pursuit.

Still, corruption and prickers apart, the principal, overwhelming reason for the accusation, prosecution and execution of witches at this time was the firm perception of the country as a whole that Scotland was undergoing a time of spiritual trial and crisis, and that Satan's agents were multiplying to a frightening extent. It has sometimes been said that the legal classes were beginning to have doubts about the whole business, and this may have been true in as much as they could clearly see a disturbing number of illegalities disfiguring the administration of justice. This is certainly the burden of Sir George MacKenzie's remarks on the conduct of witchcraft cases in Scotland, for he begins by saying that neither clergymen nor lawyers can doubt the existence of witches, the former because their death is demanded by *Exodus* 22.18, the latter because there is a statute ordaining that they be put to death. Nor, he says, should one place overmuch trust in Johann Wier's suggestion that witches are simple-minded, sick women suffering from an excess of black bile, because 'witches are [no] more deluded by melancholy than murderers are by rage or revenge'. Nevertheless, 'of all crimes, [witchcraft] requires the most relevancy and most convincing probation', and MacKenzie goes on for the rest of the long article to describe the hazards which lie in the way of establishing such proof – ignorance on the part of the suspects, prison conditions, tormenting by gaolers, false confession, immense pressure from clergymen ('ministers are oft-times indiscreet in their zeal'), personal malice on the part of accusers, and doubts which may be entertained anent the learning and integrity of some of the gentlemen to whom commissions were being granted. It all amounts to very great reservation, based on a number of personal recollections from his time as a justice depute in the early 1660s, as to the way the law was being administered in many instances. Reservation of this kind, however, does not necessarily amount to dismissal. 'I am not of their opinion', MacKenzie wrote elsewhere, 'who deny that there are witches, though I think them not numerous'.[10]

Even a brief survey of both 1661 and 1662, too, shows that the Privy Council willingly issued an unprecedented number of commissions for the trial of witches, and continued to do so throughout an eighteen-month period, and whatever doubts MacKenzie may have expressed nearly twenty-five years after the event, it is necessary to remember that granting a commission is not the same as issuing a death warrant, and that in spite of the numbers we know were executed, by far the largest number is of those whose fate is unknown. The not uncommon instances we have seen of panels being acquitted and cases being deserted reminds us that assizes were not lynch mobs, and that justice more frequently than not continued to be their aim. Thus, Agnes Williamson from Samuelston came to trial on 27 January 1662, accused of nine articles of witchcraft.[11] These included magically killing a horse and a child, making a child disappear, ruining meal, raising blasts of wind, and making a kiln and a house catch fire. It was also alleged, as part of these articles, that she had often confessed to being a witch, and that she had a reputation as one, a reputation enhanced by her saying that the Devil had come to her in the likeness of a man, had had sex with her, and given her a new name ('Nancy Luckyfoot') and a mark upon her shoulder. The assize cleared her of raising a wind and starting fires, but found her guilty of *mala fama*, of having a reputation as a witch. Her proloquitor, Nathaniel Fyffe, had successfully argued that the rest of the articles were not relevant by themselves, a view accepted by the justice deputes, so Agnes was found not guilty overall. This, in an area deeply affected in 1661–62 by the apparent upsurge in witch activity, bears testimony to the aim of advocates, judges and assizes alike to administer the law, not in tune with emotional reaction to events, but according to the evidence presented and argued before them.

If Agnes's alleged witchcraft followed more or less a standard pattern for malefices, the inclusion of the Devil exacerbated the case against her. His appearance was an indication, first, that he was taking an active interest in her, which implied he had seen some possible spiritual weakness which was worth exploiting: and secondly, that she was a person in need of spiritual help, spiritual exhortation, spiritual purging, all of which might (it could be hoped) bring her back to God, thwart the Devil, and relieve society of a dangerously feeble member whose frailty might allow the Devil access to other souls. Agnes's verdict may have cleared her of the specific charges of maleficent acts of magic, but it had left her guilty of *mala fama*, and this would have rendered her return to her community difficult, and even perilous. Satan was so ingenious. Having failed in this attempt, would he try again?

On 16 January 1662, James Welsh was delated as a witch by Janet Wast, arrested, searched for the Devil's mark (of which several were discovered), and sent from Haddington to the tolbooth of Edinburgh for close examination.[12] There he proved garrulous. He described meeting after meeting with the Devil in various places ranging from Haddington to Bolton to Tranent to Edinburgh itself. Most seem to have happened within the last three years. The first time, he was alone in the house in the evening, and went out of doors to relieve himself into a small stream, when 'there appeared to him a bonnie lass who asked him to lie with her, and he refused. Thereafter, a little from that place, there appeared to him a man who tempted him to become his servant, and said to him, "What trade do you use?" and he [James] then replied, "I seek my meat [food] as the other poor things do."' The man asked James to be his servant and promised he should be well satisfied if he did as he was told, and so James agreed and arranged to meet the man the following night beside John Rae's house. When James turned up, the man was waiting for him – and it is at this point, for the first time in the narrative, that he is called 'the Devil'.

The account so far is thus an excellent example of that mixture of natural detail shading into preternatural event, which we have noted before. It cannot be said that James lacked a sense of mischief, for he said that he once attended a meeting on Tranent Moor Brow and saw the Devil sitting with John Kincaid. One says 'mischief', but it may have been naivety, because we learn from a letter dated 17 February that James was only a boy. He had been examined by the presbytery (presumably of Haddington) and by local magistrates at Samuelston, and the documentation thus accumulated had been sufficient for Parliament to be asked for a commission to try him as a witch. The trial had been postponed because he was so young, but it was decided to send him to a house of correction for the next year and a day. The writer, Robert Ker, one of the Haddington magistrates, described James as 'a very subtle rogue' who was refusing to undergo further questioning or to repeat his earlier confession, and Robert pointed out the financial implications of keeping him under lock and key. So far, his maintenance had come from Haddington's poor box, a situation which could not be allowed to continue. Consequently, something should be done. The boy could not pay, since he was a beggar. So it was up to the authorities in Edinburgh to resolve the problem – a difficulty which was still obtaining in April, as a further letter (describing James as an 'alleged wizard') makes clear.

For us, perhaps, the situation seems fairly clear. James was a child – his exact age is not given but he is living at home with his mother, and the records refer to his 'nonage', thereby implying that he was a minor, which could refer to any age up to twenty-one, but I suspect the magistrates would not have hesitated to bring him to trial had he been other than quite a young child. If he was young, he may have been prone to fantasise, especially if he was being brought up in a circumambient atmosphere permeated by talk of witches and the Devil, as certainly seems to have been the case in Haddington at the time. Nevertheless, we ought to appreciate the authorities' dilemma. It is similar to that experienced by modern officials when dealing with child abuse. Children are known to lie and to fantasise. But they also tell the truth. Which is it in this particular case? James obviously presented the magistrates with a genuine problem. He seemed to be a rogue, he seemed to be clever – or at least 'street-wise', in modern jargon. Was there a chance he was telling the truth either in whole or in part? If so, he must be removed from society: hence, the house of correction. The magistrates were keen, apparently, to have him renew his original confession. Why? Because confession was the first step to repentance and (in the case of a child) possible reintegration into society. Therefore, if he had resiled from his first confession, he must be brought to renew it for his own ultimate good. Even if he could not be rescued socially, he could be saved spiritually, so the end was worth the effort. If, on the other hand, he was an incorrigible liar, he needed to be punished and society needed to have him removed, lest he damage people's reputations even further than he had done already by naming them as participants in his meetings with the Devil.

Distinguishing fantasy from fact was thus not easy. But if it was not easy in the case of a child, how easy or difficult was it in the case of an adult? Between 13 April and 27 May 1662, Isobel Gowdie appeared before Harry Forbes, the minister of Auldearn (a village about two-and-a-half miles east-south-east of Nairn on the Moray Firth), William Dallas, sheriff depute of the shire, and nine other witnesses, to make the first of four confessions to witchcraft.[13] She first met the Devil on an open road and covenanted with him. Then she met him in Auldearn's kirk at night, where she performed the usual ceremony of touching herself on the head and the feet, and giving all in between to Satan, who was standing in the reader's desk with a black book in his hand. He marked her on the shoulder, sucking out blood therefrom – a curiously vampiric detail which is most uncommon in Scotland – spitting it into his hand, and then sprinkling it on her head with the words, 'I baptise thee Janet, in my own name'. Not until their third meeting in the wards of Inchoch (enclosed fields not far from a baronial castle) did he copulate with her. 'He was a big, black, rough [hairy] man, very cold', she said, 'and I found his nature [penis] as cold within me as spring-wall water. Sometimes he had boots and sometimes shoes on his feet; but still his feet are forked and cloven. He would be sometimes with us like a deer or a roe'.

Thus the tone of Isobel's confessions was set. She goes into much more detail than is customary in her description of the Devil, and these details, while not in themselves unique in Scottish witch-confessions, are highly unusual when taken together. So is her vocabulary. Isobel is the first, and, as far as I know, the only Scottish witch to use the word 'coven'. She also says that 'her' coven consisted of thirteen persons – the 'her' is important; she does not say that other covens also numbered thirteen – and when she comes to describe certain incidents, her attention to graphic detail is striking. So, for example, she says that she and three others met in the kirkyard of Nairn and fetched an unchristened child out of its grave:

and at the end of Bradley's cornfield land, just opposite to the mill of Nairn, we took the said child, with the [pared] nails of our fingers and toes, pickles [grains] of all sorts of grain, and colewort leaves, and chopped them all very small, mixed altogether; and did put a part thereof among the dung-heaps of Bradley's lands, and thereby took away the fruit of his corn.

Before Candlemas (2 February), presumably 1662, since she does not indicate it was a different year, they went east of Kinloss, twelve miles or so from Auldearn, and there yoked frogs to a plough. The Devil held the plough, and John Young, whom Isobel describes as 'our officer', drove it.

The traces holding the frogs in place were made of dog-grass, and the coulter of the plough was the horn of a half-castrated ram, and a piece of the same kind of horn provided the ploughshare.

This is the kind of thing one expects from a poet, and reminds one of nothing so much as the Queen Mab speech in *Romeo and Juliet*. But there is no indication that Isobel was considered by her neighbours to be in any way unusual, nor is there any sign in the record that she was tortured or subjected to maltreatment. Indeed, it is said she 'willingly confessed'. In any case, neither torture nor maltreatment produce this kind of detail. But the more one reads her confessions, the more one discovers possible clues to her particular mindset:

> I was in the Downie Hills, and got food there from the Queen of Fairy, more than I could eat. The Queen of Fairy is beautifully clothed in white linen, and in white and brown clothes, etc; and the King of Fairy is a handsome man, well favoured and broad faced, etc. There were elf-bulls bellowing and roaring up and down there, and affrighted me.

The clerk is a nuisance with his 'etc.' He uses it a number of times during the record, and one cannot tell whether he was too impatient to note all the details Isobel was providing, or inclined to censor the narrative when it was becoming too prolix for his taste. Isobel describes how the Devil makes elf-arrowheads and then hands them over to elf-boys who shape and trim them – 'little [people], with a lean, starved appearance, looking like cakes baked with a hollow cavity'. The Devil hands out the arrowheads to the witches who then use them to kill people magically. 'We have no bow to shoot with', Isobel explained, 'but flick them from the nails of our thumbs. Sometimes we will miss; but if they touch, be it beast or man or woman, it will kill, even if they were wearing a coat of mail'.

Another notable characteristic of Isobel's narrative is her evident pleasure in listing names. On 3 May, during her second confession, she explained that each person in a coven had an attendant spirit – 'There is one called *Swain* who waits upon… Margaret Wilson in Auldearn. He is always clothed in grass-green; and the said Margaret Wilson has a nickname called, *Pickle nearest the wind*. The next spirit is called *Ruaraidh* who waits upon Bessie Wilson in Auldearn. He is always clothed in yellow;

and her nickname is *Through the cornyard*' – and so on for eight more, until the clerk became weary and wrote 'etc.' The same kind of listing takes place, not only when she is naming the members of her coven, as she does in her first confession, but also when she falls into a kind of extended chant in her third confession, describing who did what to whom and where.

> The first woman that I killed was at the ploughlands. Also I killed one in the east of Moray at Candlemas last. At that time Bessie Wilson in Auldearn killed one there, and Margaret Wilson there killed another. I killed also James Dick in Cannie cavil. But the death that I am most of all sorry for is the killing of William Bower in the milltown of Moyness. Margaret Brodie killed a woman [while she was] washing at the burn of Tarres. Bessie Wilson killed a man at the bush of Struthers. Bessie Hay in Auldearn killed a handsome man called Dunbar at the east end of the town of Forres, as he was coming out at a gate. Margaret Brodie in Auldearn killed one David Black in Darnway...

And so (to imitate the clerk) it goes on.

Isobel's narrative, then, is extraordinary in many ways, as is her manner of telling it, and I suspect that the principal reason it differs from all the others we have encountered is that she was a Highlander and thus steeped in the living oral tradition that is so much a part of Gaelic culture. 'Storytelling' here does not necessarily imply 'fiction'. It refers to a way of arranging and transmitting information, whether that information be factual or fictive. We must therefore change mental gear, as it were, when we read it and listen to the narrative through Highland, not Lowland, ears. But although many of the details are fantastic, it is perhaps possible to glimpse reality underneath, just as we have noted happening in many Lowland accounts of witches' meetings. Take Isobel's description of the Devil's tyrannical behaviour:

> When we are at meat, or in any other place whatever, the maid-servant of each coven sits above the rest, next [to] the Devil; and she serves the Devil, because he is not interested in all the old people, [who] are weak and unsuitable for him. He will be with her and us, like a stallion after mares, and sometimes [like] a man, but very eager in carnal copulation at all times; and they even so as eager and desirous of him. Sometimes,

among ourselves, we would be calling him 'Black John' or the like, and he would know it and hear us well enough; and he even then [would] come to us and say, 'I know well enough what you were saying of me!' And then he would beat and buffet us very sore. We would be beaten if we were absent any time, or neglect anything that would be appointed to be done. Alexander Elder in Earl Seat would be very oft beaten. He is a softie and could never defend himself in the least, but weep and cry out when [the Devil] would be scourging him. But Margaret Wilson in Auldearn would defend herself very well and cast up her hands to keep the strokes off from her; and Bessie Wilson would speak in a harsh, curt manner, and would be bellowing at him bravely. He would be beating and scourging us all up and down with cords and other sharp scourges, like naked ghosts; and we would still be calling out, 'Pity, pity! Mercy, mercy, our Lord!' But he would have neither pity nor mercy.

Violence was an extremely common recourse by almost anyone, as the registers of the Privy Council quickly show.[14] On 26 July 1638, for example, the Lords heard an account of how Sir George Johnston of Caskieben in Aberdeenshire assaulted Alexander Jaffrey's tenants the previous April, threatening 'to cut their ears out of their heads, to scourge them, and drag them at horses' tails'. Gender made no difference to them. Sir George and his band of thugs came to a house where they found only two women – a nurse and a servant – along with a child not yet one year old, and 'thrust them both with the bairn to the door, and so affrighted the nurse that she lost her milk: struck and wounded the other woman with hands, feet, and staffs, dragged her through the yard, [and] threatened to kill her if she delivered not the keys of the house, or told where they lay'. This was violence with a purpose, of course, but it helps to illustrate the extremities of temper which permeated society – both kirk and presbytery session records are full of male and female violence, often involving assault and the use of swords and pistolets – and local events may therefore have informed Isobel's notion of an overbearing laird. Indeed, it is always possible that she had a local laird in mind, for the laird of Park features in her confession more than once, as she and her coven fashioned a clay figure in the shape of a child with a view to killing the Laird's male children with magic, and on another occasion, she shot at him with elf-arrows as he was crossing the burn of Boath.

Another element of real life, which may have contributed to her narrative, is the apparent organisation of her coven. It had an officer and a
servant, and when Isobel underwent her diabolical baptism in the kirk
of Auldearn, the Devil was in the reader's desk with a black book in his
hands. Just so could she have remembered a kirk session with the minister
and elders and herself in attendance. The officer of the session had the duty
of keeping order during meetings and delivering messages. 'Coven', of
course, is merely a word for 'meeting'. Could the kirk session of Auldearn
have numbered twelve in 1661–62, which, with Isobel, would have made
thirteen? If so, then, was Isobel re-forming the common experience of
appearing before the elders and minister (who, as an official, customarily
wore black) into an inverted type of the institution which was likely to be
dominant in both her life and in that of her neighbours?[15]

We do not know what happened to Isobel and the forty or so names
which appear in the relevant documents. She is recorded as being penitent, but in view of her confessing to so many acts of malefice, it is quite
possible that, if she came to trial, her assize would have found her guilty.
But there is no guarantee they did, and we have seen that assizes often
produced verdicts both sophisticated and (in our view) unexpected. It
is also worth bearing in mind the purely practical point that imprisoning and executing a witch was expensive – we have already come
across petitions to the Privy Council from one or two towns asking to
be relieved of the costs – and although a witch's goods were escheat
to the Crown in order to help defray those costs, the money obtained
therefrom would not necessarily go very far, especially if the witch were
poor. A record from Edinburgh, dated 17 July 1661, makes clear the possible extent of what could be recovered by the Crown (or in this case,
William Johnston, baillie of Broughton):

all goods moveable and unmoveable, anything owed to the person, leases,
farm buildings and the ground on which they are built, rooms, possessions,
corn, cattle, furniture, household equipment, [legal] acts, contracts, bonds,
obligations, decrees, sentences, reversions, things assigned to the person,
sums of money, jewels, gold and silver whether in the form of coins or not,
and any other goods and possessions which are escheatable… [belonging
to anyone] lawfully convicted by assizes as notorious and common witches, keeping company with and resorting to devils and witches.

Unless William Johnston were lucky, however, the monetary value of anything he was likely to receive from such a concession would leave him little or nothing after the whole costs of a witch-process had been paid.[16]

Costs fell principally under three general headings: (i) maintenance of the witches in prison; (ii) incidental costs, such as sending letters and summonses, paying lawyers' bills, and so on, and (iii) the execution itself.[17] As to who should pay until the suspect had been found guilty and executed, and her or his property sold, the answer seemed to be parishioners through the kirk. Thus, when the presbytery of Lanark was asked on 12 August 1644 who was to bear the costs of such maintenance, it replied that each parish would be responsible for its own. When James Welsh was removed from Haddington to Edinburgh, the costs of his imprisonment were borne by the kirk session, the minister and elders stipulating that these should not exceed two shillings per day. Sometimes a witch might have to pay her own expenses, as happened by order of the presbytery of Cupar on 25 October 1649, or a local tax might be levied. This happened in Stow in 1630, when a tax of £2 was imposed on each plough in the parish to help maintain warded witches. On 21 June 1649, two elders from Balmerino in Fife were instructed by the presbytery to be cautioners for the charges of an accused witch during the period of her incarceration. So the burden tended to fall, one way or another, on members of the witch's community. In Lauderdale (Berwickshire) Margaret Dunhome's imprisonment and execution in 1649 cost £92 14s (of which £6 went to John Kincaid for pricking her). Margaret's estate yielded only £27. The remaining £65 14s was therefore a burden on her community.[18] It was the same elsewhere. In Spain, for example, in spite of a royal award of confiscated property, feeding imprisoned witches between 1609 and 1611 cost 40,000 *reales*, but scarcely 14,000 *reales* were taken in from all sources to offset these expenses. 'In only three of seventy-seven cases', observes Monter, 'did they receive more from these prisoners in confiscations than they spent on her or his upkeep; over half these prisoners had paid absolutely nothing'. No wonder, then, that Monter remarks 'this book-keeping exercise demonstrated how ruinous witch-hunting could be'.[19]

Old Kirkcaldy kirk session records contain an account of the expenses incurred on the execution of Alison Dick and her husband, William Coke, on 19 November 1633.[20] The costs were divided into two, those borne by the session for maintenance and so forth, and those by the town for the actual execution. The former run as follows:

To James Miller when he went to Preston for a man to try them	47s
To the man of Culross when he went away the first time	12s
For coals for the witches	24s
In purchasing the commission	£9 3s 0d
For one to go to Finmouth for the laird	6s
For harden [very coarse cloth] to make jupes [loose bodices] for them	£3 10s 0d
For making [the jupes]	3s
Total, for the kirk's part	£16 18s 0d

Compare this with the costs incurred by Dumbarton Burgh Council in connection with the imprisonment and trial of Janet Boyd in 1628.[21]

For ale and bread to Janet Boyd, witch, the 25 of August 1628	1s 4d
For coals and peat to the tolbooth for her at sundry times (and for Marion MacClintock), with some ale	11s 4d
To John Bannatyne, justice clerk depute, for making a commission granted by the Earl of Menteith, justice general, for putting the said Janet Boyd to assize	58s
And to his man for drinking money	12s
To Mr. Alexander Colville at delivery to him, as justice depute, of the said Janet Boyd's confession in writing, whereon the commission was granted, his breakfast with the magistrates	42s
To the Earl of Menteith's letter carrier that brought from his lordship the Council's ratification of the commission given by his lordship to put the said Janet Boyd, witch, to assize in November 1628: drinking money	40s
For candles furnished to the tolbooth in watching the said Janet Boyd	30s
To another letter carrier of the Earl of Menteith's that brought a letter from his lordship with the Council's commission to put Janet Boyd to assize, which was sent back again, being dated after her conviction: drinking money	24s
To John Gairdner, officer, and certain others sent to get the executioner of the sheriffdom of Renfrew	

from the Sheriff for executing the said Janet Boyd,
witch, before David Glen took the office thereof
upon him, (albeit they got not the executioner with them)   30s
To Thomas Shaw in the form of roofing turf, for sitting as
dempster to the conviction and condemning of the said Janet Boyd   4s
To Andrew Allan to run to bring [William Sempill of]
Fulwood over [the] Clyde to Janet Boyd's execution   10s

Total: £13 2s 8d

Prickers – the only people to make money, as opposed to getting wages, out of this business – also had to be remunerated. Dunfermline paid 36s to Robert MacKenzie for going to fetch a pricker in 1649, and £3 for 'those who tried the witches' mark', although we should note that this sum included charity to a poor stranger. Watchers were paid, as well. Dunfermline expended 30 shillings and then a further £6 on those watching Margaret Donald in 1645. Other expenses might include repairs to the place in which the suspect was kept, and the hire of a horse and cart to transport the prisoner to the place of execution.[22]

From all this, it will be noted that the biggest expenses were those connected with lawyers' fees, travel, and entertainment of people other than the witch. In Janet Boyd's case, for example, only 12s 8d of the total was spent on her, and some of that seems to have been for the benefit of another woman who may or may not have been confined in the same room.

When Alison Dick and her husband were executed, the town paid the attendant costs.

For ten loads of coals to burn them	5 merks
For tar barrels	14s
For ropes	6s
To him that brought the executioner	58s
To the executioner, for his pains	£8 14s 0d
For his expenses here	16s 4d
For one to go to Finmouth for the laird	6s

Total: £17 1s 4d

All in all, the episode had cost Kirkcaldy about £34. We can get some notion of what this meant if we compare the wages for harvest workers laid down by Peebles magistrates for 1656. A man was to receive 4s per day, with food, or £7 6s 8d, with food and drink, for the whole harvest period. Margaret Dunhome's costs ran to thirteen times this sum, and those of Alison Dick and her husband (imprisonment and execution together), to nearly five times the amount. Another general comparison, particularly useful for Kirkcaldy, can be made with the assessed prices per boll for oats in Fife. (A boll was a dry measure which varied in capacity from district to district). The earliest year we have for the Fife records is 1640, when the price was £5 13s 4d. Supposing the price had been more or less the same in 1633, the costs of imprisoning and executing Alison and William represent six times that sum. Prices fell dramatically between 1660 (£5 6s 8d) and 1662 (£3 13s 4d); so had they been executed in 1662, their total costs would have been ten times the oat price.[23] We may deduce, then, that pursuing and executing witches in Scotland was a very expensive business, even if the costs could sometimes be offset against the witch's property, and we may take these sums as some slight indication of how seriously everyone was prepared to regard the witches' offence.

Once 1662 had run its course, the number of prosecutions dropped noticeably. The *Source Book*, for example, gives nine in 1663 and nine in 1664, so clearly the spasm was over. What was it about 1661 and 1662 that had given rise to a frenzy of fear, not just in certain places, but all over Scotland? It was certainly not the weather. Nicoll records that 1662 was

> in all parts of it wondrous blessed, in the Spring in the summer tide and harvest, producing [a] multitude of corn of all sorts, with pears, apples, stone fruit, abundance of nuts, great and fair, the like never seen heretofore… The winter also, from November till January thereafter, [was] very kindly and seasonable.[24]

Nor was military occupation culpable. In June 1661, the army started to withdraw from Scotland and by May 1662 it had gone. Political change, to be sure, affected a small number of officials directly involved, but not the great bulk of the populace. What did convulse the country as a whole was the King's religious settlement. In summer 1660, Charles gave the impression he would retain the Presbyterian system, but an Act Rescissory in March 1661 annulled all Scottish Parliamentary legislation since 1633, and thus removed the legal basis of that system as it had existed since the National Covenant of 1638. In September, Charles let it be known to the Scottish Privy Council that he wanted episcopacy restored, and the following January a proclamation was issued, forbidding all sessions of kirk, presbytery, or synod without the relevant bishop's permission. In May 1662, episcopacy was legally restored and the clergy required to take an oath of allegiance to the new settlement on pain of being deprived of their ministries. The result we have seen already. The west of Scotland, and the south-west in particular, lost large numbers of clergy. In Galloway, for example, thirty-four out of the total of thirty-seven were thus deprived.

In the east, however, the situation was different. In spite of the fact that there were many dissenters, the clergy tended to be left in their posts, save in the presbytery of Edinburgh. This contrast is important. We have noted that East and Midlothian especially suffered witch prosecutions in 1662, whereas the west did not figure nearly as much. A community defines itself not only by what it has in common, but also by what it is against. Ministers in the west of Scotland openly expressed their opposition to the new religious settlement, and were deprived for it. They had no need to look for other ways of expressing solidarity with a particular ecclesiastical point of view.[25] But ministers in the east (and, to some extent, in the central belt), by contrast, either accommodated themselves or were accommodated in spite of themselves to the new régime, and therefore needed to demonstrate – to the government, to their parishioners, to themselves – that they still belonged to the community of the righteous. What simpler way than to unite people against known non-conformists, against those who self-evidently were *not* members of the righteous and, indeed, (again self-evidently) had pitted themselves against them? When the loyal conformists of Linlithgow wanted to demonstrate their political and religious solidarity in May 1661, the first anniversary of Charles II's restoration, they set up an arch depicting Covenant and Witchcraft and Rebellion as inextricably interlinked.

> They framed an arch upon four pillars, and upon one side the picture of an old hag with the Covenant in her hand, and this inscription

above; A GLORIOUS REFORMATION. On the other side of the arch was a Whig with the Remonstrance in his hand, with this inscription, NO ASSOCIATION WITH MALIGNANTS. On the other side was the Committee of Estates, with this inscription, AN ACT FOR DELIVERING UP THE KING. On the fourth side was the Commission of the Kirk, with this inscription, THE ACT OF THE WEST KIRK. On the top of the arch stood the Devil, with this inscription, STAND TO THE CAUSE. In the midst of the arch was a litany:

From Covenants with uplifted hands,
From Remonstrators with associate bands,
From such Committees as govern'd this nation,
From Church Commissioners and their protestation,
Good Lord, deliver us.

They had also the picture of Rebellion in religious habit, with the book *Lex Rex* in one hand, and the causes of God's wrath in the other, and this in midst of rocks, and reels, and kirk stools, logs of wood, and spurs, and covenants, acts of assembly, protestations, with this inscription, REBELLION IS THE MOTHER OF WITCHCRAFT.[26]

Witchcraft, then, offered all parties, regardless of political or religious adherence, an opportunity to demonstrate solidarity with their own particular group, and thus identify themselves to each other and to the rest of the community. After many years of foreign occupation and in the midst of the succeeding ecclesiastical turmoil, such executions also served to assure people that the natural order and balance of things was being restored. Moreover, as Jean Bodin had pointed out as long ago as 1580, God had been grievously offended, and therefore execution of witches appeased His wrath and thus obtained a renewed blessing upon the purged and revivified community. In Darren Oldridge's *aperçu*, 'the theatre of the scaffold was used to underline the natural order of creation'.[27] So these strands in the behaviour of individuals and groups of individuals during 1661–62, the years in which the Church of the Covenant found itself under threat as never before since 1638, may help to account in part for that notable upsurge in witch prosecutions, which so disfigured the period.

But such an upsurge would amount to little more than cynicism if it were not informed by a genuine fear of magic in general and witchcraft in particular, and it is also remarkable that the rise in prosecutions also seems to see a rise in the presence of Satan as a major actor in the witches' activities. Just as the Devil often appeared to individuals in moments of stress, so too, perhaps, he came to the Scottish nation during a time of particular spiritual anxiety; and we should do our ancestors a grave disservice if we interpreted this in modern terms, explaining it away as the projection of negative aspects of people's external and internal lives on to a symbol of transcendent evil. Nor does the Scottish experience coincide with Nathan Johnstone's more subtle view of that felt by the English – 'the produce of a sharpened experiential sense of intimate satanic agency and the hidden dangers of commonplace religious and secular practices, [with] its emphasis on internal temptation'.[28] In the Scottish records, Satan most often appears as a gentleman, asks the woman to be his servant (or the man to be his musician), to which she usually agrees at once and without demur – possibly an effect of the way the clerk recorded and edited the confession, possibly not. The encounter is not so much one of temptation as an offer of better employment. It is accepted by means of a ritual gesture of dedication, and the reward is equally physical in its manifestations – food and drink, good company, music, and sex without shame, sometimes in private, but frequently in sight of the woman's friends and neighbours or family. As Elizabeth Reis expresses it, 'Simply to sin implied the forging of an implicit covenant with Satan, a spiritual renunciation of God. For Puritans, to become an actual witch demanded the acceptance of a *more literal and physical invitation from the Devil*' (my italics).[29]

Calvinists, even the most godly, worried constantly about their salvation, convinced that nothing was easier than to be led astray and ultimately be condemned to Hell, a place of physical as well as spiritual torment, and these anxieties were expressed in vivid, physical terms which appealed to their actual or potential experience. Thus, John Jones, a member of Thomas Shepard's congregation in Cambridge, Massachusetts, admitted he had been happy to continue in his sins until he heard the minister 'preaching about the covenant, where he showed that everyone by nature was a prisoner in a pit and dungeon, with no comfort to be found'. It was a cast of mind which permeated Scottish society, too, to the extent that even the registers of the Privy Council often refer to the *sin* rather than the *crime* of witchcraft.

Now, of course it can be argued that Scotland was not the only country in which people had physical contact with the Devil or met together as witches in an environment of sociability coloured by defiance of God. But Scotland was different in one respect. The Kirk not only sought to govern every aspect of its adherents' daily behaviour, it possessed the machinery needed for enforcing that governance, and used it effectively. Children were punished for playing and women for drying clothes on Sunday, and everyone for cursing and swearing. Attendance at church was compulsory. Extra-marital sex was subject to heavy retribution. People's communal relationships were used as the means to enforce obedience, because public humiliation in the face of one's neighbours was the principal sanction employed against offenders; and through his regular hour-long Sabbath sermons, the minister reinforced his parishioners' sense of guilt and anxiety. If the minister was thus a controlling figure of authority, the Devil by contrast represented his opposite, a liberating master who offered guilt-free eating and drinking and extra-marital sex. In an environment of tight Kirk control, in fact, he represented the obvious mean of escaping what would otherwise be constant spiritual repression; so perhaps it was not, after all, editing by the clerk which pictured almost every witch in her confession as giving immediate consent to the Devil's suggestion of service, but the reflection of a genuine impulse reported by the witch.

Finally, was there a witch *hunt* in Scotland between 1658 and 1662? Wolfgang Behringer has drawn attention to the difficulties attendant on this kind of terminology, since it is difficult to distinguish between a hunt, a panic, a persecution, and national, extensive, or local prosecutions.[30] Nor does the terminology take into account sporadic outbursts, prosecutions with a large number of suspects but few executions, and vice versa, prosecutions spreading beyond national boundaries, prosecutions resulting from a process of chain reaction, and constant prosecutions during which the number of suspects or executed is small at any given time, but grows much larger over a longer period because the process of prosecution is more or less constant. As we have seen, prosecution of witches in Scotland can scarcely be regarded as abnormally frequent until 1661. But during 1661-62 there was undoubtedly a notable upsurge of delations, whether by ordinary individuals, or suspect witches undergoing interrogation; and in as much as these two years appear to have manifested an increase, not only in the numbers of people being accused, but also in the frequency of illegalities practised against many of them, it is fair to say that witches were being hunted at this time. In what numbers is a question which cannot really be answered. The outcome of most of the delations, for example, is not known, and therefore the number of those executed may be larger or smaller than any guess, as may the number of those acquitted, and the number of those who escaped, committed suicide, died of illness or starvation or neglect, or had their trials deserted. At a guess, one can say that there may have been about 250 executions, which is a very large number in relation to the number of executions of witches in years before and after 1660–62, but such an estimate is actually more or less meaningless when presented without reference to executions for other crimes during the same period, and such comparative work has not yet been done. Numbers by themselves thus tell us very little.

In counter-balance, however, it must also be observed that when witches came to trial, their assizes seem to have done their best to listen to the evidence presented, and to pass their verdict in accordance with that evidence, so that perhaps (although I expect not without controversy) we may say of some of them at least what Increase Mather said of the judges and jurors at Salem, that 'they are good and wise men, and have acted with all fidelity according to their light'.[31]

Notes

INTRODUCTION

1   Printed in *Acts of the General Assembly of the Church of Scotland*, Vol. 1, (Edinburgh 1843), 220.

2   Name-calling, consulting, charming, witchcraft: CH2/141/3; CH2/1157/1; CH2/799/3; CH2/100/2; CH2/299/3; CH2/24/1; JC26/24.

3   See Gibson & Smout: *Prices, Food, and Wages in Scotland*, 265.

4   *Disquisitiones Magicae*, Book 5, section 15; Book 1, chapter 1.

5   Text given in J. Lumsden: *The Covenants of Scotland*, 228.

6   *Diary* Vol. 1. 156-7; Vol. 2. 296-7, 125.

7   *Witchcraft and its Transformation*, 21, 22, 23, note 63.

8   *The Witches of Fife*, 25, 28, 188-90.

CHAPTER ONE 1657: NEITHER DEVIL NOR HUNT

1   Name-calling, superstition, and charming: CH2/122/3; CH2/1157/1; CH2/84/2; CH2/62/1; CH2/188/1; CH2/716/5; CH2/716/6; CH2/400/2; CH2/592/1; CH2/1173/3. Cramond: *Records of the Kirk-Session of Elgin*, 284-5. CH2/458/1; CH2/111/1; CH2/389/1 (September 1649). Cf. a case of charming in Kinnaird in July 1658. This consisted of drying up cows' milk, a magical action clearly coming within the usual definition of 'witchcraft', CH2/418/1. J.M. MacKinlay: *Folklore of Scottish Lochs and Springs*, (Glasgow 1893), 86-107, 188-212.

2   Cramond: *The Church and Churchyard of Ruthven*, 22-5. Maxwell-Stuart: *Satan's Conspiracy*, 72-87, 98-107. CH2/52/1; JC26/20/7.

3   JC26/22/5/1-7; CH2/424/4; JC6/5.

4   JC26/22/3/3-5; JC26/23.

5   JC26/22/3/1; JC26/22/4/39; JC26/23.

6   CH2/420/2.

7   Sanderson: 'Scottish families of all social groups are notable for the number
      of servants they maintained, some of whom would be dependent relatives',
      A Kindly Place? 34, cf. 126-7. See also Whyte: *Scotland Before the Industrial
      Revolution*, 165.

8   JC26/22/5/31; JC26/22/5/39; JC26/22/5/42; JC26/22/4/1; JC26/22/4/10;
      JC26/22/2/27; JC26/22/6/40. *RPC* 3rd series, 1.11-12.

9   JC26/23; JC26/20/1; JC51/6.

10   CH2/636/34.

11   *Acts of the Parliament of Scotland* 2.539.

12   *Malleus Maleficarum*: 'The category in which women of this kind are includ-
      ed is called "the category of women who prophesy or foretell the future"
      [*Pythones*]. In these women, an evil spirit either speaks or works marvels'
      (Part 1, question 1). The title *Pytho* is derived from that given to the ancient
      priestess at Delphi, through whom the god Apollo answered questions put
      by clients to the oracle. Cf. 'the ritual practices of workers of harmful magic
      belong to the second type of superstition, namely, to divination' (Part 1, ques-
      tion 2).

13   JC26/21/1. On Sir Robert Grierson, see A. Fergusson: *The Laird of Lag*
      (Edinburgh 1886).

14   JC26/19/2; JC26/22/5/35 and 37.

15   JC26/22/3/22.

CHAPTER TWO 1658: THE INITIAL STORM

1   Numbers extracted from Larner: *A Source-Book of Scottish Witchcraft*, 16-21,
      55-6, 211-12. See also Larner: *Enemies of God*, 35-9.

2   *Cromwellian Scotland*, 221-2.

3   *Culture of Protestantism*, 408.

4   JC26/25.

5   CH2/100/2. Cf. George Sutherland, who came before the presbytery of
      Caithness on 6 July 1658 'and confessed consulting with a witch that now is
      dead, in burying of a cock', CH2/47/1. Incidences of animal sacrifice are not
      uncommon at this period and are likely to date back perhaps to pre-Christian
      times.

6   JC26/25. The various papers in this box of documents unfortunately have
      no separate numbers to distinguish them from one another. Cf. commis-
      sions issued for Caithness, Fife, Forres, Inverness, Ross and Forfar in July 1655
      which adopt the same phraseology, JC26/17.

7   *JC26/25*, Aberdeen Roll.

8   *Institutions of the Laws of Scotland* (1681), Book 1, title 3.

9   *JC26/18A/1-3, 6-10*. The death penalty was prescribed by an Act of 1563, subsequently repeated in 1581 and 1650. See *Acts of the Parliament of Scotland* 2.539; 3.213; 6 part 2.593b.

10   *JC26/25; JC51/6; JC26/24; JC26/25. CH2/592/1*.

11   *Depositions and Other Ecclesiastical Proceedings from the Courts of Durham*, (Surtees Society, London & Edinburgh 1845), 21.99-100.

12   *The Life and Wonderful Prophecies*, 5.

13   *The Spiritual Warfare, or, Some Sermons concerning the Nature of Mortification, Right Exercise, and Spiritual Advantages thereof* (Edinburgh 1693), 48, 124. Gray died in 1656. This sermon was first published posthumously in 1676.

14   *King or Covenant*, 155.

15   *Analecta* 1.349-50.

16   *JC26/26*.

17   *JC26/24; JC10/1*.

18   See Firth: *Scotland and the Protectorate*, 382. *JC51/6; JC10/1; JC26/25*.

19   *JC26/25*.

20   *Enemies of God*, 117.

21   *JC51/6; JC26/25; JC10/1*.

22   *JC26/18A/6*. An attached document shows that on 6 May, Katharine Smyth's husband entered into a bond of caution for her release.

23   *JC26/24; JC26/25*, Kirkcudbright Roll; *JC10/1*.

24   *CH2/1284/1*.

25   Janet MacMurdoch: see Larner: *Enemies of God*, 120-5.

26   *JC26/25; JC6/5*. Geographical references in the text identify this as Liberton near Edinburgh rather than Libberton in Lanarkshire.

27   *CH2/722/6. JC26/24; JC6/5; JC10/1; JC26/26*. Geographical references in the texts identified Alloa (spelled 'Alloway' in the records) as the town in Clackmannan, not 'Alloway' in Ayr.

28   *CH2/48/23; CH2/1026/1; Extracts from the Records of Lanark*, 177.

29   See R. Mandrou: *Possession et sorcellerie au xviie siècle: textes inédits* (reprinted Paris 1997), 236.

30   *Disquisitiones Magicae*, Book 1, chapter 2. Clark: *Thinking With Demons*, 19-23.

31   *Diary*, 216.

32   *JC26/24; JC26/26; JC10/1; JC26/27*

33   Del Rio: *Disquisitiones Magicae*, Book 5, section 6. MacKenzie: *Laws and Customs of Scotland*, title 26, para. 10.

34   Nicoll: *Diary*, 208, 222. Behringer: 'Weather, hunger, and fear', 69-82. Morrison: 'Evidence of climatic changes in Scotland', 11.

CHAPTER THREE 1659: THE DEVIL ENTERS THE PICTURE

1   Glaber: *Historiarum libri quinque* 5.2. Fra Angelico, *Hell*, in the Museum San
Marco, Florence. Wier: *De praestigiis daemonum*, Book 2, chapter 5. *CH2/383/1*.
Roper: *Witch Craze*, 90 and 3. MacWilliam, *JC26/20/4*. Jackson: *Treatise* 5,
164-5. Germany, see Roper: *Witch Craze*, 44, 82, 85-8, 96, 97. Wier: *De praes-
tigiis daemonum*, Book 6, chapter 11. Dommartin, see L. Pfister (ed.): *L'enfer sur
terre* (Lausanne 1997), 203, 221, 223, 241. Lorraine, see N. Jacques-Chaquin &
M. Préaud (eds): *Le sabbat des sorciers*, (Millon, Grenoble 1993), 169. Devon: *A
True and Impartial Relation* (1682). See further U. Valk: *The Black Gentleman*,
51-63. K.G. Rosenfield: 'Monstrous generation: witchcraft and generation in
Othello' in L.H. MacAvoy & T. Walters (eds): *Consuming Narratives: Gender and
Monstrous Appetite in the Middle Ages and the Renaissance* (University of Wales,
Cardiff 2002), 222-34.

2   *JC26/8/1/1; JC26/8/1/2; JC26/19/3; JC26/26*. See also Larner: *Enemies of God*,
147-8. *CH2/124/1* (19 August 1649). On 6 September 1626, William Lamb in
Kirkcaldy said that Helen Birrell had told him she saw a large black man come
into her house. He had cloven feet with buckles on them, *CH2/636/34*. The
cloven feet are most unusual in Scottish accounts of meeting the Devil. But
Helen's alleged admission is unusual altogether, for she was also supposed to
have said that she brought Satan two hens because she was his tenant, and had
supper with him, along with her husband, son, and daughter.

3   John Grant: *Statistical Account of Scotland* 16.300, 302. Cf. a letter by Edmund
Burt, an Englishman travelling in Scotland in 1730, in which he describes a
hill west of Inverness and the local belief that 'the fairies within it are innu-
merable, and witches find it the most convenient place for their frolics and
gambols in the night time', *Burt's Letters from the North of Scotland*, ed. A.
Simmons, (Birlinn, Edinburgh 1998), 124. *CH2/523/1* (1632); *CH2/1157/1*
(1657); *CH2/890/1*.

4   Harry Wilson: *CH2/113/1*. Cargill: *Wonderful Prophecies*, 10. Blair: *Life*, 65-8.
Todd: *Culture of Protestantism*, 394-6, 94, 95. These personal stimuli were the
principal motives for writers' undertaking further investigation of demonic
phenomena. Cf. Christoph Ehinger whose interest was strengthened because
one of his parishioners was suffering assaults by the Devil, *Daemonologia, oder
etwas neues vom Teufel* (Augsburg 1681).

5   See E. Graham, H. Hinds, E. Hobby, H. Wilcox (eds): *Her Own Life:
Autobiographical Writings by Seventeenth-Century Englishwomen* (Routledge,
London & New York 1989), 197-210.

6   Ecclesiastical sessions (January-June): *CH2/212/1*; *CH2/1100/1*; *CH2/383/1*;
CH2/546/2; *CH2/101/2*; *CH2/1284/1*; *CH2/722/6*; *CH2/89/2*;
CH2/96/1/2; *CH2/153/1*; *CH2/225/1*. Cf. Margaret Taylor who declared in

John Rynie's hearing that 'she hoped God would never let beast nor body prosper that had taken any part of her land away', a simple curse without any overt hint of witchcraft, but one which could have been reinterpreted had any misfortune fallen subsequently upon those she had cursed, *CH2/1115/1* (2 May 1659); and Janet Finlayson in Dunblane, who was accused of casting sickness on Katharine White's son. John Buchanan, giving supporting evidence, told the session that Janet had come in to see him, and did no more than take him by the hand – 'but such a grip, he never saw the like'. He accused her both of making him ill in the first place, and then of taking it off, a circumstance which altered his experience of her strong grip and made it deeply suspicious, *CH2/101/1* (25 September). *CH2/799/3*. (July-December): *CH2/1026/4*; *CH2/229/1*. Isobel Jackson from Edinburgh was just as foolish when she said she would renounce herself, soul and body, to the Devil before she would agree to undergo ecclesiastical censure, *CH2/141/3*, Trinity College Church.

7   *Diary*, 145, 158, 169-70, 195, 243.

8   *A Discourse of the Damned Art of Witchcraft* (London 1608), 156.

9   *Diary*, 264.

10 *JC26/26; JC10/1*. In March, Barbara Erskine confessed and was therefore convicted. She was due to be executed on 1 April. James Kirk was convicted by plurality of votes, but merely had to find £20 caution for his future good behaviour. We do not know the details of their cases.

11 *JC26/26; JC10/1*.

12 *JC26/26; JC6/5*.

13 *Enemies of God*, 153.

14 *Diary*, 228, 233.

15 *JC26/26; JC51/18/1*.

16 Martin: 'The Devil and the domestic', 81.

17 See further Maxwell-Stuart: *Witch Hunters*, 107-14. On the Cleveland affair, it is worth noting that the following year, Stuart Bell, MP for Middlesbrough, overtly likened that scandal to a witch-hunt, *When Salem Came to the Boro* (Pan Books, London 1988), 12. On reflex anal dilatation, see Bell, 50.

18 *Instruments of Darkness: Witchcraft in England 1550–1750* (Hamish Hamilton, London 1996), 141-2.

19 *JC6/5; JC26/24; JC26/26; JC10/1; JC10/15/1-2; JC51/6*. John Shennan's experience of a ghostly or demonic hand illustrates the difficulties people sometimes had in assessing certain experiences with any exactitude. On 21 February, for example, the presbytery of Dumbarton heard that James Foyar had confessed to seeing several 'apparitions', but it is not clear from the record what nature of apparition these may have been, *CH2/546/2*.

20 *Deadly Words: Witchcraft in the Bocage*, English trans. (Cambridge University Press, 1980).

21 Giving a witch an object: cf. the case of Jean Thomson empanelled before Dumfries circuit court in spring 1659. Item 4 of her dittay tells us that Geillis Young, servant to James Thomson, tried to stop one of Jean's lambs from suckling promiscuously by hobbling it with one of her garters. Jean threatened her with the falling sickness which, indeed, she contracted a year later, and for twelve or fourteen years she sought a cure from various people. One of these lived over the border in England, and she told Geillis that because her garter had been used to hobble the lamb, Jean had got hold of it and was thereby enabled to have power over her body. Otherwise, she would have had none. *JC26/27: Dumfries Roll.*

22 Measuring: see Wilson: *The Magical Universe*, 175, 330, 336, 347, 366.

23 *Letters and Journals* 3.395. See also 3.375-81.

CHAPTER FOUR 1660-61: THE DEVIL CONTINUES HIS WORK

1 *Cromwellian Scotland*, 247.

2 Kirk and presbytery sessions, 1660: *CH2/52/1*; *CH2/471/3*; *CH2/242/5*; *CH2/1173/4*; *CH2/153/1*; *CH2/141/3*; *CH2/122/3*; *CH2/424/4*. The information relating to Seal may be found in *CH2/389/1*.

3 *CH2/890/1*.

4 See further Wilson: *Theatres of Intention*, 184-215.

5 Both these quotations come from Levack: 'Decline and end of Scottish witch-hunting', 174, notes 31 and 32. Levack conflates torture and maltreatment, using these quotations to assist his point. See also Unsworth: 'Witchcraft beliefs and criminal procedure', 96.

6 *Laws and Customs of Scotland*, Part 2, title 27.

7 *The Witches of Fife*, 126-7, 137-8.

8 *Domestic Annals*, 219.

9 See Dow: *Cromwellian Scotland*, 29 and 285, note 83.

10 *JC26/20/8/1-5*. Cf. the case of Mary Cunningham and her daughter, who complained to the Privy Council in August 1644 about similarly barbarous (and illegal) maltreatment at the hands of the clerk to the baillies of Culross, *RPC* 2nd series, 8.101.

11 Magical assemblies: (a) and (c) are taken from Medway: *Lure of the Sinister*, 316, 146. (b) comes from *JC26/27*.

12 *CH2/234/1*; *JC10/1*; *CH2/799/3*; *Records of the Burgh of Lanark*, 205-6; *JC26/26*; *GD103/2/176/4*; Nider: *Formicarius* 5.4; *CH2/141/3*; *CH2/592/1*. Cf. Cook: *Annals of Pittenweem*, 49.

13 Quoted in D. Oldridge: *Strange Histories* (Routledge, London 2005), 106.

14   This is the subtitle of a book, *Witches*, by Evelyn Heinemann, English trans. (Free Association Books, London 2000). cf. A. Llewellyn Barstow: *Witchcraze* (Harper Collins, London 1995), M. Hester: *Lewd Women and Wicked Witches: A Study of the Dynamics of Male Domination* (Routledge, London 1992), C. Rehberger: 'Die Verteufeung der Frau als Hexe in den Hexenverfolgungen des späten Mittelalters und der frühen Neuzeit', *Evangelische Theologie* 52 (1992), 65-75, and a critique of this kind of approach by D. Purkiss: *The Witch in History* (Routledge, London 1996), 7-29.

15   Appearances at kirk and presbytery sessions: *CH2*/188/1; *CH2*/1284/1; *CH2*/1100/1.

16   Ekirch: 'Sleep we have lost', 364 (quotation), 369-70. *CH2*/799/3 (3 January and 7 February 1660); *CH2*/420/1 (24 May 1664); *CH2*/591/1 (11 July 1677); *CH2*/799/3 (4 September 1659).

17   Ekirch: *art.cit.* 373, 381.

18   *JC26*/27.

19   *JC26*/27/9/5.

20   *CH2*/1120/1.

21   *Reading Witchcraft*, 21-5. See also *Ibid.* 76-7 for a very useful methodological checklist of questions for anyone reading witchcraft documents.

22   *JC26*/25/bundle 3/20.

23   Assizes' voting: for detailed examples taken from the two trials of Janet Cock from Dalkeith in September and November 1661, see Maxwell-Stuart: *Witchcraft: A History* (Tempus, Stroud 2000), 103-4, 106.

24   Witches, 1660: *DO* 31/1/2/8 and *DO* 31/4/3; Larner-Lee-McLachlan: *Source Book*, 214. *JC26*/26;

25   Ecclesiastical witchcraft records, 1661: *CH2*/424/4; *CH2*/145/7. The session also heard that Elspeth Allan, alias 'Fool Eppie', had been delated 'for going dancing during the night on the streets with alleged witches'. *CH2*/424/4; *CH2*/105/1; *CH2*/122/4; *CH2*/276/4; *CH2*/84/3; *CH2*/799/3; *CH2*/1100/1. MacKenzie: *Laws and Customs*, Part 2, title 26. *CH2*/647/1; *CH2*/285/4; *CH2*/62/1; *CH2*/15/1; *CH2*/1463/1; *CH2*/716/6; *CH2*/338/2; *CH2*/113/1.

26   Acts of the Privy Council: 7.199. *RPC* 3rd series, 1.11. Cf. 1.16-17 (1 August).

27   Records: *RPC* 3rd series, 1.11, 34, 62, 90-1.

28   1.48. Cf. Jean Gyllor who was also in the Canongate tolbooth, and had been there for a long time, 1.64 (3 October); 1.73, 74.

29   1.25 (2 August). On 7 November, the Council also heard from the Earl of Haddington, who asked them to relieve him of Agnes Williamson who had lain in prison at his expense since about March, and was costing him money and his tenants inconvenience, 1.78. On the same day, the Lords were told

that Adam Robertson, a maltman in Eyemouth, had been in the tolbooth of Duns for the past six weeks because malicious information had dubbed him a witch, and order was given that he be set free on caution, 1.74.

30   *RPC* 3rd series, 1.647-51; Anderson: 'Confessions', 248. *JC*2/10.

31   Forfar witches: Anderson: 'Confessions, 246-52. GD103/2/176/1,3,4,8 (2 January 1662).

32   *The Witches of Fife*, 179.

33   T. Dömötör: *Hungarian Folk Beliefs* (Indiana University Press, Bloomington 1981), 130, 204.

34   *JC*2/10 (3 August); (20 August).

35   *JC*2/10; GD103/2/3/11.

36   RPC 3rd series, 1.71 and 75, 26, 64. *JC*17/1.

CHAPTER FIVE 1662: AFTERMATH

1   Grinlaw & Howison: 1.151-2. Cf. Garvie & Honiman who were suffering in similar fashion, 1.52. They had been in prison since mid-December. Janet Hood from Eyemouth had remained 'in a vile and ugly dungeon' since November, and wrote to the Council on 10 April to ask for her liberty, 1.200. Mary Rhind and Helen Alexander petitioned the Privy Council for release on 13 February 1663. They had been imprisoned in Forfar tolbooth for eighteen months, and no one had yet come forward to initiate their process, 1.336. On 20 February 1662 John Aitkin complained he had lain long in Pentland, 1.70. Whatever 'long' means, it may take his arrest back to late 1661, too. Likewise, John Purdie had been 'several weeks' in the tolbooth of Ayton in Berwickshire, 1.70, and Beatrix Ford in the tolbooth of Duns 'this long time past', 1.181. Agnes Williamson: *JC*26/28.

2   Illegalities: *RPC* 3rd series, 1.12, 188-9, 195, 197, 222, 265.

3   Proclamation: 1.198.

4   1.221. Cf. Muriel Gillipatrick and Isobel Duff (26 June), 1.234.

5   Kincaid: 1.132, 187, 210, 224, 226-7. See also Maxwell-Stuart: *Witch Hunters* (Tempus, Stroud 2004), 107-11.

6   Convinth & Dickson: 1.233, 210.

7   MacLean: 1.237.

8   'Hunting the rich witch in Scotland: high-status witchcraft suspects and their persecutors, 1590–1650' in Goodare (ed.): *The Scottish Witch-Hunt in Context*, 106-21.

9   Janet Cock: *JC*26/27/9/20.

10   *Laws and Customs* Part 1, title 10; *Pleadings Before the Supreme Courts of Scotland*, no. 16. We have an example of the ignorance which could exist, despite the clergy's efforts. On 27 January 1652, James Naismith, the minister of Hamilton

in Lanarkshire, complained to the kirk session that Robert Naismith was so ignorant that he did not know how many gods there are, nor which person of the Trinity is Jesus Christ, *CH2/465/7*.

11   *JC2/10; JC26/28*.

12   *JC26/28*.

13   Pitcairn: *Criminal Trials* 3.602-16.

14   Violence: *RPC* second series 7.49.

15   Kirk session: Isobel's account of witches meeting in a church with the Devil calling an attendance-register is not unique. It appears in accounts of the witch-craft conspiracy of 1590–91, describing witches assembling in the kirk of North Berwick. These accounts, however, lack Isobel's specific terminology of 'coven' and 'officer'.

16   *Extracts from the Records of the Burgh of Edinburgh, 1655–65*, ed. M. Wood (Oliver & Boyd, Edinburgh 1940), 249. Cf. Larner: 'The likelihood of financial gain was of importance in some urban areas where the suspects were substantial people. It could be a reasonable estimate, however, that the prosecution of ninety per cent of witch suspects was an expense to the local though not necessarily the central government concerned', *Enemies of God*, 197.

17   Maintenance costs: *CH2/234/1*; *CH2/799/3* (22 December 1661). Cf. the expenses of Bessie Kennedy imprisoned in Haddington tolbooth, which amounted to £10 (24 December 1661). *CH2/82/1*. T.C. Brown: *The History of Selkirk or Chronicles of Ettrick Forest*, 2 vols (Edinburgh 1886), 1.449. *CH2/82/1*.

18   A. Thomson: *Lauder and Lauderdale* (Craighead Bros, Galashiels 1902), 210.

19   *Frontiers of Heresy* (Cambridge University Press 1990), 273.

20   *CH2/636/34*. Making such upper garments is also recorded in Kirkcaldy on 2 May 1626 when £2 4s 6d was spent on green cloth for two witches imprisoned in the kirk steeple.

21   *Dumbarton Accounts*, 61-2. Dunfermline: *CH2/592/1* (18 December 1649 and 29 January 1650, so the two entries cover a single summons). E. Henderson: *The Annals of Dunfermline and Vicinity* (Glasgow 1879), 314.

22   Other costs: *Dumfries Burgh Treasurer's Account*, 24 November 1649.

23   Comparative wages and prices: Gibson & Smout: *Prices, Food and Wages in Scotland*, 280, 85.

24   *Diary*, 386-7.

25   Solidarity: Cf. Todd: 'At Perth in March of 1638, the whole congregation, men and women, gathered and swore the Covenant 'by upholding of their hands' at a communion 'in the old manner', sitting round the table rather than kneeling, as a ritual gesture of solidarity in the face of the English enemy', *The Culture of Protestantism*, 119. Attitudes among the self-consciously godly had not changed twenty-four years later.

26　　J. Kirkton: *Secret and True History of the Church of Scotland*, ed. R. Stewart (Edwin Mellen Press, Lampeter 1992), 68.

27　　Bodin: *Démonomanie des sorciers*, Book 4, chapter 5. Oldridge: *Strange Histories* (Routledge, London & New York 2005), 51.

28　　'The Protestant Devil', 205.

29　　'Witches, sinners, and the underside of Covenant theology', 104, 106, 107.

30　　*Witches and Witch-Hunts*, 49.

31　　*Cases of Conscience concerning Evil Spirits personating Men, [and] Witchcrafts* (Boston 1693), postscript.

Select Bibliography

MANUSCRIPT SOURCES

National Archives of Scotland

(a) *Kirk Session Records*
CH2/24/1 Dysart
CH2/48/23 Cambusnethan
CH2/52/1 Canisbay
CH2/62/1 Carrington
CH2/82/1 Cupar
CH2/84/2-3 Dalkeith
CH2/101/1 Dunblane
CH2/100/2 Dunbarney
CH2/122/3-4 Canongate
CH2/122/69 Canongate
CH2/124/1 Corstorphine
CH2/141/3 Trinity College Church, Edinburgh
CH2/145/7 Elgin, St Giles
CH2/153/1 Fetteresso
CH2/188/1 Inchture and Rossie
CH2/196/1 Inverurie
CH2/206/1 Kennaway
CH2/225/1 Abbotshall, Kirkcaldy
CH2/276/4 Newbattle
CH2/285/4 North Berwick
CH2/338/2 Stow

CH2/383/1-2 Liberton
CH2/389/1 Humbie
CH2/400/2 Falkirk
CH2/418/1 Kinnaird
CH2/420/2 Peebles Old Kirk
CH2/458/1 Petty
CH2/465/7 Hamilton
CH2/471/3 Lasswade
CH2/523/1 Burntisland
CH2/531/1 Inveresk
CH2/542/1 Kemnay
CH2/592/1 Dunfermline
CH2/636/34 Old Kirkcaldy
CH2/647/1 Dunbar
CH2/716/5 & 6 South Leith
CH2/799/3 Haddington
CH2/890/1 Rothesay
CH2/1026/1 Stirling
CH2/1100/1 Shapinsay
CH2/1115/1 Boharm and Dundurcas
CH2/1157/1 Dirleton
CH2/1173/3-4 Kelso
CH2/1463/1 Innerwick

(b) *Presbytery Session Records*
CH2/15/1 Arbroath
CH2/47/1 Caithness
CH2/89/2 Deer
CH2/105/1 Dunfermline
CH2/111/1 Dunoon
CH2/113/1 Duns
CH2/234/1 Lanark
CH2/242/5-6 Linlithgow
CH2/295/4 Peebles
CH2/299/3 Perth
CH2/424/4 Dalkeith
CH2/546/2 Dumbarton
CH2/722/6 Stirling
CH2/1082/2 Orkney
CH2/1120/1 Turriff
CH2/1284/1 Dumfries

(c) *Court of Justiciary, High Court Minute Books, and Circuit Courts*

JC2/10

JC6/5

JC10/1

JC10/15/1-3

JC17/1

JC26/20/1, 7

JC26/22/2/27

JC26/22/3/1, 3-5

JC/26/22/4/1,10, 39

JC26/22/5/1-7

JC26/22/5/31, 39, 42

JC26/22/6/40

JC26/17

JC26/18A/1-3, 6-10

JC26/23

JC26/24

JC26/25

JC26/26

JC26/27

JC26/28

JC51/6

JC51/18

(d) *Gifts and Deposits*

GD 103/2/3/11

GD 103/2/176/1-7

Orkney Archives

DO 31/1/2/8

DO31/4/3

PUBLISHED PRIMARY SOURCES

Acts of the General Assembly of the Church of Scotland, vol. 1 (Edinburgh 1843)

Anderson, J., 'The confessions of the Forfar witches (1661), from the original documents in the Society's library', *Proceedings of the Society of Antiquaries of Scotland* 10 n.s. (1888), 241-62

Anon., *The Life and Wonderful Prophecies of Donald Cargill* (Glasgow n.d.)

Ayr Burgh Accounts, ed. G.S. Pryde (Edinburgh 1937)

Baillie, R., *Letters and Journals, 1637–1662*, ed. D. Laing, 3 vols (Edinburgh 1841-2)

The Life of Robert Blair, Minister of St Andrews, containing his Autobiography from 1593 to 1636, ed. T. M'Crie (Woodrow Society, Edinburgh 1848)

Chambers, R., *Domestic Annals of Scotland*, 3rd ed., 3 vols (Edinburgh & London 1874)

Cramond, W., *The Church and Churchyard of Rathven* (Banff 1885)

– *Records of the Kirk-Session of Elgin, 1584–1779* (Elgin 1897)

Dumbarton Common Good Accounts, 1614–1660, ed. F. Roberts & I.M.M. MacPhail (Dumbarton 1972)

Extracts from the Records of the Royal Burgh of Lanark, ed. R. Renwick (Scottish Burgh Records Society, Glasgow 1893)

Firth, C.H. (ed.), *Scotland and the Protectorate: Letters and Papers relating to the Military Government of Scotland from January 1654 to June 1659* (Edinburgh 1899)

Hay, A., *Diary, 1659–1660*, ed. A.G. Reid (Edinburgh 1901)

Johnston, A., *Diary of Sir Archibald Johnston of Wariston*, vol. 1 (1632–39), ed. G.M. Paul (Edinburgh: Scottish History Society 1911)

– *Diary of Sir Archibald Johnston of Wariston*, vol. 2 (1650–54), ed. D.H. Fleming (Edinburgh: Scottish History Society 1919)

Nicoll, J., *A Diary of Public Transactions and Other Occurrences Chiefly in Scotland from January 1650 to June 1667* (Edinburgh: the Bannatyne Club 1836)

Pitcairn, R. (ed.), *Criminal Trials in Scotland*, vol. 3 (Edinburgh 1833)

Register of the Privy Council of Scotland: 2nd series, vols 7 & 8

Register of the Privy Council of Scotland: 3rd series, vol. 1

The Statistical Account of Scotland, 1791–1799, vol. 16 (reprint EP Publishing, Wakefield 1982)

Wodrow, R., *Analecta, or, Materials for a History of Remarkable Providences mostly relating to Scotch Ministers and Christians*, 4 vols (Maitland Club, Edinburgh 1842–3)

SECONDARY SOURCES

Behringer, W., 'Weather, hunger and fear: origins of the European witch-hunts in climate, society and mentality', in D. Oldridge (ed.), *The Witchcraft Reader* (Routledge, London & New York 2002), 69-86

– *Witches and Witch-Hunts* (Polity Press, Cambridge 2004)

Bostridge, I., *Witchcraft and its Transformations, c.1650–c.1750* (Clarendon, Oxford 1997)

Campbell, J.G., *Gaelic Superstitions and Witchcraft*, ed. R. Black (Birlinn, Edinburgh 2002)

Clark, S. (ed.), *Languages of Witchcraft: Narrative, Ideology and Meaning in Early Modern Culture* (Macmillan, Basingstoke 2001)

Cook, D., *Annals of Pittenweem, being notes and extracts from the ancient records of that burgh, 1526–1793* (Anstruther 1867)

Dalyell, J.G., *The Darker Superstitions of Scotland* (Edinburgh 1834)

DesBrisnay, G., 'Twisted by definition: women under godly discipline in seventeenth-century Scottish towns', in Y. Galloway Brown & R. Ferguson (eds), *Twisted Sisters: Women, Crime and Deviance in Scotland since 1400* (Tuckwell, East Linton 2002), 137-55

Dow, F.D., *Cromwellian Scotland, 1651–1660* (John Donald, Edinburgh 1979)

Ekirch, A.R., 'Sleep we have lost: pre-industrial slumber in the British Isles', *American Historical Review* 106 (April 2001), 343-85

Findlay, J., *All Manner of People: The History of the Justices of the Peace in Scotland* (Saltire Society, Edinburgh 2000)

Gibson A.J.S. & Smout T.C., *Prices, Food and Wages in Scotland, 1550–1780* (Cambridge University Press 1995)

Gibson, M., *Reading Witchcraft: Stories of Early English Witches* (Routledge, London 1999)

Goodare, J., 'Witch-hunting and the Scottish state', in J. Goodare (ed.), *The Scottish Witch-Hunt in Context* (Manchester University Press, 2002), 122-45

Henderson, L. & Cowan, E.J. (eds), *Scottish Fairy Belief* (Tuckwell, East Linton 2001)

Hodgkin, K., 'Reasoning with unreason: visions, witchcraft, and madness in early modern England' in S. Clark (ed.), *Languages of Witchcraft, q.v.* 217-36

Hufford, D., *The Terror that Comes in the Night* (University of Pennsylvania, Philadelphia 1982)

Johnstone, N., 'The Protestant Devil: the experience of temptation in early modern England', *Journal of British Studies* 43 (2004), 173-205

Kristóf, I., 'Elements of demonology in Hungarian Calvinist literature printed in Debrecen in the sixteenth and seventeenth centuries', *Cauda Pavonis* ns. 16 (1997), 9-17

Larner, C., *Enemies of God: The Witch-Hunt in Scotland* (Blackwell, Oxford 1983)

Larner C., Hyde Lee C,. McLachlan H.V. (eds), *A Source-Book of Scottish Witchcraft* (Glasgow 1977)

Levack B.P., 'The great Scottish witch-hunt of 1661–1662', *Journal of British Studies* 20 (1980), 90-108

– 'The decline and end of Scottish witch-hunting' in J. Goodare (ed.), *The Scottish Witch-Hunt in Context*, q.v. 166-81

Lumsden, J,. *The Covenants of Scotland* (Paisley: Alexander Gardner 1914)

MacDonald, S., *The Witches of Fife: Witch-Hunting in a Scottish Shire, 1500–1710* (Tuckwell Press, East Linton 2002)

– 'Torture and the Scottish witch-hunt: a re-examination', *Scottish Tradition* 27 (2002), 95-114

Martin, L., 'Witchcraft and family: what can witchcraft documents tell us about early modern Scottish family life?', *Scottish Tradition* 27 (2002), 7–22

– 'The Devil and the domestic: witchcraft, quarrels and women's work in Scotland', in J. Goodare (ed.), *The Scottish Witch-Hunt in Context, q.v.* 73–89

Maxwell-Stuart, P.G., *Satan's Conspiracy: Magic and Witchcraft in Sixteenth-Century Scotland* (Tuckwell Press, East Linton 2001)

– *Witch Hunters* (Tempus Publishing, Stroud 2003)

Maxwell Wood, J., *Witchcraft and Superstitious Record in the South-Western District of Scotland* (1911, republished EP Publishing, Wakefield 1975)

Medway G.J., *Lure of the Sinister: The Unnatural History of Satanism* (New York University Press, 2001)

Mentzer, R., 'The persistence of 'superstition and idolatry' among rural French Calvinists', *Church History* 65 (1996), 220–33

Miller, J., 'Devices and directions: folk healing aspects of witchcraft practice in seventeenth-century Scotland', in J. Goodare (ed.), *The Scottish Witch-Hunt in Context, q.v.* 90–105

– *Magic and Witchcraft in Scotland* (Goblinshead, Musselburgh 2004)

Morrison, I., 'Evidence of climatic change in Scotland before and during the age of agricultural improvement', *Scottish Archives* 1 (1995), 3–16

Muchembled, R., *History of the Devil from the Middle Ages to the Present*, English trans. (Polity Press, Cambridge 2003)

Oldridge, D., *The Devil in Early Modern England* (Sutton, Stroud 2000)

Purkiss, D., *Troublesome Things: A History of Fairies and Fairy Stories* (Allen Lane, London 2000)

– 'Sounds of silence: fairies and incest in Scottish witchcraft stories', in S. Clark (ed.), *Languages of Witchcraft: Narrative Ideology and Meaning in Early Modern Culture* (Macmillan, Basingstoke 2001), 81–98

Reis, E., 'Witches, sinners and the underside of Covenant theology', *Essex Institute Historical Collections* 129 (1993), 103–18

Roper, L., *Witch Craze* (Yale University Press, New Haven & London 2004)

Rushton, P., 'Texts of authority: witchcraft accusations and the demonstration of truth in early modern England' in S. Clark (ed.), *Languages of Witchcraft, q.v.* 21–39

Sanderson, M.H.B., *A Kindly Place? Living in Sixteenth-Century Scotland* (Tuckwell Press, East Linton 2002)

Stevenson, D., *King or Covenant? Voices from Civil War* (Tuckwell Press, East Linton 1996)

Tolbooths and Town-Houses: Civic Architecture in Scotland to 1833, Royal Commission on the Ancient and Historical Monuments of Scotland (Edinburgh 1996)

Tucker, M-C., 'Sir George MacKenzie of Rosehaugh, procureur du roi, défenseur de la sorcière Maevia en 1672', *Etudes écossaises* 7 (2001), 175–81

Unsworth, C.R., 'Witchcraft beliefs and criminal procedure in early modern

England' in T.G. Watkin (ed.), *Legal Record and Historical Reality* (London 1989), 71-98

Valk, U., *The Black Gentleman: Manifestations of the Devil in Estonian Folk Religion* (Academia Scientiarum Fennica, Helsinki 2001)

Valletta, F., *Witchcraft, Magic and Superstition in England, 1640–70* (Ashgate, Aldershot 2000)

Waite, G.K., *Heresy, Magic, and Witchcraft in Early Modern Europe* (Palgrave, Basingstoke 2003)

Walker, D.M., *The Scottish Jurists* (Green & Son, Edinburgh 1985)

Whyte, I.D., *Scotland Before the Industrial Revolution: An Economic and Social History, c. 1050–c. 1750* (Longman, London 1995)

Wilson, L., *Theatres of Intention* (Stanford University Press, 2000)

Wilson, S., *The Magical Universe: Everyday ritual and magic in pre-modern Europe* (Hambledon & London, London & New York 2000)

Yeoman, L.A., 'The Devil as doctor: witchcraft, Wodrow and the wider world', *Scottish Archives* 1 (1995), 93-105

List of Illustrations

Index